Anjali Deshpande is a journalist and activist. She has participated in many campaigns and movements including the women's movement and the Bhopal gas tragedy survivors' struggle for justice. She is also a novelist and writes mainly in Hindi. This is her first non-fiction work.

Nandita Haksar is a human rights lawyer, teacher and campaigner. She has represented contract workers as well as trade unions in the Supreme Court, including those in the public sector such as telecommunications and at Bharat Electronics. She writes extensively and has published several books, including on the trade union movement in Kashmir and migrant workers from the Northeast.

She is the author of *The Many Faces of Kashmiri Nationalism: From the Cold War to the Present Day* (2015; revised edition, 2020), *The Flavours of Nationalism: A Memoir with Recipes for Love, Hate and Friendship* (2018; revised edition, 2022), and *The Exodus Is Not Over: Migrations from the Ruptured Homelands of Northeast India* (2016), among other books.

JAPANESE MANAGEMENT, INDIAN RESISTANCE

The STRUGGLES of the MARUTI SUZUKI WORKERS

Anjali Deshpande
and Nandita Haksar

SPEAKING TIGER

SPEAKING TIGER BOOKS LLP
125A, Ground Floor, Shahpur Jat, near Asiad Village,
New Delhi 110049

First published by Speaking Tiger Books 2023

ISBN: 978-93-5447-444-6
eISBN: 978-93-5447-450-7

10 9 8 7 6 5 4 3 2 1

Typeset in Garamond Premier Pro by SÜRYA, New Delhi
Printed at Chaman Enterprises, New Delhi

Contents

Timeline of Important Events

June 1971: Maruti Motors Limited incorporated with Sanjay Gandhi as the first managing director

1978: The company goes into liquidation

16 December 1977 to February 1979: Maruti investigated by commission headed by Justice Alok Chandra Gupta; they conclude that 'Maruti...brought about a decline in the integrity of public life'

24 January 1981: Indira Gandhi nationalizes assets of Maruti Motors Ltd and incorporates it as Maruti Udyog Limited; V. Krishnamurthy of BHEL asked to head the project

2 October 1982: Licence and joint venture agreement signed between the Government of India and Suzuki Motor Corporation

1982: First workers' union, affiliated to INTUC, led by K.K. Datta

14 December 1983: PM Indira Gandhi hands over keys of first car commercially produced to Mr Harpal Singh, an employee in Indian Airlines, selected through a lucky draw

1986: First independent union, the Maruti Udyog Employees Union (MUEU), registered in the Gurgaon factory

April 1986: Mathew Abraham suspended

1987: The success of the joint venture leads Suzuki to increase its equity from 26 to 40 per cent; it goes up to 50 a few years later in 1992

1987: Krishnamurthy leaves Maruti Udyog and goes back to BHEL

1988: Mathew Abraham becomes general secretary of MUEU; serves till 1989

1995: Old incentive scheme withdrawn; new productivity cum profit-based scheme introduced

1994: Mathew Abraham again becomes general secretary; suspended in 1996 for calling a strike

1 January 2000: Jagdish Khattar appointed as managing director after S.S.L.N. Ravela Bhaskarudu is forced to step down

September 2000: MUEU rejects revised incentive scheme

October to December 2000: First long strike in the Gurgaon factory

13 December 2000: Strike continues in front of Udyog Bhawan, New Delhi; lasts till 8 January 2001

2000: Scab union called Maruti Udyog Kamgar Union (MUKU) formed at Gurgaon factory

2001: The first voluntary retirement scheme (VRS) for workers implemented by management

2001: First elections to MUKU held with a show of hands in a small group

2003: Second round of VRS implemented; MUKU remains sole representative of workers

2003: Maruti Udyog Ltd sold to Suzuki Motor Corp

2006: Manesar factory set up; starts operation in 2007

17 September 2007: MUL becomes Maruti Suzuki India Limited

2011: Manesar workers asked to join MUKU of Gurgaon; they refuse

3 June 2011: Maruti Suzuki Employees Union (MSEU) formed by Sonu Gujjar at Manesar; application for registration filed but rejected

4 June 2011: Thirteen-day occupation of Manesar factory starts

5 June 2011: Management seal off the gates

8 June 2011: Trade union federations AITUC, CITU, HMS, INTUC and UTUC form action committee in solidarity

10 June 2011: Strike declared illegal by Haryana government

17 June 2011: First occupy strike ends; work begins after verbal assurance that dismissed workers will be reinstated

18 June to 28 August 2011: Work resumes but resistance of the workers continues

14 August 2011: Application for registration of MSEU rejected

29 August 2011: Management imposes lock-out on those who refuse to sign a 'good conduct' bond

1 September 2011: Various unions gather in front of Manesar factory in solidarity

14 September 2011: Strike at Suzuki Powertrain Ltd, Suzuki Castings, in Manesar, and at Suzuki Motorcycle in Gurgaon in solidarity

16 September 2011: HMS union negotiates an end to strike at Powertrain

30 September 2011: End of lock-out; workers sign 'good conduct' agreement; many permanent workers remain suspended

7 October 2011: Second occupy strike begins at Maruti Suzuki

in Manesar, Suzuki Powertrain, Suzuki Castings and Suzuki Motorcycle

21 October 2011: Management agrees to take back sixty-four permanent workers; thirty, including MUEU leaders, remain suspended; Sonu Gujjar leaves Manesar factory

October 2011: New union, Maruti Suzuki Workers' Union (MSWU), formed at Manesar; application filed for registration

1 March 2012: MSWU gets registration number; union celebrates flag day

18 April 2012: Charter of demands given to management

April to July 2012: Negotiations on demands but the management stalls

18 July 2012: Anger explodes in Manesar factory after a worker has an altercation with a supervisor and is suspended; factory shuts down; FIR registered under several sections including murder, with fifty-five workers named in it

2 August 2012: Union leaders surrender; throughout the month of August, a total of 146 workers arrested

22 August 2012: Factory reopens; 2,500 workers dismissed of whom 546 are permanent

February 2017: Thirty-three convicted of lesser crimes and sentenced but released because they had already served their time; 117 acquitted

17 March 2017: Thirteen workers sentenced to life for murder, including MSWU leadership and one worker

2022: All sentenced to life out on bail; appeals pending in the High Court; dismissed workers continue their struggle for justice both in court and on the streets

Prelude

The Fateful Day

I dreamed I saw Joe Hill last night
Alive as you and me
Says I, 'But Joe, you're ten years dead,'
'I never died,' says he
'I never died,' says he

And standing there, as big as life
And smiling with his eyes
Says Joe, 'What they can never kill
Went on to organize,
Went on to organize.'

—stanzas from 'Joe Hill',
a folk song named after labour
activist Joe Hill, by Alfred Hayes, 1925

For Jiya Lal, 18 July 2012 began just like any other day at the Maruti Suzuki factory in Manesar, Gurgaon district, Haryana. Like the other workers, he had punched in his card and got to work at the assembly line. He had no premonition of things to come.

The first shift began early in the morning. Many of the workers hadn't had time to have a cup of tea before boarding the factory bus; some hadn't had time even to go to the toilet. When the alarm sounded for the tea break, like the other workers, Jiya Lal too hurried off to grab his glass of tea and snacks and rush to the toilet. He knew he had just seven and a half minutes to do it all.

It was during those seven and half minutes that Jiya Lal had an altercation with the supervisor, Sangram Kumar Majhi. Jiya Lal, who was Dalit and known to be even tempered, objected to a casteist slur made by Majhi and there was a hot exchange of words between the two. But Jiya Lal went back to work and finished his shift.

The management suspended Jiya Lal; the trade union took up the matter. It was just another minor dispute. It should have been settled within the course of the day. The union agreed to the suspension if the supervisor too was suspended for making casteist remarks. But the management did not settle.

The union could not have imagined that the negotiations with the management over a suspension would lead to the events that followed. The workers' frustration and anger, which had been building up over the past months over several issues, erupted like a volcano and the lava that flowed destroyed everything that came in its path.

By the end of the day the factory was on fire and the flames claimed the life of one manager, Awanish Kumar Dev. The management immediately blamed the workers for the murder; and the media demonized the union and the workers. But the question that should have been asked was: why would the workers target Awanish Dev? He was a human resource manager, well-liked by the workers. He had even accompanied them to Chandigarh to help them register their independent union.

Awanish Dev was aware of the discontent among the workers, and apprehending trouble, he had put in his papers. But his resignation had not been accepted and he had been forced to stay on by the management; and now his family got back a charred body identified by his teeth.

The cause of the mayhem is still not known. Many conspiracy theories have come up, including some which suggest that competing car manufacturers were behind the arson, and others which say that factionalism within a section of the management led to the violence.

Awanish Dev's family demanded a CBI enquiry; the workers demanded a judicial probe. The contents of the factory's internal enquiry were never made public, so we do not know how a manager could be burnt alive with so many policemen and security guards present.

Instead, the management terminated the services of 2,500 workers, of whom 546 were permanent workers; 146 workers were arrested and thirty-three were convicted; of those convicted, thirteen were given life imprisonment—the twelve trade union leaders and Jiya Lal.

The workers found themselves in jail, their families running from courts to lawyers' chambers to jail—and all the while struggling to find the money to survive.

The workers of Maruti Suzuki continue their struggle in the courts. But they find the scales of justice weighed against them. As Rajendra Pathak, a lawyer who has been taking up Maruti workers' cases, says: '*Chit bhi meri, pat bhi meri, anta mere baap ka.*' In other words, Suzuki and the government have it all: heads they win, tails the workers lose, and if there is a little change left, that, too, Suzuki takes.

The story of the workers of the Maruti Suzuki factory is not only that of a union fighting for workers' rights; it is a glimpse into the new India which is emerging: a welfare state transforming into a corporate state; a state in which profits trump the rights of citizens.

One

Death of a Manager

The real problem of humanity is the following: we have Paleolithic emotions, medieval institutions, and god-like technology.

—E.O. Wilson (1929–2021), in a debate
at the Harvard Museum of Natural History,
Cambridge, Mass., 9 September 2009

It has become appallingly obvious that our technology has exceeded our humanity.

—Albert Einstein (1899–1955)

On 18 July 2012, a part of the Maruti Suzuki factory in Manesar was set on fire. One manager died and more than ninety managers were injured, as were many workers. This violence was unprecedented in the history of the company.

The manager who died that day was Awanish Kumar Dev. In an interview a few days after his death, his brother told *The Economic Times*: 'There was simmering tension at the Manesar plant for quite some time and Awanish had put in his papers. He was very stressed out and could have seen this coming. He was all set to join another organization but had finally decided to give in to the persuasion of senior officials of the company.'

The brother went on to say: 'We are now definite that the attack on my brother was pre-planned. It wouldn't have been possible otherwise to summon over 3,000 people in such a short time. Our eighty-year-old father, Rameshwar Saha is demanding a CBI probe into the incident.'*

The workers say that the people who instigated the violence were some 100 to 150 bouncers who came during the second shift. These bouncers entered in workers' uniform and started the fire and beat up the managers. The workers alleged in a case they filed that Awanish was killed at the instigation of another manager with whom he had serious differences. That manager, they said, told the bouncers to break Awanish's legs and set the room on fire. The workers' petition was dismissed.†

So far, we do not know who planned the violence and with what motive. The management had called the police and there was a substantial police presence there; why did they not intervene and stop the violence? Why was the security force employed by the company not able to rescue the manager? And, worst of all, why did no one want to know what the grievances of the workers were?

Whoever was responsible for inciting the violence knew that there was simmering resentment among the workers because the management had stalled the negotiations on the union's charter of demands; that, therefore, the workers could be instigated and this could be used as a cover for something else.

* 'Deceased Maruti HR manager Awanish Kumar Dev had resigned 6 months back', *The Economic Times*, 21 July 2012 (https://economictimes.indiatimes.com/deceased-maruti-hr-manager-awanish-kumar-dev-had-resigned-6-months-back/articleshow/15068741.cms, last accessed 11 January 2023).

† Unfortunately, we could not get a copy of the complaint, but the reference is in the 2018 report by the People's Union for Democratic Rights, 'A Pre-Decided Case: A Critique of the Maruti Judgment of 2017'.

The Japanese management was shocked by the violence but refused to admit that the workers had genuine grievances. Shinzo Nakanishi, managing director and chief executive of Maruti Suzuki India, said this type of violence had never happened anywhere in Suzuki Motor Corp's global operations—it had never happened in Hungary, Indonesia, Spain, Pakistan, Thailand, Malaysia, China, the Philippines.

Nakanishi announced: 'We are going to de-recognize Maruti Suzuki Workers' Union and dismiss all workers named in connection with the incident. We will not compromise at all in such instances of barbaric, unprovoked violence.' When asked whether Suzuki Motor intended to close down their factory in Manesar, he categorically denied the rumour. Nakanishi declared that they would continue to manufacture in Manesar, and that the Suzuki factory being set up in Hansalpur, Gujarat (which finally opened in 2017), was in addition to the Manesar plant, not an alternative to it.

Osamu Suzuki, chairman of Suzuki Motor, in an interview to Aroon Purie of *India Today*,* a month after the incident, said: 'I don't consider this a union–management labour issue; I term it as a criminal act, and, of course, it shocked me.'

He also told journalists that 'all those who indulged in this violence—there were 546 people—have been identified and [their services] have been terminated'.

In fact, the number of workers whose services were terminated was 2,500; of these, 546 were permanent workers while the rest were contract workers.

One year after the 2012 violence in Manesar, Kenichi Ayukawa, who became the chief executive officer of Maruti Suzuki India Ltd on 1 April 2013, refused to accept that the violence reflected any genuine grievances of the workers. He

* Print edition, 30 September 2012.

said in an interview that the events were 'orchestrated mob' violence that didn't seem to stem from a dispute over wages or working conditions.*

Ayukawa said his top priority was to 'delete' memories of the riot.

An internal enquiry by Suzuki Motor Corporation had found 'miscommunication and management failure' among the reasons for the 2012 violence. The events of 18 July 2012 thus gave the Japanese an opportunity to tighten their grip over the Indian subsidiary.

Three executives were stripped of their powers: S.Y. Siddiqui and M.M. Singh, who were directly in charge of the situation at Manesar at the time, and S. Maitra, who was in charge of the supply chain. The three affected executives were the seniormost Indians in the company, besides R.C. Bhargava, who was at the time the non-executive chairman.†

Suzuki deputed two Japanese officials to keep a close watch on the plant and production activities in the company. Toshiaki Hasuike was named the joint director of Maruti while Toshio Ozawa was brought in as advisor for human resources. Now, the Japanese were in full control of the Indian subsidiary.

It is not clear who in the management decided to hire a Bangalore-based 'Vedic astrologer' to sort out *vaastu* issues at the Manesar plant. The astrologer, Daivajna K.N. Somayaji, was brought in to ensure that the violence of 18 July 2012 did not occur ever again.

---

* 'The Great Comeback: How Kenichi Ayukawa revitalized Maruti after its dark days of labour unrest in 2013', Value Research, 7 June 2016 (https://www.valueresearchonline.com/stories/31243/the-great-comeback/, last accessed 11 January 2023).

† 'Maruti Suzuki strips three COOs of executive powers', *Livemint*, 2 May 2014 (https://www.livemint.com/Companies/7A8POI8hQdEkAYmGiNNs6I/Maruti-Suzuki-strips-three-COOs-of-executive-powers.html, last accessed 11 January 2023).

According to this astrologer, the problem was rooted in the fact that a part of the 600-acre plant site had once served as a burial ground. Besides, he said, three temples which existed at the site had been razed to set up the plant. There was too much negative energy at the site.

The astrologer was asked to purge the site of all negative energy through a series of rituals spread over two to three weeks.

A visit to the astrologer's website revealed that he 'specializes in advising the young professionals and business executives on various key projects and career aspects, such as venture capital, portfolio management, and primary/secondary market, International trade, banking, diversification, reviving the sick industries, I.T. companies and various industrial issues. He is an expert advisor on issues such as Marriage, Education, Children, Domestic relationship and Commercial Aspects.

'He has travelled extensively across India and constantly travels to Russia, European Countries, U.S.A., Middle East, Bangladesh, Nepal, Singapore, Hong Kong, Malaysia, Sri Lanka, Canada and Australia.'*

These special skills do not make him an expert on issues of wages, working conditions of workers and the right of workers to form trade unions—issues that the management should have been seeking advice on.

The management also called in Brahmakumaris to deal with the rage of the workers. Groups of workers were made to learn meditation; and yoga was made compulsory for workers. The meditation was supposed to help workers deal with their anger.

However, according to the charge sheet filed by the Special Investigation Team (SIT) formed to probe the incident, the

---

* See Official Website of K.N. Somayaji (http://www.somayajikn.com/indian-astrology-consultant-in-bangalore.html, last accessed 11 January 2023).

violence at Maruti Suzuki India's Manesar plant was not instigated from outside, but was due to internal issues between management and workers.

Justice for Workers

All the workers we interviewed, without exception, expressed genuine grief on the death of Awanish Dev; they did not condone the crime in any way.

The workers, their family members and trade union leaders said that Awanish Kumar Dev favoured the workers and had even accompanied the union leadership to Chandigarh to register the Maruti Suzuki Workers' Union. They felt no animosity towards the manager and had no motive to harm him in any way.

The trade union leaders and workers maintain that they have been wrongly accused of a crime they did not commit or condone. Independent fact-finding reports by civil rights groups have said that the workers did not get a fair trial. ('A Pre-Decided Case', PUDR, 2018; the report has an analysis of the judgement sentencing the thirteen workers to life imprisonment.)

The workers feel that they stood little chance of justice being done to them because the government and the corporation would not allow it.

Sarabjeet Singh, the general secretary of the Maruti Suzuki Workers' Union, who has been sentenced to life imprisonment, said, 'Even if we had got the best lawyers, and we did get some of the best, but even if we had got senior lawyers, we would still have been defeated. We *had* to lose the case. Maruti is a very big company. How could we have matched their resources? The management and government were hand in glove. How could we have won?'

The question that arises is this: Can workers in India get justice in the courts; can they go against the interests of big corporations which have the backing of the government?

The thirteen workers, of whom twelve were office-bearers in the trade union, were:

1. Jiya Lal, Dalit worker who was suspended on 18 July 2012.
2. Ram Meher, the President of the Maruti Suzuki Workers' Union;
3. Suresh Dhull, Treasurer of the Union;
4. Sandeep Dhillon, Chief Patron;
5. Sarabjeet Singh, General Secretary;
6. Ajmer Singh, Legal Advisor;
7. Yogesh Kumar Yadav, Secretary;
8. Pawan Kumar Dahiya, Joint Secretary;
9. Pradeep Gujjar, Executive Member;
10. Sohan Kumar, Vice-President;
11. Dhanraj Bhambi, Executive Member;
12. Amarjeet Kapoor, Executive Member; and
13. Ram Vilas, Executive Member.

The dismissal, termination and convictions have had a devastating effect on the families of the workers. The workers, all of whom were young men at the time, belong to villages near the factory; most of the others are from Haryana and Rajasthan, and some from further away—Himachal Pradesh and Uttar Pradesh. Most of them were first generation workers whose families had small holdings, while some of their parents worked as agricultural labourers. The families had sacrificed much to put their sons through school and then the industrial training institute (ITI). They were proud that their sons were educated and skilled; and all their hopes and aspirations rested on the shoulders of these young workers.

The workers told us that, to begin with, working in the Maruti Suzuki factory was a status symbol and the uniform was greatly respected. After all, they worked in one of the most modern factories in the country alongside 2,500 robots. Women in the villages aspired to have husbands who worked in the factory and the men worked hard so that they would become permanent workers, which would ensure a secure future for themselves and their families.

Many had worked as contract workers before becoming permanent. And that is why they had a deep sense of solidarity with the contract workers and had taken up their cause. They knew how contract workers suffered from anxiety and stress given the precarity of their employment, fearing they may never escape this uncertain, insecure situation.

Their fears were not unfounded; in its single largest human resource initiative, Maruti Suzuki announced after the violence of 2012 that it would stop hiring contract workers for production work. Till then, as we shall see, these contract workers made up a significant portion of the company's total workforce. The entire recruitment process is now routed through the company's own human resource department. While it would appear that the decision to stop hiring contract workers is a positive development, in fact, when they used to be hired by a contractor, the same contract workers would get the job with breaks of a few months; at least that ensured they had more-or-less regular employment. Now, the same contract workers are not taken after a break. While they were substituted to some extent with robots, the management also hired 'temporary' workers and apprentices who were paid less. Besides, the training period of trainee workers was increased.

Over time, especially after privatization (which we will discuss in chapter two), the number of permanent workers saw a decline and the number of contract or temporary workers grew; although the two categories of workers did the same work, the difference in their wages also increased enormously. Despite the handsome increment offered by Maruti Suzuki in the new wage agreement, the company's wage bill remains the lowest among listed automobile companies.

Among the workers at Manesar were a few that had relatives who had worked in the first Maruti factory at Gurgaon and had memories of the factory when it was still owned by the Indian government. The latter had been witness to the slow and steady privatization of the company—Suzuki Motor Corporation, a minority partner when Maruti Udyog Limited was founded in 1981, became the sole owner in stages by 2012.

The young men who joined the Maruti Suzuki factory were not revolutionaries seeking to change society. Most of them had a conservative outlook and were focused on working hard and providing for their families. Their dreams extended to having a home and enough money to educate their children and pay medical bills.

However, with increasing privatization, as Suzuki bought more and more shares in the company, work conditions became worse, with greater pressure being put on the workers to work faster and increase production—till they reached a point where every 45 seconds a new car was being completed on the assembly line! The speed would vary according to the target set for the day. It was one of the demands of the workers to decrease the speed of the assembly line, to give them a little more time to fit the parts into the body of the car. (It was after intense struggle that this allotted time was increased from 45 to 58 seconds.) The pressure was such that the workers were not even allowed a toilet break.

Under such pressure, the workers realized the need to organize themselves to fight for better working conditions.

They wanted a reliever so they could take a toilet break; they felt that the huge deductions from previously agreed upon incentives made by the management were unfair; they needed factory transport to cover those workers who lived at a distance from the factory; and they felt that the punishments meted out even for minor mistakes were humiliating.

The testimonies in this book document how Suzuki turned young village youth into machines; the Japanese culture they wished workers to imbibe consisted of measuring time in units of seconds and micro-seconds. A worker tasked with installing the driver's seat in the body of the car, for example, given his allotted time of, say, 46 seconds, was, in his eight-hour schedule, installing some 580 car seats!

Celebrating Japanese Work Culture

The usual hagiographic accounts of Suzuki the company, portray it as a runaway success: a company which makes more than a million cars a year that price conscious Indian middle classes aspire to own. The facts and figures relating to production are awe inspiring indeed—some 4,000 trucks drive into the two facilities every day carrying 39,000 consignments of metal, plastics, rubber, and glass that eventually come together as Maruti Suzuki cars. The company came to control around 50 per cent of the country's passenger car market.*

Suzuki is touted as a success story in Japan as it is in India. As Kazuyuki Motohashi points out in his book on global strategies of Japanese companies: 'Amid the global economic downturn precipitated by the Lehman Brothers bankruptcy, Suzuki's subsidiary in India, Maruti Suzuki, was experiencing

* Maruti Suzuki India slimmed its market share to an eight year low at 43 per cent in the financial year ending 31 March 2022.

spectacular success. Thirty percent of Suzuki's overall profit on a consolidated basis came from India. As the "people's car of India", Suzuki's Maruti 800 established a strong brand recognition. In 2007, Osamu Suzuki, the president of the company, received the "Padma Bhushan" award from the Indian government for the company's contribution to the Indian economy.'

The Indian CEO of Maruti Suzuki India, R.C. Bhargava, was awarded the 'Order of the Rising Sun, Gold and Silver Star' by the Emperor of Japan for his contribution to the promotion of economic and bilateral relations between Japan and India. Bhargava was also given an audience with the Emperor. Bhargava has written about how Suzuki introduced Japanese work culture in the Maruti factory in his book *The Maruti Story: How a Public Sector Company Put India on Wheels* (June 2013).

Japan is known for its work culture: efficient, diligent and loyal. And it is this work culture which is credited to be the secret behind Japan's success as an industrial powerhouse. It is ostensibly based on a philosophy which values 'smaller, fewer, lighter, shorter and neater'.

From Japanese culture, the Maruti factory imbibed practices such as an open office, a common uniform for workers and managers (except for the colour of their helmets), and a common canteen for managers and workers.

In the beginning, Indian workers were not very particular about work hour schedules, making it difficult to implement production lines with routings managed in seconds. By training these employees in Japanese factories, the company was able 'to elicit a desire to master automobile production management systems'. The workers' testimonies show how ruthlessly this culture was imposed on Indian workers.

Japanese work culture had critics among the Indian management. For instance, V. Krishnamurthy (1925–2022), known as the father of the Indian public sector, in his memoirs, *At the Helm: A Memoir* (2014), wrote critically of the Japanese management. V. Krishnamurthy was known for turning public sector undertakings into profit-making enterprises that are able to compete globally. He was the first chairman of Maruti Udyog Ltd. In his book, he speaks of the disagreements he had with Suzuki. For example, he was keen on the introduction of new technology to make working conditions for the workers better as opposed to the Japanese who were more interested in cutting costs and also in dumping old technology.

Kazuyuki Motohashi notes that, although in the beginning Suzuki held only 26 per cent of the shares, it insisted on having veto rights for major management decisions. He writes: 'Suzuki also ensured that its approval of important policy matters, such as CEO changes, was included as a condition in the Joint Venture (JV) agreement, thereby allowing Suzuki to instil Japanese management styles into the JV, despite its hold as a minority participant.'

Suzuki went to the extent of objecting to the executive nominated by the Indian government to head the joint venture in 1997. Motohashi quotes Osamu Suzuki from an interview with a *Nihon Keizai Shimbun* reporter: 'We'll have an abacus in our left hand and come out punching with our right. We don't need to compromise.' (*Nihon Keizai Shimbun*, 25 September 1997, p. 24)

Suzuki went so far as to take action against the Indian government in both the Delhi High Court and London's International Court of Arbitration. Finally, in 1998, the two parties settled. However, Suzuki managed to get his way and overrule any decisions by the Indian management even though he did not as yet have full ownership.

This book traces the history of how Japanese work culture was introduced into the Maruti Suzuki factory and what impact it had on the lives of the workers and their families.

The Maruti factory was embroiled in controversies from the start, even before Suzuki took it over. It was a project of Sanjay Gandhi, the spoilt son of Prime Minister Indira Gandhi. A pamphlet entitled 'Maruti to Mafia: The Sanjay Gandhi Story', published by *Mainstream* in 1977, documents the sordid beginnings—from the acquisition of land to the loans obtained through pressure tactics from nationalized banks. The corruption also had an impact on institutions which form the bedrock of Indian democracy: courts, media, and the working of the Constitution of India. The full pamphlet is included as Appendix 1.

This book does not pretend to be objective as described by academia, eschewing the kind of objectivity which invariably works against the weaker, less politically powerful section of people. However, if we think of objectivity as truth, verifiable facts and justice, then this book is objective and takes the reader to 'the other side of appearance'. It challenges the reader to look at the shiny Maruti car and the technology which goes into its making from another perspective—the perspective of the workers who work in the Maruti Suzuki factories. This book hopes to challenge the perception of Maruti Suzuki as a success story.

Listen, first, to the testimony of Manish. He spoke to us on condition of anonymity because there is still fear that anyone who speaks out could be framed in a false case, or have his services terminated.

Manish (name changed)

Active in the Maruti Suzuki Workers' Union, he was neither accused nor arrested, but was still fired. He was interviewed on 18 July 2021 at the home of a friend.

Let me tell you straight away that Manish is not my real name. I am scared of speaking out after the way the union leaders have been framed.

When I got into Maruti, what a reputation it had as an employer! That was when getting a job in Maruti was a matter of great honour. A Maruti worker held his head high. He got many offers of marriage. He got a good dowry. He suddenly rose in the esteem of his villagers. When he went into the market in his uniform, people used to stand and stare at him with envy.

I am from Jhajjar district. I am of the barber caste. I went to a government middle school in the village. After class 10, I joined an ITI and I studied for class 12 and the ITI course together. At that time the Haryana Education Board had a scheme under which you could do both the courses together. After the tenth standard I studied through distance learning. You'll be surprised to learn how much I worked in those days. I used to study, I worked in a workshop, and I used to travel long distances in buses for this.

My father was a contract labourer. He was never made permanent. Some days he worked, some days he had no work. He worked for a plywood factory as a loader; loading and unloading goods into trucks. The contractors were from our village. They would take him along with other villagers for the work.

We also kept buffaloes. He used to sell milk in Delhi by catching the morning train. Buffaloes also mean a lot of work.

Bathing the buffalo, taking it out for grazing, bringing fodder, cutting the fodder, milking the buffalo—it's a lot of work.

I have one brother, two sisters. My brother also did a course from an ITI and works on the lathe machine in a company. I trained as a motor mechanic in the ITI. They taught only theory. Book knowledge. They charged fees, but now I don't remember how much; maybe 600 rupees for a year. There were not many teachers either. There was a teacher for drawing and one for maths too. In the last six months of the course, a teacher of diesel mechanics came to teach us. Teachers were few but teaching was good. Drawing teachers used to teach how to draw parts. Parts are based on drawings. Every tool has a drawing. That is what I learnt.

I went to the ITI because most of the boys in my school and many of my friends were doing the same thing. Some 128 boys had passed with me in class 10 and fifty or sixty of them went to an ITI. This is what happens at that age—you do whatever a friend does.

You can't even imagine how hard my life was. Sunday used to be a holiday in the ITI. That day I used to go to a workshop in Bahadurgarh. One of my father's acquaintances ran this workshop there. They worked on four-wheeled vehicles only. I was hired to work there. They did not pay me. But I got my first training there. From servicing to overhauling, I learnt everything there. I learnt how to straighten dents in the body of the vehicle. Many boys with me were doing the same thing. We didn't take a single day off. Every Sunday I used to go up to Bahadurgarh and learn to work from the master there. Sometimes I used to go two days in a week—on Sundays, and any other day that happened to be a holiday.

Many people from our ITI, from the batch before us, were employed in Maruti. I also wanted to get work there.

I passed the ITI course in July 2006. I had been thinking of joining Maruti in Gurgaon for a year. The salary was good. At that time, a permanent worker used to get anywhere between Rs 40,000 to Rs 80,000 depending on his seniority.* I worked so hard only to land that job.

The recruiting was done at the ITI campus in Rohtak. People from many companies would flock to that campus in Rohtak looking for recruits. Not only Maruti, all the companies that made vehicles, or parts of vehicles. ITI students from all over Haryana had come to the Rohtak ITI to take the exam. Four to five thousand students took the test. It was like a *mela*. I took the test too. The test was to be conducted during the day and its result was to be declared in the evening on the same day. In the evening, announcements were made on the loudspeaker as to who had been selected by which company. I was breathless with apprehension. My name was announced towards the end. I had been selected by Maruti! My joy knew no bounds.

However, when I reported to Maruti's Gurgaon plant in September, they sent me back and asked me to come back the next month. A batch before mine had also joined and it was not yet decided whom to place where. At the time, Maruti's Manesar plant was coming up. Maybe that's why the decision was taking so long. When I went again in October, I was employed in the Gurgaon factory.

It was time to become an apprentice. Without an apprenticeship the ITI diploma is not given to you. I was sent to the research and development department or the R&D. I got no salary but Rs 3,000 as a monthly stipend.

Five or six of us rented a room near the bus stand for

* The figures were higher in the Gurgaon factory than the one at Manesar, where contract workers were the norm.

Rs 3,000. With the electricity bill, it used to cost us Rs 4,000 a month. Each one of us had to put in 700 or 800 rupees. We used to cook the food ourselves. This room was eight kilometres away from the factory and I used to take a bus to the factory. The bus fare was ten rupees.

My department was very good. I had to work in the general shift from nine to five. For this I had to reach the factory at quarter to nine.

The work was also very interesting. There were no strict timings there. You could go for lunch whenever you wanted, spend as much time as you wanted. This was work in the lab and there was no rush. In the lab, a number of tests were run on motor parts. We used to see whether the part was made according to the drawing or not, check its quality, calculate the percentage of titanium, aluminium, iron, etc. Many such investigations were done.

I was put to work in the polymer lab. Three apprentices were working in it. The work was negligible. Some permanent workers also worked in it. They were highly experienced senior workers and they would teach us how to do the tests, how to ascribe values in quality testing. The atmosphere was great. I got to learn a lot. An MTech engineer also used to come over and he taught us how to assess whether a part is made to the design and drawing or not.

There I learnt metallurgy, learnt to test aluminium and iron. I also learnt about the impact of weather and changes in weather on various things and how to minimize those impacts. I learnt the effect of weather and friction on different parts of the car. I had not learnt all that in the ITI.

For example, rubber. We would take two pieces of rubber and put both of them in environments of different levels of humidity and temperature and see the effect of sunlight, and moisture in the air. There were machines to do all this. We only punched in different levels of temperature and humidity into the machine. It created the kind of atmosphere we wanted and we would place the rubber in it and leave it for two hours, then check it against the quantities given in the manual. The amazing part was that one hour in the machine equalled several hours outside in the actual world and there was also a manual for it. There were all kinds of charts. It was great fun.

We got to know the effect of every season in the same way. It was not necessary to keep the part in the machine for two hours if you wished to see the effect of two hours of exposure. A short time would be enough and equal to several hours. Everything could be adjusted in the machine. What fun it was! That is why it is said that such and such effect was seen in the lab. In reality the effect could be slightly different because the exact situation on the road cannot be replicated in a lab each time. This is just an example. I learnt so many interesting things like this.

With the help of all those charts we used to make reports. In the beginning we gave the data to the senior who prepared the report. In six months I knew enough to start preparing the reports myself. I really liked this work. There was no pressure. We worked comfortably. It was a small department. There were four apprentices among a total of six or seven employees. I was the only one in my polymer lab and seniors kept coming and going. One of them was a supervisor. We all got along and used to work cheerfully.

This was not production work, so there was not much stress. The working conditions were good. The labour was not hard. There was no boredom. There was something new every day. We used to have the model of every vehicle, not only what our factory used to make. Maruti used to buy all models of vehicles made in the whole country. Other factories also do the same thing. We used to have a treasure trove of vehicles. There I saw all kinds of cars and different models of all cars.

When my apprenticeship ended, I was put on training for three years. With this, I began to get a salary and it also started increasing every year. The first year I used to get Rs 6,400 per month, the second year Rs 7,200 and the third year Rs 8,500 per month.

Meanwhile, the boys I was sharing the room with got married so they moved out and others shifted into my room. For the two-year training period I lived in the same room with four friends and used to go to Manesar from Gurgaon. In my third year, I went back to the village and started commuting to work from there.

Eight or ten of us workers got together and pooled in money to hire a regular cab. The cab used to pick us up from a point in a place called Sampla. We all reached there and went to Manesar in the cab. It cost us 40,000 rupees a month! I had to get up at 2.30 am to reach in time for the morning 'A' shift. I had to leave the house by three in the morning or a little later. I had to pay five thousand rupees every month for the cab which was more than half my salary.

But it didn't matter, I had started living with my parents again so I did not need to buy milk or rations, or cook food; the wheat was from our own farm, the milk from our buffaloes. Good food was available.

When I became a trainee and was posted in Manesar for the first two or three days, I just stood there idling. Each labourer used to get five to six parts to fit in the car. I used to watch my seniors to see how they worked at it. Some parts had to be fitted under the car, some on the side and some over the head... and the car turned on the line accordingly.

If you have to place something underneath, the car starts moving uphill and if you want to put something on the side, then it sort of lies down. Accordingly, the worker also has to turn. If the car is moving up, then he has to walk along under it while fitting the part and if it is to be placed on the side the worker has to bend from the waist to do so. This is called assembly line. You have to walk at the speed of the body of the car on the line.

Some parts have to be installed in 15 seconds, some in 12, some in 17...everything is done in seconds. There are no minutes there, only seconds.

In the factory everything is measured in seconds; no, it's measured in micro seconds. There are 1,000,000 nanoseconds in a millisecond; the machine can measure perhaps a tenth or maybe even a hundredth part of a second. You can see the second hand on a clock and its ticking but the machine counts the fractions within that movement of a second. The machine can tell how long the work stopped—one tenth of a second or more. Trust the machine to know.

The worker has to pick up the component and fit it into the body of the car which is moving towards him; he has to walk along with the moving car and at the same time fit in the components, nuts or screws within the given seconds. Sometimes the worker is not able to get the work done within the stipulated time. He can't do the job so fast. The car keeps moving, it overtakes him, goes out of reach, and he can't handle it. In such a situation, he can also sound an alarm. There is an alarm that you can pull. The assembly line stops.

When the alarm rings, the whole factory gets to know. It rings even in the HR department. There, on a monitor, a light blinks. Everyone gets to know where the work has stopped.

As soon as the alarm sounds, the supervisor in charge of

the shift rushes to the place from where it was sounded to see why the work stopped.

A car has hundreds of parts. Some parts are such that they have to be installed the moment the body of the vehicle arrives and they are all kept in the right spot for this. If the car slips forward, those parts cannot be fitted, but the car will go on moving without them. The worker cannot run behind it and quickly place the missing parts because another car is headed his way. He has to pull the alarm. The car has to be stopped. He also cannot simply let the car go on with the missing part because all parts fit into each other and at the next station it will be discovered that a part is missing. All parts are interconnected. Good system. It should be so. But it could be adjusted to give the workers a little more time; a few more seconds. We had to fight just to get a few more seconds for each task.

Then there are some parts named 'Maru A'. This is a list of parts that are extremely important. These are the parts that if missing or not fitted properly can endanger people's lives. This is a very responsible job and is handled by very experienced workers. If the rubber of the window glass is not fitted properly, that too will be considered a defect in the car, but it does not endanger the life of the driver or passengers or others on the road. But what if something is missed while fitting the brakes?

It is sometimes necessary to sound the alarm. But details are noted about who raised the alarm and how many times. If someone does it three or four times, he is hauled up, called to the HR, given a dressing down and told that he will get a bad annual CR (confidential report).

That's why there is a lot of pressure to do the work quickly and accurately. We are human beings, sometimes mistakes happen. So we should also get a chance to correct them without getting bad reports. There is a heavy burden of work and to work accurately on workers all the time. It is very stressful.

I used to do engine mounting. The thing on which the engine rests is called a mount. I used to lift that mount and put it on the chassis and fit the nuts in it with a 'gun'. The car arrives, I lift the mount, dump it on, pick the nuts in one hand, gun in the other hand, drive them in and torque them with the gun. There is a certain limit to which the nut has to be screwed in and that level is referred to as torque.

Within a few days, I had become so proficient that, almost automatically, up the mount would go, and my hand would come up with nuts and the gun, and the torquing would be over. I became a machine; every time my hand picked up exactly as many nuts as required—if I wanted four nuts, only four nuts would appear in my hand from the box below; if I wanted three, only three would. Never one less or one more.

Everything had become automatic. I had become automatic. Hands would go up and down, guns would move, nuts would fit the grooves...the car would go ahead, another car would reach my station, hands would go down, come up... My body's rhythm matched the speed of the car on the assembly line. I didn't even have to think. The brain had nothing to do with it. The hands moved on their own. Continuously. And I kept walking in the same rhythm, at the same speed, the same steps up and down for the whole of eight hours. I became a part of a huge machine.

Initially, when I became a trainee, I used to install the hose [pipe] of the air conditioner. It is found in the grille of the roof of the car. In the beginning, I was not used to doing this. My whole arm went numb on the first day. For a long time I could hardly lift my arm. There was so much pain in raising, lowering or moving it that I kept groaning. I could not knead dough. Cooking became difficult. I couldn't even sleep because of the pain. Friends cooked for me. The company had a dispensary. But what would the doctor do? Just gave me painkillers. Somehow I would manage to work the next day. I would come home and rest. Hot compresses helped. In the morning somehow I would push myself to go to work. It was bad for two months. Slowly, I got used to it and then the pain disappeared.

We had to reach the factory fifteen minutes before the start of the shift. Do some yoga first. Then take out the helmet and gloves from the locker, put them on and take out our glass too, which we would use for tea or water. Having done all this we had to stand at the station a second before the shift started. All the clocks used to keep track of it.

Despite these working conditions I did not think of quitting the job. I had worked very hard to get it. What options did I have? There was no other work. If you came from a well-to-do family, why would you go out to do all this? Fellow workers used to say, 'Endure it for three years. Then you'll become permanent. You'll get used to the work. Just think of the handsome salary you'll get.' It was true too. We used to get the appointment letter on the day we joined as trainees. They had to be confirmed after three years. Then you got a good salary and some other facilities too. Insurance cards were given as soon as we became trainees. I got it too. But that covered treatment only if we were admitted in the hospital. My limit of medical expenses was fifty thousand a year.

The Manesar factory started in 2006 and I joined in 2007. At that time there were only trainees in it. It ran because of us. Some people from Japan had come to train us. Among local people there was no permanent worker. All the Japanese workers were from Suzuki Motor. All of them were put up in a good hotel. Some lived in a hostel. They were nice to us.

We had a language problem. We could not talk to each other properly, but we used to understand everything related to work.

Some Japanese worked on the assembly line, many in the paint shop. There may have been a hundred Japanese in the whole plant. They work so fast that we can't even imagine. Even after working for many years, we could not work at that speed. Their hands moved incredibly fast.

I think that despite this friendship, they used to be informers of the management. I myself noticed how sometimes, when I made a mistake or damaged some small part or broke it and threw it away, the management would get to know. The boss always knew. He used to ask me what happened and why. They demanded explanations. The question was: How did they know who did it? Who was giving this news to them? It seemed to me that the Japanese would go tell them. Whoever snooped for the management got rewards. They were given coupons to shop. The Japanese kept getting such coupons.

Apart from this, it was also necessary to make suggestions on how to improve production in the plant. It felt like it was compulsory to give two suggestions a week. Forms were kept there for the purpose. Suggestions had to be made about changes in the methods of work so that production could be faster, better. Sometimes a worker came up with very good suggestions, only for the manager to take credit for it, claiming that he had made the suggestion. That also happened.

There was no way to complain. It probably wouldn't have helped. We were trainees, so we could not be members of the union—not that there was a union at that time. We had a manager called P.K. Roy. He used to say, 'I have looked through everyone's mouth. No one has teeth in their mouth!'

This was true at that time too, in the beginning when we were just trainees. We heard such taunts occasionally.

When the process of confirmation started, we suddenly got the membership of the union. Thanks to the management!

What happened in Manesar was that when the letter of confirmation was received, a form for union membership was also given to us. Along with that, a fee of ten rupees towards union membership was deducted from the salary. But that was the *jebi* union,* not a real union.

Many permanent workers lived in the same area in which we lived. Some were from our own factory, some were from Honda, some from the vendor companies. We heard of the AITUC† from them and we began to think that once we have an AITUC union all will be fine with us.

In those days Honda had a militant union in Gurgaon. It was associated with AITUC. We were very impressed by that union. We used to think that AITUC was a big thing. We thought that AITUC was very powerful, that the management was afraid of it. Joining a union affiliated to AITUC was akin to acquiring or building an army of our own. We used to think that, just like the defence forces of the country protect us, the AITUC union will protect us. Our voices would be heard.

Some of us got together and started thinking of forming a union. A separate union that would raise our issues and work in our interest. For a while we only talked and did nothing to form the union. Then we decided, come what may, we will definitely form one. We named it Maruti Suzuki Employees Union. We tried but we could not get it registered. Then we renamed it Maruti Suzuki Workers' Union.

---

* The workers call a trade union which is essentially a stooge of the management a pocket, or 'jebi', union because it is *in the pocket* of the management.

† AITUC is the oldest trade union federation in India. It is associated with the Communist Party of India. According to provisional statistics from the Ministry of Labour, AITUC had a membership of 14.2 million in 2013. It was founded on 31 October 1920 with Lala Lajpat Rai as its first president.

All we were doing was asserting a right given to us by the Constitution of India and the labour laws. Then why did the management deny us this basic right?

The Constitution of India, international labour standards and Indian labour laws recognize the right of workers to collectively bargain for their rights. This was the right that the workers at Manesar were trying to exercise, and this was the right they were being denied.

This book tells the story of how it came to pass that Indian citizens, working in the most modern automobile factory in independent India, could be arbitrarily thrown out of their jobs, framed in false criminal cases and sentenced to life imprisonment without a fair trial.

Two

The Inevitable Privatization of Maruti Udyog

When you buy a brand new car it smells good, but drive it off the lot and it drops in value by 30 per cent... Nothing you will do in your lifetime, realistically, will waste more money than buying a new car. It's the single worst financial decision millennials will ever make.

—David Bach, bestselling financial author

The Indian freedom movement against colonial rule emphasized the need for self-reliance and self-sufficiency, and India promised to build a socialist and democratic country for the people. That was the reason why in the early days after Independence, dependence on consumer goods was discouraged. At that time owning a car was not thought to be a necessity, but a luxury. At a price of Rs 12,000 for the Hindustan Ambassador (Rs 11,554 plus taxes), the car represented forty years of an average Indian's salary then!

The year 1951 was a landmark for the industry, when the Industries (Development and Regulation) (IDRA) Act was enacted. The Act required an entrepreneur to get a licence to set up a new unit, to expand it, or to change the product mix.

In 1954, there were sixty-odd models of cars, mostly imported, selling in a market which barely aggregated 20,000 sales per year. The import of automobiles and their components was a serious drain on foreign exchange. The government imposed high import tariffs on automobiles and components to support the indigenous automobile industry. Consequently, General Motors and Ford stopped their assembly operations that year.

The government set up a committee in April 1959 under L.K. Jha, an additional secretary in the commerce ministry, to look into the possibility of making a 'low cost' people's car for Rs 5,000–7,000, after soliciting proposals from both Indian and foreign manufacture.

The Jha Committee concluded that it would be possible to make an inexpensive 'people's car' at a target price of around Rs 5,000 to Rs 6,000 (the equivalent of Rs 1.8 lakh in current value)—this was about half the prevailing price of cars then—and that the demand for such a car could well be over 10,000 units per year.

The Jha Committee submitted its report in February 1960. While it said that, yes, a small car was feasible, it did not recommend a particular model. It did state, however, (and rather vaguely) that the small car should be 'roomy', 'sturdy' and 'capable of carrying an average Indian family'.

The conclusions of the Jha Committee had the Indian government enthused enough for the then minister of industry to announce in Parliament that 'we will have the people's car, of the people, manufactured by the people, for the people of this country'.

In 1975, the Planning Commission stated: 'The profit motive and exploitation of workers for private gain have no significance in State-owned enterprises. The undertakings have no doubt to show the same, if not greater, efficiency of working as private-owned undertakings. They have also to show profits...

[but] the profits which these undertakings make are not profits intended for any individual or group of individuals, but are extra wealth for the whole country."*

However, all these lofty ideas and Constitutional promises were undermined when Indira Gandhi declared a national emergency in 1975 and India witnessed countrywide human rights violations, with her younger son being directly responsible for violations under a horrific population control programme.

For the purpose of our book, we will focus only on her son's project of making a 'people's car'.

The Beginning

Sanjay Gandhi (1946–1980), the younger son of Indira Gandhi and grandson of Nehru, gave a proposal in 1970 for an entirely indigenized two-door model for a car powered with a 552cc engine. The next year Prime Minister Indira Gandhi's cabinet proposed the production of a 'people's car', a vehicle which had to be cheap, affordable, efficient, and more importantly, indigenous. Remember the last word.

So, a company by the name of Maruti Motors Limited was incorporated in June 1971 with Sanjay Gandhi as the first managing director. Sanjay Gandhi had no previous experience of manufacturing automobiles, yet he was awarded the license to manufacture India's first indigenously built people's car. Land was duly allocated for the factory in the Gurgaon district of Haryana.

---

* Quoted in the speech given by Chandrajit Yadav, Minister of Steel and Mines on 24 May 1975, Institute of Development Studies, Mysore.

Why Haryana?

Bansi Lal Legha (1927–2006), was a former chief minister of Haryana, former defence minister of India, and the architect of modern Haryana.

Lal served three separate terms as chief minister of Haryana: 1968–75, 1986–87, and 1996–99. Bansi Lal was a close confidante of former Prime Minister Indira Gandhi and her son Sanjay Gandhi during the Emergency era of 1975–77. It was Bansi Lal who brought the Maruti car project to Haryana, where he provided over 297.3 acres of land for the Maruti factory in the district of Gurgaon, of which 157 acres belonged to the Ministry of Defence, and 140 acres were highly fertile and populated land that belonged to local farmers. Some 15,000 farmers were evicted for it. He also provided Maruti a government loan to cover the costs of this purchase.

Thus, Bansi Lal laid the foundation for the development of corporate India. By 2011, the Gurgaon-Manesar-Bawal belt would be declared an auto hub.

Gurgaon, or Gurugram as it is now called, is a city developed by the corporations and not the government. Haryana is one of the most industrialized states in India with 34 per cent of the GSDP coming from industries.

Delhi Land & Finance (DLF Limited) is a commercial real estate developer founded in 1946. One of India's largest real estate developers, DLF builds residential, office and retail properties. It has developed residential colonies in Delhi such as Model Town, Rajouri Garden, Krishna Nagar, South Extension, Greater Kailash, Kailash Colony and Hauz Khas.

But in 1957 the Delhi Development Act was passed. The local government assumed control of real estate development in Delhi and banned private real estate developers. As a result,

DLF began acquiring land at relatively low cost in Gurgaon. It was instrumental in the creation of this modern city. Around 1995, it built the first large office space for General Electric. It went on to build gated colonies, luxury shopping malls and high-rise buildings there. Ravindra Chandra Bhargava, the former CEO of Maruti Suzuki, describes Gurgaon as the 'epitome of new India'.

Large corporates thus got cheap land from the villages all around. Instead of waiting for the Haryana Urban Development Authority (HUDA) to set up the services they needed, the multinational companies improvised, bringing in private builders to pave roads and drill borewells, and buying privately owned backup diesel generators. Private companies, they felt, would do the job faster and better than the government could.

Maruti Factory

The first factory for Maruti came up in Gurgaon after Sanjay Gandhi's death. Sanjay Gandhi did not manage to make a single car. There were serious allegations against him and his company of abuse of public policy irregularities in land allocation and money laundering. The company went into liquidation in 1978.

The land scam was not the only scam that the Maruti project was mired in. After the Emergency was lifted and Indira Gandhi held elections, she was defeated and the Janata Party came to power.

The Janata government set up a commission of enquiry to enquire into the working of the Maruti company. Justice Alok Chandra Gupta, who headed the commission, investigated into Maruti from 16 December 1977 to February 1979, and the report of his findings was officially submitted on 31 May the same year. *India Today* too carried a report in its issue of 30 September 1979 on the findings of the commission.

In its 471-page report, the Maruti Commission documented in all its sordid details the story of Sanjay Gandhi's dream of building an automobile empire gone awry.

Justice Gupta concluded: 'The affairs of the Maruti concern appear to have brought about a decline in the integrity of public life and sullied the purity of public administration.'

Workers too had been recruited for the factory but there was little work as Sanjay Gandhi did not have the technical know-how to make a car. The workers began to demand the nationalization of the factory for irregular payments of wages and want of job security. Workers once gheraoed Sanjay Gandhi. He was let go on the condition that he would never come back. He never did visit the factory again. (Bhargava 2013, p. 24)

In 1980, the Congress was elected to power again but Sanjay Gandhi died soon after when the glider he was flying crashed. Indira Gandhi nationalized the assets of Maruti Motors Ltd and incorporated it as Maruti Udyog Limited, in a joint venture with Suzuki Motor Corp as minor partner, on 24 January 1981 to realize her son Sanjay's dream of manufacturing a small car.

When Maruti was nationalized, Indira Gandhi asked V. Krishnamurthy to take over the project. Krishnamurthy wrote in his memoir that 'allegations were flying thick and fast at the time that the nationalization was a cover for the Gandhi family and for the original shareholders to get their money out of the company'.

Krishnamurthy had been given the humongous task of building a new company with a capacity to produce 100,000 passenger cars a year and 40,000 light commercial vehicles a year. He writes that the project was seen as being born in sin. Maruti had such a negative image that 'my wife stopped socializing, except when it was absolutely unavoidable, because she was hesitant to face remarks about my wisdom or lack thereof in accepting the assignment'.

He writes: 'In the initial stages, when we faced innumerable obstacles, which I thought were beyond human endeavour, in the execution of the project, I realized divine dispensation was required. Besides organizing multi-religious *poojas*, I publicly announced that the first car would be offered for the services of the Lord at Tirupati. Realizing that none of us had the authority to donate company property, I requested those of the believers amongst the employees, vendors and dealers to contribute towards the price of the car.'

The licence agreement on the transfer of technology between Maruti and Suzuki and the joint venture agreement between the government and Suzuki were signed on 2 October 1982. There was much to celebrate for Suzuki. R.C. Bhargava says in *The Maruti Story* that despite being a dry day, being Mahatma Gandhi's birth anniversary, a suite was booked in the Ashok Hotel and champagne bottles were procured and uncorked.

In an elaborate ceremony held in New Delhi on 14 December 1983, Prime Minister Indira Gandhi handed over keys of the first car commercially produced to Mr Harpal Singh, an employee in the Indian Airlines, who won the ownership rights through a lucky draw. The first car produced had, of course, already been donated to Lord Balaji at the Tirupati temple!

The first model produced was the Maruti Suzuki 800. It was a small city car that was manufactured by Maruti Suzuki in India from 1983 to 2014. The first generation (SS80) was based on the 1979 Suzuki Alto and had an 800cc F8B engine, hence the moniker.

The success of the joint venture led Suzuki to increase its equity from 26 to 40 per cent in 1987, and to 50 per cent in 1992, and further to 56.21 per cent as of 2013. When the Atal

Bihari Vajpayee government decided to relinquish control of Maruti Suzuki in 2002, the firm was valued at Rs 4,339 crore.

In 2003, Maruti Udyog Ltd was sold to Suzuki, and became known as Maruti Suzuki India Ltd, a subsidiary of Suzuki Motor Corporation, Japan. The Gujarat plant which opened in 2017 is wholly owned by Suzuki, a foreign company.

While Suzuki made more and more profits, the workers experienced a steady deterioration in their conditions of work as the factory got privatized and Suzuki increased the level of automation. The number of robots grew and so did the dehumanization of the production process. Workers complained of the working conditions. Most of these workers did not know that the Japanese have a word for a phenomenon that distinguishes Japanese work culture: *karoshi* (過労死). This word means 'death from overwork'.

Interviews with the older workers show that, despite the scams and irregularities that sullied the name of the original company, the permanent workers who worked in the Maruti factory during the time it was a public sector enterprise were on the whole happy with their working conditions.

When it began, the Maruti company had a decisive impact on the lifestyles of the workers. As a public sector company, it paid workers handsome salaries, and their children began to attend good private schools. A job in Maruti became the highest position a worker could aspire to; landing a job in the factory became the prime ambition of first-generation skilled workers of Haryana. One of the older workers whom we interviewed said: 'You know, my wife told me that she used to pray that she should get married to a worker in Maruti.'

All this began to change as the shares of Suzuki in the joint venture went up, as Maruti ceased to be a public sector company and came under the total control of Japanese management.

Mangeram Jatav (name changed)

An old worker who started working when Maruti was a public sector enterprise; he remains loyal to the company. Interviewed in his relative's home in Gurgaon on 12 June 2020.

I am a Dalit, a member of the Scheduled Caste. I belong to the Jatav community and to a landless family.

My father used to work in Rewari as a labourer. We belong to Kotkasim, a village in Rewari. Then he got a job in the Municipal Corporation of Delhi. He did not like the work so he quit and became a *raj mistri* [mason].

I did not want to be a worker. I had passed my twelfth with commerce and maths as my subjects. I enrolled in a graduate course and did my BA too through correspondence with history and political science as my subjects.

But I joined the ITI in Palwal because I thought that if I didn't get any other job I would at least have acquired a skill and would have another option for earning a livelihood. I opted for welding because two of my friends had also joined the same course. There are many kinds of welding—arc welding, metal welding, inert gas welding. The ITI taught us just the theory and that was all. We did not have practical experience at all.

Two men from my village had been working for Maruti since 1984. They made good money. After passing my tenth standard I had applied for a job in Delhi Police and I had even been selected. They had a pay scale of Rs 950 as the basic salary. I would have got a total salary of 3,000 or 3,500 there. I did not join the police. At the time Maruti had a scale of 1,200 a month. That was so much better. Workers got 6,000 rupees a month. It was about double of what I could make as a policeman.

I went for the test for Maruti in 1994. It was then a factory of the Government of India and the test was in the Khel Gaon stadium. I think more than four thousand took the test. We were tested on our knowledge of maths, general knowledge and science. I was one of the 800 they selected.

I became an apprentice in Maruti. They placed 400 in the first batch and another 400 in the second batch. I was in the second batch.

Maruti has a centre to train apprentices. It is called Maruti Suzuki Training Academy or MSTA. It was established in 2012. I have also been there for additional training. I also learnt typewriting. I was acquiring all these skills only to get a job later in life. I saw my first computer in Maruti. Those days there were not so many computers in the country. Now you can find them in every house.

I was stunned by the factory. I had never seen anything like it. This training was for three weeks, and I used to get only Rs 480 as a stipend. I also got extra allowances for night duty and to wash my uniform. I used to make a total of 800 or 900 a month in 1994. I felt happy. I watched videos of welding work. I saw all the safety precautions they took for welding work.

The assembly line and welding shops worked in two shifts. Those days the 'A' shift, or morning shift, began at 7.30 am and ended at four in the afternoon. The second, or 'B' shift, worked from 4 pm to 12.30 am. They mostly made Maruti 800 those days. It had a very large market.

They also made Omni and Gypsy but their lines were still not fully functional so their production was limited.

The car arrives in the welding shop from the press shop. In the press shop they cut the sheets of steel into cars and send it onwards to the welding shop. I was on the Maruti 800 line and there were some four robots there. It was the first time I had seen robots and they were gigantic.

The robots were cordoned off, their area of work was separated from ours so that we did not get in their way and injure ourselves. I found it quite normal that they picked up huge sheets and cut out the bodies of cars. We worked in the same shed where they worked. After a point we stopped noticing them. Now the factory has many, many robots, but those days we were the privileged ones who had seen and worked alongside [a robot].

I started working in December 1994 and was an apprentice till 1995 and after that they gave me a break. After a while they called me back and sent me to LWC. It is short for Learning, Working in Company or some such thing—I have forgotten. For nine months I worked there. This LWC is not counted in the service period. Those days apprentices and workers in LWC got twelve leaves and we got an off on all the gazetted holidays. If you took leave over and above these allowed to you, money was deducted from your salary. Also, the period of learning is extended accordingly.

We got half the salary of whatever the permanent workers got. I used to get Rs 4,000 a month. At the end of nine months we were made to take another test. I passed and I became a permanent worker. I began to bring Rs 8,000 home every month. I got other perks too. EPF, medical insurance.

I used to live in Dakshinpuri in Delhi those days. I used to go to work in the company bus and come back in the company bus. Early in the morning at 6.30 I would leave home to get to Khanpur from where the company bus fetched us. The bus dropped us at the main gate and I had to walk a kilometre inside to reach my work station. We then had to wear our gloves, don our helmets and be ready and at the work station a minute before work started. We used to have a card that we inserted in a slot at the main gate to mark our presence. Now they have a biometric system.

Now a lot of things have changed. Even the shift timings have changed. Now the morning shift begins at 6.30 and works till 3 pm and the second shift begins then.

I will retire at the age of fifty-eight which is what the government rules decided then. All those government rules apply to me. And people like me who were employed when the factory was in the government sector.

I am a member of the Maruti Udyog Kamgar Union or MUKU. Earlier, we used to have a separate SC Association but after the company became private this Association was dissolved.

As a Dalit, I noticed that there was hardly any discrimination in the work itself but our Indians still have the old mindset. The Japanese never discriminated between workers of different castes. I did work with some. They were very nice.

Those days, when I joined, and the company was a government company, Maruti also had reservations. I don't know if they have any such provision now. And how will I know? They have not employed new workers in a long while now. Those days it was compulsory to employ a certain percentage of Scheduled Castes and Scheduled Tribes and they did.

While nobody abuses you with casteist abuses there are other forms of casteism that prevail in the factory. Like the boss will not give you the same kind of good annual confidential report that he will give to upper castes. The way they put it, you cannot really pin it on casteism, but as a Dalit I know. However hard you work you are not considered as good as the others. They will find some flaw or deficiency to put in the reports. It affects promotion.

Right now the numbers of Dalits in the company is quite good. The union president is also a Dalit. When the union elections are held factions along caste lines emerge. But that happens everywhere. Overall, it is a nice place and the work atmosphere is good. I am still working in Maruti but in the Gurgaon factory.

I am now at L11, that is eleventh level. Every three or four years we get promoted in accordance with government rules. I was actually being promoted to the supervisor level but I refused. I do not want to become part of the management. Work at that level means too much stress. You have to bring the work home, think of the target and how to meet it all the time. I don't want to do it.

I like my work. I am happy where I am. For a long time I was on the assembly line. Then I got transferred to office work. I am in layout now. I have to check quality. It is part of quality control. We have some set standards and every product must meet at least 95 per cent of those standards. Reports are made on the computers. That is what I do. I work in an air-conditioned office, away from the hustle and bustle of the assembly line. When you go up to higher levels your salaries go up. Supervisor is a post, not a rank, so even though I refused to be one I draw the salary of the same level. If I had become a supervisor the colour of my helmet would have changed. From the colour of the helmet you can figure out who is what. A worker wears a yellow helmet, supervisors wear blue, managers have a white helmet and safety personnel wear green helmets.

My salary is good. Every year I get Rs 15,000 for treatment in OPD. I get coupons for Rs 800 once a year to take my children to a restaurant. I get allowances for my children's education. I have worked really hard to get where I am. For about some years in the beginning I got Rs 20,000 to 25,000 a month. For nine years now I earn a lakh a month. I have a car. I own my house. I am happy. Maruti has given me a lot. In fact, whatever I have is because I work in Maruti. It has given me a lot.

Ramesh Dalal

He is older than Mangeram, but unlike him, active in the union supported by the All India Trade Union Congress (AITUC). He was forced to take voluntary retirement under a voluntary retirement scheme (VRS) brought in by the management. Interviewed in his home in Neelkanth Colony, Sohna Road, Gurgaon in the first week of March 2020.

Dalals are a *gotra* among Jats. I come from Ghuskani village in Bhiwani district. I belong to a landed family. We are three brothers and five sisters. Ours is a family of farmers and I did farming, too.

Nobody in my family was educated. My father had passed the fifth standard. My grandfather was in the army. I wanted to join the army too and was preparing for it but I could not get recruited because I could never pass the maths test.

So after passing out from school I joined the Meham ITI and enrolled in a course of a fitter. This was in 1983. All the while I kept trying to get into the army.

A fitter is like an 'all in one' course. If you are a fitter you know almost everything. Every assembly needs a fitter. Fitters don't do die-casting, but they maintain dies. They do almost everything else too. There were twenty-one or twenty-two students in my batch and of them five or six joined Maruti.

It was a two-year course. We learnt theory and we had practicals too. The Meham ITI was a good industrial training institute. I worked for a rolling mill where they made steel from iron. I used to get 240 rupees a month. This was a stipend and this was given by the government. Every ITI student has to work as an apprentice in a factory for a year and gets this stipend. You do not get the diploma without the apprenticeship. The stipend was given by the National Council for Vocational Training.

I passed out in 1985. By that time Maruti Gurgaon had begun production and they were looking for trained workers. Those days the engine of the Maruti car used to be brought from Japan. Some major parts too were imported from Japan.

It so happened that about a month before my apprenticeship was over Maruti people came to our ITI to recruit workers. They told us that soon they would hold tests. They then held the test in the PHD House, a venue for meetings here in Delhi. Our whole batch took the test. I had not even heard of Maruti. I had no idea what it was. About three months before that I had heard that something called Maruti had come up as a new factory but that is all I knew.

I passed the test. Then I passed in the interview too. On 13 August 1986 I joined the Maruti factory as an apprentice. Now, I was someone who had never even sat in a car. Those days there were not so many cars. When someone got married, they rented one if they had money.

The first day I went to the factory I was astounded. I had never seen such a huge factory. Where could I have seen it? My jaw dropped. There was probably only one robot then and it worked in the press shop. I had never seen such machines.

The human resource department was on the mezzanine, meaning neither the first floor nor the second floor—somewhere in between. It had glass all around it and you could see the whole plant from there. I was stunned to see such a factory.

It did not scare me though. I did not get the feeling that I couldn't work there. Jats are never scared of anything. They have a lot of confidence. Especially the son of a landed Jat is never afraid of anything, not even ghosts. We go out into the fields to irrigate them at night and we face all kinds of danger. The factory did not scare me, but I was endlessly amazed. For a long time my amazement knew no bounds.

Gradually, I learnt the job. I had been made an apprentice for a year. By that time the Japanese had stopped training us. Locals taught me everything. When I went to the factory they sent me straight to the assembly line. The workload was heavy and it was also difficult work. I did not find it too difficult. Farm work is tougher. In farms you have to work in all kinds of weather—in the blazing summers, during rains and in bitterly cold nights too. Comparatively speaking, this was easier work. My stipend was Rs 480 a month.

I had a distant relative in Gurgaon so I stayed with them for three days before I could find a room to rent in Dundahera. It is not far from the factory. Actually, it is one of those villages whose land had been acquired for the factory. I and a classmate got together to rent the room. We paid Rs 60 as monthly rent. We used to walk to the factory and back. It was a fifteen-minute walk.

Every week our shift changed. We would work the 'A' shift for a week, the 'B' shift the next week. There were only two shifts. Three assembly lines were then in operation: one for Maruti 800, one for the Omni and one for the Gypsy. I was on the Omni line.

It took me about twenty days to get used to their speed of work. We used to get to the factory early in the morning and even those who cycled or came by cars were made to park outside. Nobody could take the vehicle inside the premises of the factory. From there we would go to the department we were attached to. We had to walk. Those lucky to have their work station or department close to the gate could arrive a bit later but those who had to walk a long distance inside to report for duty had to arrive earlier. I was lucky. My department was close to the gate. At the gate of the department the cards of each worker hung in a line and we had to look for our cards, pick them up and insert them in a machine slot. It would make a round inside and pop back out. That was called punching. Nowadays you have to use your thumb. Press the thumb on a biometric machine. Those days we punched cards, manually. Then we entered and the first thing we did was PT or physical training. For five minutes. For that we used to go to the exercise area. Then we would go to the work area.

In the work area each of us had a locker, a set of clothes, our uniform, and a glass, all of which we stored in the locker. So I would open the locker, take out the uniform, get dressed and then wear gloves. Every day we got fresh gloves. New ones. A supervisor would be standing there to see that we wore everything properly and looked neat and trim. We had to do all this and stand at the work station at least a minute before 7.30 am for the 'A' shift. At exactly 7.30 am the line would start moving. Delays were not tolerated. Nowadays there is greater strictness but even in those days the work began punctually.

Supervisors explained the day's work to us. I had to work two stations, suspension and tie-rod. The car would keep moving and I had to go on fitting these things into it. It was hard work. The car emerged from the paint shop and kept moving on the assembly line. When it moved up I had to work in its underbody. Axle, radiator, engine—everything is fitted from the underbody side. The car is above you and you are fitting stuff in it. I have fitted everything in a car. I learnt everything; I could do everything. From the trim to the final stages, I have done all the work over the years. Trim means when it comes from the trim line—an empty body. In the final stage when it leaves it is a full car with everything inside it.

Those days we were young. We had no problems staying up at night, working all day. We did not feel tired.

I used to enjoy it. The work atmosphere was very nice. Till Bhargava remained MD the atmosphere was very amiable. He used to think of the worker. When he came to the canteen he ate what everyone else ate. He also got Maruti Vihar built. He had the welfare of workers at heart. My seniors live in Maruti Vihar. Later, Maruti Kunj was also built.

Till the time Maruti Udyog Ltd was a public sector enterprise, all rules applicable to the public sector were applicable to Maruti too. Salary structures, pay scales, allowances and other perks for all employees from the shop floor level to top management, all were fixed.

Despite this the workers' union had to fight to get some of the amenities they were entitled to under the law. This included the right to housing. In the initial stage Maruti had made no provisions for housing. And no money was earmarked for it.

Mathew Abraham, who became the general secretary of the Maruti Udyog Employers Union (MUEU)* after he won the union elections in 1988 raised the issue of housing. After prolonged negotiations, the management finally proposed a new kind of scheme for workers' housing. Under this scheme, flats were to be constructed for workers who would buy them and become owners instead of only living in them during the period of employment. This was a new experiment.

The workers were told that at the time of retirement, instead of vacating the house the company allotted them, they would own their house and would not have to worry about making alternate arrangements. After the workers agreed to the proposal the union had to consent to it.

---

* The MUEU was the only registered union functioning in the company, initially as an ad hoc body, since 1984 and the office bearers were elected democratically every two years. It had a hundred per cent membership of the workforce of Maruti Udyog Ltd.

How much money the company saved on housing for workers through this scheme, since the workers were paying for their housing from their salaries, is well worth studying. It is also true that those who bought the first flats built in Maruti Vihar gained financially from the rising prices of land and real estate in Gurgaon and a number of them had something to fall back on when they were sacked later.

This first colony of Maruti employees came up in Chakkarpur village in Gurgaon district. Workers were encouraged to buy flats and for that the company provided them loans on low interests.

This model of housing was easy to implement when the prices of land were relatively low and the government of Haryana was willing to oblige with acquisition and allotment of land for its pride, the Maruti factory, in the initial years.

When the time for the construction of the second such residential colony came the government threw up its hands and asked the management to buy land at market price. The company eventually bought a piece of land in Badshahpur where Maruti Kunj came up as a cooperative group housing society. It is very far from the factory in Gurgaon unlike Chakkarpur. The workers of Maruti Kunj complain of many irregularities and not having freehold possession of their flats.

At present, Maruti is building a third residential colony in Dharuhera in which anyone can buy a flat from management personnel to workers.

Ramesh Dalal continues...

I had also bought a flat in Maruti Kunj. This may have been in 1992. They were booked then and in 1995 we got possession. We were given an option of one-, two- or three-bedroom flats and it wasn't as if only managers could buy the three-bedroom ones, anyone could. The price of course would be different for different sizes of flats. If you could pay you bought the bigger flat. It is true that very few managers bought flats in Maruti Kunj. It was very far from the factory. I think the one-bedroom flat was for two lakhs and the three-bedroom ones were for five lakhs each.

I became a permanent worker and my salary became Rs 1,250 a month. That was my total salary. It was not a bad wage for those days.

When I became permanent I also became a member of the union affiliated to the INTUC [Indian National Trade Union Congress]; it was supported by the Congress party. I had no idea what a union meant or anything about them. I knew some people in INTUC so I joined that union.

Those days there were two unions: one was affiliated to the INTUC and the other with HMS [Hind Mazdoor Sabha]. K.K. Datta was the leader of the INTUC-affiliated union and Sombir Singh led the HMS union.

The union used to negotiate with the management and arrive at a settlement on wages, DA and other such things. Earlier, the HMS union did such negotiations; then the INTUC began to do it.

The two existing unions were always at loggerheads and quarrels broke out very frequently. The management did not like it at all. Both the unions were political, affiliated to some political party, and they kept fighting. And the management wanted a union that wasn't connected to any political party other than the ruling Congress party.

After a while some people formed a separate union which was not affiliated to any outside body. This was an independent union. It was the Maruti Udyog Employees Union or MUEU.

I also joined it. Only when there would be a nationwide strike we would put down our tools. We did not have protests or demonstrations around our local issues in those days.

Every day we had a tea break of seven and half minutes at 9 am. In that period you had to have your tea, snacks, use the toilet, smoke your *beedis*. You had to go to the locker, open it, take out your glass, take your tea, and by the time the break was over, you had to wash and lock up your glass, wear your gloves and be back at the work station. The eatables they served with tea used to be very tasty—*samosas*, jam sandwiches, bread *pakoras*, bread and butter...different things on different days.

We used to arrive at work so early that by the first tea break we would be ravenous but there was hardly any time to enjoy them. The second tea break used to be in the afternoon but then they only gave us biscuits with tea.

Even our lunch break used to be of only half an hour. In that limited time, we had to use the washroom, run to the canteen, stand in the queue, quickly gobble the food and also smoke and then get back to wear our gloves and be ready to work. Those days we also got only four *rotis*. Nowadays there is a buffet. You can eat whatever you want and however much. Back then they handed us limited quantities of food. The canteen was small. I must say that everyone got the same food. Sometimes we would even spot Bhargava eating there. He ate the same food.

Also everybody wore the same uniform. I used to like this culture. It was like a big joint family and Bhargava was our head of the family.

The uniform of Maruti commanded great respect those days. People in the market recognized the uniform and treated us with respect. It was a great feeling.

You can't imagine how clean our workplace used to be, so

spick and span. The clothes we wore to work never got dirty. Only our gloves got dirty but they were changed every day.

We worked with great concentration.

Our first strike took place in the year 2000. The government had started privatizing the enterprise. In other words, selling off the factory to the Japanese. The central government privatized Maruti in 2002 and Suzuki became the majority owner of Maruti Udyog Limited.

A.K. Sharma

He is one of the older workers dismissed after he became active in the Maruti Udyog Employees Union, which was close to the AITUC, though not formally affiliated to it. He has a flat in Maruti Kunj. Interviewed on 8 February 2020.

I was stupid enough to have quit a job in Uptron, which was a Central Electronics Ltd venture, to join Maruti in January 1985 because there was some slight difference in the basic pay. It was higher in Maruti. That was a mistake. The work in Maruti was so hard that I could not even turn my head. It felt like someone had tied a band around my head and held it in place. I was only twenty-four, had moved from Ghaziabad to Gurgaon and was regretting my decision. But what choice did I have?

I had attended the Pusa ITI and had never been told that I would have to work like this.

I soon joined the union in 1985. Then there was only one union, affiliated to INTUC and led by K.K. Datta. He had come from Bharat Heavy Electricals Ltd or BHEL (a public sector enterprise) along with other BHEL officials and was close to them. They hardly did anything for workers.

Soon, I began to realize that the workers were more scared of the union than of the management. If a management personnel noticed some fault he would choose to ignore it sometimes and correct the worker in a kind manner but the union was unforgiving. It harassed workers no end to prove, I think, that it could discipline workers. By the end of the year workers were furious and in January 1986 workers began raising slogans against the union. Buses that brought workers to the factory used to enter the outer perimeter and offload workers there. Workers would stand there and raise slogans of *murdabad* ['down with'] against the union. We also had silent protests on some days.

The management was in a fix. It did not want any other union. They offered to set up a joint management committee of workers and management. I was then Process & Quality Control Inspector. I was elected unopposed. This JMC had some twenty members. Each shop had two representatives of workers. And every department of the management also had representatives in it like HR, Production, Manufacture and Administration. It used to have monthly meetings. We used to raise issues of workers in those meetings.

Those days the canteen served only two *rotis* to workers. Imagine, after such hard work, you could not get to eat as much as you needed. The contractor of the canteen was perhaps given some limited amount of money and they would keep our plates ready with limited portions of food. We raised this issue and got things improved but it took a long time for the buffet system to be established which is what they have now.

Soon, the management realized that they could not co-opt us. They were in a quandary. They did not want to offend the ruling Congress party and INTUC so they wouldn't recognize the HMS-affiliated union that had gained a lot of support. They even dismissed the HMS union's elected president and general secretary. Those days the management used to be diplomatic and generally well behaved, and when we raised the issue of these dismissals in the JMC, after some resistance, the two were taken back. By that time it was clear that workers did not like K.K. Datta and the INTUC hardly had any support.

From 1986 we started thinking of forming a new and independent union. Mathew Abraham will have greater knowledge of how the union got registered. In the beginning the management did not allow us to register it. However, after Mathew became the leader things changed a lot.

Mathew stood for elections for the HMS union and in the 1986 elections he was chosen president; Sombir Singh became the general secretary. But there were strong differences between us and the HMS so Mathew and other leaders decided to fight for our own independent union.

In 1989, elections were held again. This time we had our own union, the Maruti Udyog Employees Union. I became an executive member of the Maruti Udyog Employees Union or the MUEU from 1989 onwards. After that we had elections every two years.

We fought long and hard to get the new union registered. You should know that even a registered union, recognized by the Ministry of Labour, is not automatically recognized by the company management; the recognition of the union is not obligatory. It all depends on the sweet will of the management.

In 1998, we had a wage revision settlement too. I was in the wage revision committee in 1998 and we had prepared a presentation on the basis on which our wages should be revised and by how much. It was such a good presentation and made on such solid basis that the economist who had been brought in by the management was also impressed and he was surprised that we, the workers, could prepare such well-argued presentations.

That was the time when Inder Kumar Gujral was the prime minister. Bhaskarudu was our MD. Mr Suzuki disliked Bhaskarudu. I will tell you just how the Japanese used to insult him all the time. He was a technocrat. He understood technology and technical matters well and he was a staunch nationalist. He was insisting that Suzuki transfer the gear box technology to Maruti which had been promised in the joint venture agreement. Suzuki kept postponing it on one ground or another. Suzuki used to send old dies from Japan, painted freshly to make them look new. Bhaskarudu could not be fooled. He used to object to this.*

Meanwhile, we had given a charter of demands and the management agreed to meet most of them. Our wages had a 52 per cent upward revision. This was fantastic. Of course, Suzuki did not like it.

Suzuki even went to the High Court against the appointment of Bhaskarudu but the government won the case.

When Suzuki sent letters to Bhaskarudu, they never addressed the letters to the MD but used only his name, as in, they would write 'Mr Bhaskarudu'.

V. Krishnamurthy, in his book, says that Suzuki gave a public statement saying the government's choice of S.S.L.N. Ravela Bhaskarudu as Bhargava's successor as managing director was not suitable. Suzuki took the government to court and international arbitral institutions to ensure that their man was made the CEO. Krishnamurthy says that he thought it was unbecoming of a Japanese partner to comment so harshly on

* Krishnamurthy (2014), says in his book that Bhaskarudu was clueless about technology and it was R.D. Deshpande, whom he had appointed, who would brief him.

someone who had been the director of production until the other day and had been nominated by the Government of India to the managing director's position.

In August 1999, the media reported that Bhaskarudu had decided to resign four months before his tenure was due to end. It was reported that Bhaskarudu's tenure as managing director was mired in controversy, with Suzuki Motor Corp expressing reservations over his appointment. However, the government wanted Bhaskarudu for the job and had appointed him despite opposition from Suzuki. One newspaper reported that in 'a fit of pique, Suzuki had halted the transfer of technology for new car models that hurt the car maker at a time when several companies entered the market with spanking new models.'*

The issue was resolved finally when the Bharatiya Janata Party led government reached a compromise with Suzuki and cut short Bhaskarudu's tenure as managing director and decided to appoint Jagdish Khattar to the post from 1 January 2000. Bhaskarudu resigned after an out-of-court settlement was reached between the government and Suzuki Motor Corp which signalled the end of this fractious relationship between the two equal partners in Maruti Udyog.

A.K. Sharma continues...

Whenever they had board meetings the directors of Suzuki would leave at exactly 6 pm even if the meeting continued and the MD was sitting there. These directors would leave the meeting before the MD to insult him.

---

* 'Bhaskarudu Resigns as Maruti MD', *The Telegraph*, 16 August 1999 (https://www.telegraphindia.com/business/bhaskarudu-resigns-as-maruti-md/cid/915315, last accessed 11 January 2023).

When the Vajpayee government was formed, Bhaskarudu was sacked and Jagdish Khattar was made MD.

I have seen what nationalism means. I am proud of having worked under Bhaskarudu. He was insisting on saving the country's foreign exchange reserves; he wanted us to learn and acquire new technology and make things in the country. Our union supported the government when he raised the issue of indigenization. He also supported us and was good to the workers.

Those days Gurudas Dasgupta and Indrajit Gupta of the CPI also were in our favour. They supported us and they also made sure that we got better wages. But our incentive scheme was a major issue of controversy then. Bhaskarudu couldn't do much about it either. It was to be revised and we were objecting to some of the clauses in the revised proposal.

When Khattar became MD we asked him to start negotiations on the revision of the incentive. He first said that he was new and needed time. Then after four months, when the union insisted, he began to raise the issue of allowances instead. The middle management was in our favour but the top management chose to side with Suzuki, and Khattar was on that side, on the side of the Japanese.

Mathew used to negotiate on our behalf and Khattar used to negotiate on behalf of the management. How we know all the details is that Mathew used to come back from the meetings and tell us everything in his speeches at the gate. He believed in keeping workers informed. He didn't want to cut a deal behind our backs and he paid a heavy price for it.

So what happened was that whenever the union wanted to talk about the incentive scheme, Khattar would insist on discussing allowances. These allowances were some perks attached to our salaries. Like House Rent Allowance. It had nothing to do with production and incentives but Khattar always raised this matter. He talked about reducing the HRA which used to be 30 per cent of our basic salary. That meant that we needed to first agree to a reduction in our wages, only then would he talk of incentives.

They probably asked the dealers too to go slow on selling cars so that they could show some losses. They wanted share prices to go down so Suzuki could buy more shares. There was propaganda in the media that the cars were not selling, that Maruti was making losses.*

It was an awful time. Our union was also playing it smart and adopted a calibrated strategy. We did everything to build pressure. We stopped eating in the canteen; it was a kind of hunger strike. Then we wore black badges and shouted slogans and then on 3 October the union started a tool-down strike for two hours in each shift.

We began our protest in by a go-slow, then we had a tool-down strike, and finally we sat on a relay hunger strike. Mathew and Dinesh Kumar, who was the union president, sat on a hunger strike. The police dragged them to prison. Several workers were dismissed.

The police began to visit our Maruti Kunj colony and terrorize the families of workers. This is a private colony but the police came in without our permission or invitation.

The company wanted us to sign a good conduct form. We refused. Then things came to a head. The company got an order from the High Court that we should stay 500 metres away from the gate of the company. We would then hold meetings in a public park. We had refused to sign the good conduct undertaking.

---

* This was also given as a reason for depriving the workers of incentives based on production.

Finally, we all went to Udyog Bhawan near India Gate and sat there in the freezing cold for three months. Nothing helped us.

All this for what? To save some money for Suzuki. That is the way some of our top managers went against our country's interest, and they got awards and honours here and in Japan too.

After the strike ended all the active members of the union were targeted. The management issued charge sheets to selected workers and then held no enquiry, keeping the worker on tenterhooks.

They used other tactics too. I think they wanted to reduce the permanent workforce and throw out the older workers and keep only the young and fit. So what they would do was to show a dismissal letter to a worker with the place for the name of the worker left blank and tell him it was meant for him. And then he would be scared. Sometimes they would charge a worker with not having fitted a part properly and haul him up and tell him that he was endangering people's lives on the road. How could he prove that he had not done anything of the sort?

I was thrown out. I knew I would be. Like Mathew. They charged me with threatening a manager. It was a false charge. That they had done even before we had gone on strike. I got the charge sheet on 12 August 2000. The enquiry was held on 29 May 2001. Mathew was terminated. I was terminated.

This Maruti Kunj is built on 101 acres that the company had bought for us. We set up a cooperative housing society and many of us are still paying our instalments. When they bought the land in 1989 the going rate here was 60,000 to 80,000 rupees an acre. Those days managers too were part of the cooperative society. Later, they withdrew. The industry ministry had not approved of the sale and it seems the *kisans* were paid less. They had shown that each and every *kisan* had been paid 3,80,000 an acre. It was quite a scam. R.C. Bhargava was MD at the time.*

It got into the media. And some officers were suspended too. That is another story. You know that the management built residential buildings here without getting the land use changed. It was illegal. Some office bearers of this society, who were workers like us, were also involved in the scam. We, the society, derecognized the president of the society.

More horrible things were done to us. The management became a guarantor and it took a loan of thirty-five crores from HDFC and also usurped the right to operate the accounts of the society, and those accounts were never audited. Many managers had cases against them.

They had the Delhi Public School here for our children. Bhargava boasted that his workers were sending their children to DPS. In the beginning it ran from the flats here. Then they got a building made and wanted us to contribute to it. Every year the school management would hold an annual function here and they told Mathew that workers should contribute money for holding the function, which used to be like a *mela* with games and competitions. Mathew said no. After the VRS we were no longer Maruti employees. Then the management of DPS said that we should contribute to the building fund. We protested because by then the building was ready. Why should we have been asked to contribute to something that was not even under construction? But we no longer had the same power and we were made to pay because our children were studying in the school. The annual functions stopped! Now

---

* For the dispute over the ownership of the land on which the Maruti Kunj is built, see the December 2022 press note put out by the Maruti Employees Co-operative Housing Building Society (Appendix 2).

we pay every year and we do not even have the fun and games we had once a year.

We have many, many stories to tell. We have suffered a lot. Some of us quit our jobs under the VRS and lost a lot of money towards the housing loan. Till then only five years of EMI had been paid, so a substantial sum was deducted from what they got [under the VRS settlement]. The EMI was to be paid in fifteen years. We paid in five because of the VRS, but we got no discounts; we did not have to pay less.

I had joined Maruti when our uniform in the market earned us respect and envy. Only regular workers used to have uniforms. Now even causals are given uniforms because the company wants to keep them happy. So they give money to contractors to give even casual workers uniforms. But the uniform has no respect now.

Maruti Udyog Ltd was slowly being taken over by Suzuki Motor Corp. But it dictated terms to the management even before it took over. There were disagreements between the different sections of management over the method of this privatization, the lack of technology transfer and the need for indigenization of components. But there was never any serious debate on the working conditions of the workers. Even those managers who seemed pro-worker were really just making a case for the union from the management's point of view. Sathya Narayanan, a former manager at Manesar who agreed to give an interview (produced later in the book), says that he thought Awanish Kumar Dev's apparent pro-worker stance was really a management ploy not a reflection of empathy for the workers.

In 1992, Suzuki was allowed, through a shareholder agreement, to raise its equity to 50 per cent following which

Maruti Udyog Ltd ceased to be a public sector enterprise. A decade later, MUL was privatized with the government selling the controlling interest to Suzuki. There is a story about the corruption in the disinvestment process but it does not belong to this book.

The privatization of the company was a brutal process by which a living human being was turned into a machine, denied his basic right to dignity and self-respect.

Jitendra Kumar

A dismissed worker, not among the accused in the 18 July 2012 case, who took to law to fight for worker's rights. Interviewed in the premises of Gurgaon courts on 26 February 2020.

You must have seen Chaplin's film, *Modern Times*. It was about us. Making a man a machine. They don't give you time even to eat or even to go to the toilet.

The health of many got compromised with that strict adherence to the clock. Like getting no time off in the middle of work to go to the toilet. Some people can stay without using the loo for long hours, some cannot. I've seen the men working with urine flowing down their trousers and making a puddle on the shop floor.

There was the case of a worker who passed blood in his urine. He took leave. Then at home he pissed blood again so we got an ambulance and took him to a hospital. The doctor told him not to keep holding back and urinate when he had the urge to. Unfortunately, he met with an accident soon after the incident and had to take a fortnight off. He was summarily dismissed. He was a trainee. We could do nothing for him. We felt awful.

The Japanese could not have introduced their work culture without the active help of the Indian managers, and they richly rewarded those Indians who were loyal to them. Their strongest ally in the entire enterprise was of course R.C. Bhargava. Bhargava has been felicitated innumerable times for the Maruti success. In his book and in his interviews he has credited the success to the Japanese, the Indian managers and himself. There is never any mention of the contribution of the workers who actually manufacture the cars.

In his interview to *Autocar India* on the occasion of seventy-five years of independence and the fortieth anniversary of Maruti, workers were not mentioned even in passing.

Bhargava sees the success from the point of view of rich consumers and export markets but never from the viewpoint of the dismissed workers, who have been thrown out of their jobs unfairly, some even sentenced to life imprisonment in false cases without the possibility of ever seeing justice done to them. This is a battle between people versus profits.

Three

Haryana's Automobile Hub

I am the man, the very fat man
That waters the workers' beer
I am the man, the very fat man
That waters the workers' beer
And what do I care if it makes them ill
If it makes them terribly queer
I've a car, a yacht, and an aeroplane,
And I waters the workers' beer.

—'The Man that Waters the Workers' Beer',
Paddy Ryan (1938)

Osamu Suzuki of Suzuki Motor Corporation had been so happy with his success, he committed that every yen Suzuki invested in India would be in Haryana. True to his word, all Suzuki investments were made in Haryana.

After the events of 18 July 2012, Suzuki did start a factory in Hansalpur in Gujarat, but they are back in Haryana, building another factory in Kharkhoda village in Sonipat district. One plant in the Sonipat factory is expected to have a capacity to manufacture 2,50,000 vehicles per annum by 2025.

Maruti Suzuki's existing facilities in Gurgaon and Manesar have a cumulative production capacity of fifteen lakh units per annum. It also has access to an additional 7.5 lakh units from the Gujarat facility of Suzuki Motor.

While the dismissed workers of the Manesar factory struggle to survive and make rounds of the labour courts in the hope of getting their jobs back, the Haryana Enterprise Promotion Board (HEPB), headed by Chief Minister M.L. Khattar, has allotted Suzuki 900 acres of land for the new enterprise. According to media reports, the company has been given an SGST (State goods and services tax) reimbursement for fifteen years by the government.

This is a part of the government's policy of encouraging transnational corporations to enter India. The justification for encouraging foreign investors, especially big corporations, to come into our country is that they bring much needed capital and help in the development of the country.

The central and State governments have provided all kinds of incentives to multinational corporations to improve the investment climate. These incentives basically boil down to ensuring that the corporations do not have to pay too many taxes and that the workers are not able to form trade unions so that 'industrial peace' is maintained.

Haryana has the most SEZs in the country, of which seven are operational and twenty-five have acquired formal approval according to a Ministry of Commerce and Industry notification dated 10 March 2021.* SEZs, or special economic zones, in effect mean corporate tax exemptions and a promise that the labour would be cheap and compliant. Labour laws do not apply in the SEZs. This is one of the attractions for the corporates that choose to invest in Haryana.

In 2011, Haryana's Gurgaon-Manesar-Bawal belt was declared an 'Auto Hub' to facilitate industrial progress in the

* See Ministry of Commerce and Industry press release shared by the Press Information Bureau (https://pib.gov.in/PressReleasePage.aspx?PRID=1703791, last accessed 11 January 2023).

automobile sector in the region. The belt, which is within seventy-five kilometres from the national capital, already has automobile plants of three auto giants—Maruti Suzuki, Hero MotoCorp and Suzuki Motorcycle.

The Indian automobile industry saw rapid growth since the early 2000s. The output of cars in India grew from 1.3 million to 4.1 million cars between 2001 and 2012, making India the world's sixth biggest car passenger and commercial vehicle producer. Maruti Udyog Limited (MUL) had a quasi-monopoly on the production of passenger cars until 1991. In that year, India liberalized its economy and allowed foreign companies to enter. With the opening of the market for passenger cars in the 1990s, Hyundai was the first foreign company to begin operating in the open market. It took up production in 1998. However, MUL continued to dominate the market with a 49 per cent market share in 2013, and 44 per cent in 2012. (Nowak 2016)

Haryana is in fact home to an increasing number of corporate offices of many Japanese companies. They include Nidec, Somemiya Holdings, Keihin, TDK, Terra Motors, MUFG, SMBC, SoftBank, Fast Retailing, Nitto Denko, Panasonic, Daikin, Toshiba, Hitachi, Suzuki, Honda, NEC, Toyota, Murata, Mitsui Chemicals and Rohto Pharmaceuticals, to name a few.

Having attracted investment running into millions of dollars from Japanese industry, the Haryana government has announced that it would set up a Japanese township in the State. A consortium of Japanese companies is involved in the building of Smart Communities or Eco-Cities along the Delhi–Mumbai Industrial Corridor (DMIC) region—the country's showpiece for a futuristic development model.

Despite the presence of so many manufacturing companies,

Haryana has been placed at number one for its unemployment rate. While 85.11 per cent are unemployed in the 20–24 age bracket, 36.07 per cent are unemployed in the 25–29 age group.

These figures were released as part of the report on unemployment rates for May–August 2021, by the Centre for Monitoring Indian Economy (CMIE), a leading business information company established in 1976 as an independent think tank. However, the chief minister, Manohar Lal Khattar, has refuted the CMIE report on unemployment on the floor of the House.

Automobile Production

In order to understand the grievances of the workers, and the problems of organizing trade unions within the Indian automobile industry, it is essential to understand the changes that have taken place in it.

Among the significant changes the industry has witnessed over the years is the structure of automobile production itself. In a 2018 study titled 'Changes in Production and Labour Regimes and Challenges before Collective Bargaining', Amit Chakraborty and Nayanjyoti explain how India's automobile production began with knock-down production, or a simple assembly of imported parts. The change from that structure of the production process has had a very direct impact on the collective bargaining mechanism.

In the old production process, a car and all its components are assembled under one roof, in what is called knock-down kit assembly. For instance, the Hindustan Ambassador was manufactured by the Birlas from 1957 in knock-down assembly plants. Mahindra and Mahindra too had begun business in 1947 with complete knock-down kits for their jeeps. This was what is called the Fordist model. The advantage the worker had in the Fordist model was that there was a single employer and one wage policy negotiated with the workers' union.

This changed to a structure where 'there is a seemingly vertical structure of production networks, where OEMs (Original Equipment Manufacturers) form 'nodes' or 'hubs'. OEMs are assembler plants where no production of components takes place. In a 'just-in-time' or 'lean' production model, where there is hardly any inventory in the assembler plants, the...supplier companies supply components continuously in batches.'

In the case of the Ambassador, for example, the 1,800 components of the car were all produced under one set-up, in their own foundry and forging shops. In contrast, on average a Maruti car has approximately 10,000 components and sub-components under nearly 1,500 categories. These components of Maruti Suzuki cars are manufactured by different vendor, or supplier, companies. The main factory only assembles these components sourced from the various vendors.

Maruti Suzuki factories can spin out a car in seconds because most of their components are made elsewhere under different managements with different wage structures. Even the engine is not made in the main factory; it is produced by Powertrain (which has now merged with Maruti Suzuki). The automobile plant plans its targets and places orders with vendors. The vendors then order what they need to their vendors. They in turn source their material from smaller vendors till we get to a tiny workshop-level supplier in unregulated urban slums. Thus, the production network has deep backward linkages, extending to informalized production in small workshops and home-based production.

Thousands of trucks enter and leave the two plants every day. The two plants receive raw materials and components from the 2,500 vendors in more than 3,400 trucks daily and send out 650 trailers loaded with cars every day. Such a production technique dictates the emergence of the automobile hub.

Amit and Nayanjyoti explain that the new model of production also outsources the management of a large workforce. That helps to keep production costs low. That is one of the secrets of producing an affordable car. So, while the production process is awe inspiring and the figures are mind boggling, in effect, all this helps in preventing workers from getting fair wages. Their capacity 'to control production and affect production by using the weapon of strike action [is] to some extent blunted'.

Broadly, these are the factors Amit and Nayanjyoti identify which have had an adverse impact on the collective bargaining capacity of the workers, quoted here in extenso for they have broader relevance to youth unemployment and the economy and politics in general:

- The increased mobility of capital and the setting up of multiple units of the same company in the industrial belt and the easy shifting of production from older to newer units (with more flexible labour regimes), and even closure of old units, have reduced workers' control over production, effectiveness of strikes and bargaining capacity of unions in the older units. It has reduced the associational bargaining power of workers.
- New technology has made workers more disposable and has given management more control over production. Mechanization and automation have made skill and experience increasingly redundant and have threatened job security. Intensification of work demands a young, docile workforce instead of older, experienced people. Continuous industrial restructuring has reduced

structural bargaining power of workers. By 2017, there were around 2,500 robots at the Manesar facility. In total, including the Gurgaon plant, there were an estimated 5,000 robots.

- Crises of agriculture, jobless growth and India's demographic dividend has created a large pool of unemployed youth waiting outside the factory gate, and ready to work even under worsening working conditions.
- Infomalization of work in a formal sector like automobiles has shifted the burden of production from permanent to various categories of temporary workers. Permanent workers have become a minority. Their union thus has less control over production. The new categories of workers like Diploma trainees, Student trainees, Diploma Apprentices are not even recognized as 'workers' and thus they have minimal connection with the union process.
- The increasing connectivity inside production processes under 'just-in-time' and 'lean' production and the competitiveness in the auto sector cannot tolerate any form of worker subjectivity that influences the production process and creates uncertainty. It has resulted in projecting the union process and 'collective bargaining' of workers as an 'act of indiscipline'. Thus, the 'labour dispute' is now seen as a 'law and order' problem. It has led to criminalization of labour struggles and repression, in place of reconciliation and mediation mechanisms.
- The BJP government in Haryana, Rajasthan and in the centre after 2014 and its pro-corporate policies have had an impact too. The gradual dismantling of

> labour protections, pro-corporate changes in labour law and the weakening of institutions such as the labour department, labour court, tribunals, have led to a weakening of the framework of collective bargaining.

Amit and Nayanjyoti conclude by stating that the trade union movement, which was rooted in the Fordist production regime and the labour laws of a welfare state, faces challenges in this new era of globalization of capital, the roll back of the welfare state and the emergence of corporate governance.

Suzuki typifies the new era of corporate rule.

Who Is Mr Suzuki?

Suzuki is a Japanese family name; much as Tata or Birla are Indian family names. So, who is this Mr Suzuki?

Osamu Matsuda was born on 30 January 1930. Osamu started his career as a loan officer in a local bank. His life took a turn when he married Shoko Suzuki, the granddaughter of the patriarch of Suzuki Motor Corporation, Michio Suzuki. As the Suzuki family did not have a male heir, Osamu was married into the family, and following Japanese custom, Osamu took up the family name of Suzuki to become Osamu Suzuki.

An avid golfer, Suzuki said he golfed forty-seven times in 2020 when he was ninety years old.

Suzuki has made a name for himself and achieved celebrity status among middle-class Indians; they have been seduced by the myths of Japanese work culture and Japanese success. But what this means for the workers employed by Japanese corporations is rarely talked about—even after the events of 18 July 2012.

During the 2001 Tokyo Motor Show, some Indian journalists were thrilled by their chance encounter with Osamu

Suzuki, and one of them wrote of the meeting: 'The Suzuki Chairman was indulgent enough to pose for pictures before ambling away. Though a brief interaction, it was awesome to spend time with someone who had spearheaded the Maruti small car revolution in India from the mid-1980s.'*

Suzuki never behaved as a minor partner in the company from the beginning of the joint venture. He imported the Japanese style of work and management and made many far reaching decisions. Suzuki was obsessed with keeping production costs low.

V. Krishnamurthy and R.C. Bhargava, the first chiefs of MUL had visited the Hamamatsu plant in Japan. It was hot and humid but they were shocked to find that the factory did not have an air conditioner and even top officials worked in sweltering heat.

At the initial stage when the Maruti factory was under construction, this attitude of Suzuki led to serious arguments that almost endangered the Indo-Japanese partnership.

In the Gurgaon factory Suzuki was not prepared to even invest in a conveyor belt to move parts from one place to another and Krishnamurthy, the then founder vice president of the company, had to tell Suzuki that if he was going to use trolleys to move material inside the factory, India could do without their help. Only after being ticked off like this did Suzuki install a conveyor belt.

Krishnamurthy writes in his book that he found Suzuki avoiding the introduction of some automated processes that were in use in Japan, in order to keep costs low, even if it meant exposing the workers to poisonous paint fumes.

* 'A brief encounter with Osamu Suzuki', *The Hindu Business Line*, 20 January 2018 (https://www.thehindubusinessline.com/companies/a-brief-encounter-with-osamu-suzuki/article8710441.ece, last accessed 11 January 2023).

Suzuki seemed to give priority to cutting costs over welfare of the workers. And he was reluctant to make investments or transfer technology to his Indian partners.

Some managers, executives and supervisors were sent to Japan and later some workers were too. Suzuki also deputed Japanese employees to train Maruti workers at the factory in the operation and maintenance of machines as well as shop floor culture. Such on-the-job training by experts ensured productivity levels were high and there was 100 per cent capacity utilization.

But what does 100 per cent capacity utilization mean when you're talking about a worker, a human being?

Between 1999 and 2000 production had crossed 4,00,000 units. In other words, every worker was producing on an average 107 cars each year, which means he was actually working 2.5 times as fast as agreed upon in 1988. ('Freewheelin' Capital', PUDR, 2007, p. 3)

Bhargava describes Suzuki's first visit to India in his book. The first time he came he was shocked by the work culture. Suzuki wanted every worker to enhance quality and productivity and reduce costs. In order to achieve this, he wanted to ensure that the eight-hour shift meant that not a second was wasted.

In India, a worker was deemed to have arrived on time for his shift if he entered the factory gate. Suzuki changed this practice; he wanted the worker to be at his work station, ready to work, when the shift started and leave only when the shift ended. He wanted the duration of the lunch break (which was not included in the eight-hour shift) to be controlled so no working time was lost due to workers returning late from lunch.

During those early days the factories had ten- to fifteen-minute breaks but Suzuki introduced two seven-and-a-half-minute tea breaks during a shift, something unheard of in Indian manufacturing at that time.

Khushi Ram, a dismissed worker who was active in the Maruti Suzuki Worker's Union, listed all the things that a worker has to do within the seven-and-a-half-minute tea break:

The hooter sounds. Countdown begins.

Finish whatever you are doing. Ten to twenty seconds gone.

Put the tools down in their places. All tools have specified places at the work station.

Take off your helmet. Take off your gloves. Take off your apron. Put them away at a specified place.

Go to the rest area which is ten or fifteen steps away.

Go to your locker, open it, take out your glass for tea.

Get into the queue in the rest area with around twenty-five to thirty-five people.

The trolley is already there. Get your tea. Pick up a *samosa* or bread *pakora* or jam-and-butter sandwich in your hands. You can have a second *samosa* if you gobble the first very quickly.

Walk to the loo holding your glass of tea and *samosa*. Washrooms are not too far because every rest area has a large bathroom with some ten to twenty cubicles for peeing and about five cubicles with toilets.

After peeing, wash hands and wash the glass. Get back. Open the locker.

Place glass in locker. Lock it. Go back to the work station.

Put on the apron. Put on the gloves and helmet. Pick up your tools.

If you are delayed and the line has started then the line will stop for you and HR will know at which point the line stopped and who was late.

Khushi Ram added: 'I should tell you that from 2008 they started to give us disposable glasses but we were not given plates.' This meant that workers could not take two *samosas* or whatever snack was on offer, since they did not have a plate.

Another worker, let us call him Junaid, since he did not want to give his real name, said in his interview on 13 February 2022:

'In the beginning when I was told that I would get only a seven-and-a-half-minute break for tea I did not know how to manage. It used to be so tough in the beginning. I would run to the bathroom and then pick up my snacks and take my tea and go sit near my line and gulp it all down. The moment the hooter sounded I would dump the half-finished food into the dustbin. That is how I had my breakfast in the mornings at work. It took me nearly six months to get used to shoving food into my mouth so quickly. I kept working half fed for so long. And it was hard work.'

Jitendra Kumar

We work for eight hours, with only two seven-and-a-half-minute toilet breaks and a thirty-minute lunch break. Both the canteen and the toilets are half a kilometre away.*

They don't even give you time to eat.

When I worked for Maruti, I had developed a habit of swallowing food at great speed. I had become such a machine that I didn't taste any food. I simply did not know what I was putting in my mouth. At home too I used to gobble food the minute it was put on the plate. I drank piping hot tea in such a hurry that people used to stare at me, struck speechless. It never took me more than a minute to down a cup of hot tea. I used to literally pour it in my mouth.

---

* This distance would also depend on where in the factory they worked. Some said the rest area was not too far away while others had to walk much longer.

For several years after I lost my job I continued to eat and drink in the same way as I did while working in the Maruti factory. It has taken me years to kick the habit.

I am now fighting the cases in the labour court on behalf of workers dismissed by Maruti. After the tragedy on 18 July 2012 in Manesar, 546 workers were fired from work. I was one of them. That is why I became a lawyer and am working in the campaign for labour rights. I have been associated with the campaign ever since I was fired by Maruti in 2012 after the tragedy in Manesar.

Khushi Ram

Not accused or arrested, but dismissed from work; member of the provisional committee of the MSWU formed after the incident and still associated with the struggle. Interviewed the first time in October 2019 in the union office in Rajiv Nagar, Gurgaon and subsequently over several phone conversations.

I am from Ghuskani village in Bhiwani district which is about 100 kilometres from Gurgaon. I do not wish to state my caste because I am opposed to the caste system.

We are two brothers. The family has some land and we did only farming. Our family's financial condition was not good. We tried growing cotton also but did not get a good crop. Now we grow wheat and paddy.

I took admission in the ITI in Meham in 2004. It was a government institution. The fee was negligible. I was just an average student; I scored 48 per cent in class 12 although I got 68 per cent marks in class 10. I did not want to do farming. I wanted to get a job somewhere. A farmer has neither an income nor any respect. In villages only people with jobs are respected.

I had noticed that even a peon in the city would be invited everywhere in the village.

I started participating in sports not because I had any interest in them but for my career. Government jobs have a quota for sportspersons and I thought that was one way to get a job. So I started running races. In the 2006 district tournament in Bhiwani, I ran 400 metres in 52 seconds. I thought I could join the army. I could have joined the police force also but my height was less than that required for the force.

There was one Rameshji* in the village. He used to work in Maruti. After talking to him it seemed to me that even the job of a worker in a factory was not a bad option. So I joined an ITI.

In 2006, I took the test in the Rohtak ITI and got selected as an apprentice in Maruti. My family was thrilled. They said that if I become permanent in Maruti I would get a handsome salary. I stopped running races.

I started living in Rajiv Nagar in Gurgaon. Two more workers shared the room with me. We were all from Haryana. I had to pay 1,200 rupees towards the rent. One of my roommates was an apprentice like me in Maruti and the other worked for a vendor company of Maruti. This company provides car seats to Maruti. We used to walk to the factory. Actually some fifty or sixty people from my village used to work in many of the companies here. Some were permanent workers in Honda.

The shift used to start at seven in the morning. We would leave at six o'clock so that we could reach by 6.30 am.

At that time I used to get only 3,000 rupees a month. I used to bring *atta*, pulses and rice from the village. I had all sorts of conventional ideas those days. I thought that cleaning, cooking,

* Ramesh Dalal, whose interview is included in this book.

washing clothes, all these household chores are women's work. In the village men never do these things. My mother did all this and if she went away for some reason or fell ill, any other woman from the village did it for us. I was very young then. Now I am thirty-three years old.

When I came here to work my attitude changed. The friend who shared the room with me taught me how to cook. He was from my own village.

When I was in the ITI, there was a strike in Honda and there was a big lathi-charge on the workers. I had heard about it. In the village you get to hear these stories. Earlier, when there was a prolonged agitation in Maruti in 2000, Rameshji was in the union [that led it]. He used to talk to us about it.

When I became an apprentice, he told me that I should not join the union till I become a permanent worker. Ramesh had lost his job after that agitation of 2000. He was very active in the union. He too had been compelled to quit as part of the so-called voluntary retirement scheme or VRS.* He got some money but how long does a few lakhs last? Now he is a property dealer.

When I joined as an apprentice I was very upset. The working conditions were very bad. I used to feel exhausted all the time. I was in the engine assembly. I had no time to even drink water. Even if I kept a bottle of water next to my work station I did not have enough time to pick up the bottle and put it to my mouth.

I worked at fitting pistons. As long as I stayed in the factory, I kept fitting pistons. I did not see the whole factory even once, the press shop, weld shop or paint shop. Nothing.

* Voluntary retirement schemes for employees are a management strategy to downsize the labour force; sometimes referred to as 'right-sizing manpower' by the management as a euphuism for pressurizing the workers to leave their jobs.

I saw them only when we went on strike! That is when I saw the whole factory.

I had to fit a piston in 5 seconds. In the beginning I had a lot of pain in my arms. I also had to bend on one leg to place the piston. I had pain in the back. There was pain all the time. Yes, there was a dispensary in the factory. There was a doctor. But what could they do? If it got very bad, they gave me enough medicine to enable me to work. They gave Combiflam or some such tablet. Sometimes I would get injured; then they bandaged the hand or foot. That is all. The first few days I worked only with the help of Combiflams.

We used to have half an hour for lunch. I had to run to the canteen 200 metres away, stand in a queue and run back to my work station. My training as a sprinter came in handy!

All these claims of the manager and the workers eating together, eating the same food in the same canteen is all talk. Our *rotis* would be cold and stiff and half done, our salad used to be pieces of onion and cucumber chopped up roughly. Officers got hot *rotis* and their salads were nicely sliced and presented beautifully. We got *saunf* [fennel seeds] and *misri* [rock sugar], but our *misri* used to be nearly powdered and the managers got good fat crystals. We did not even go near the area where the managers sat. Old workers used to tell us that earlier the food used to be good. They would say, 'Earlier there used to be a union, and now there are Japanese!'

We have never had any direct encounter with the top management. We had contact with only the supervisor and shift in-charge. Only sometimes did we have to face the manager of the department. I was not even aware of the structure of the management, their ranks and who is below whom.

I went and complained to Ramesh uncle. I asked him why he had misled me, praising Maruti when it was not a good place.

He told me that when they had a union conditions were really better and if we wanted to improve conditions we would have to form a union. He advised me to first get my job confirmed and then think of the union.

He told me something very significant. He said, 'Remember, you will be heard only when you have control of production. So, first seize control of production. First, do not budge from the machine; sit there and if you are evicted from there then sit inside the factory. If you are removed from there too sit at the gate of the factory. If you are evicted from there as well, then you have lost the battle. That is when you should know that you will not be successful!'

In July 2007, my apprenticeship was over. I had to leave. Then I went to work in Honda as a casual worker. Honda had a union. A bus was available to reach the factory. The food was better there too. There was less work. The pace there was not as fast. The speed was slower. And if you needed to drink water, or go to the toilet you could ring a bell, a reliever would come and you got your break. Things were much better than in Maruti.

In Maruti, everyone had to work for an extra fifteen minutes. Everyone had to do it. It was the case that if you were in the 'A' shift then you had to keep working till the 'B' shift worker took over. They always joined fifteen minutes after the end of the 'A' shift. That used to be their starting time. You have to put in these extra fifteen minutes in lieu of the two tea breaks of seven and a half minutes. It is worked into the schedule. The break we get for tea has to be compensated for. Only lunch breaks are not to be compensated for. How lucky for us!

And if the worker of the 'B' shift arrives late then you have to keep working beyond those fifteen minutes. That worker will lose money—it will be deducted from his salary—but you will not get extra money for the extra work you have done.

Actually, the 'C' shift was the shortest. You had to work only six and a half hours in the 'C' shift. It is the night shift. Production work did not take place at night. Maintenance work is done during the night. Utility works, electrical work and other such works which are necessary for the running of assembly lines.

We were supposed to have an eight-hour shift but in reality we had to spend nine and a half hours in the factory.

One, we had to reach half an hour before the shift began. There would be an early morning meeting of fifteen minutes in which some speeches were made about how we should think of the factory as ours and that all of us workers and managers were one happy family!

Then the supervisor would tell you the plan for that day, give you targets, and if there had been any tardiness that too would be talked about.

Then you need another fifteen minutes to put on all the safety gear, pick up your tools. In this way the factory takes an extra forty-five minutes. Then you have to give fifteen minutes to the production line over and above the eight hours.

We got one day of leave after enough of those extra fifteen minutes had been taken from you. You couldn't choose the day you wanted to go off on leave; they gave you a day off.

In this Maruti factory, a car was ready every 46 seconds. This is not only India's but Asia's fastest car manufacturing plant. Please remember that Japan is also in Asia.

The whole process of making this car is streamlined. Firstly, steel sheets will be cut according to the design of the vehicle in the press shop. Many dies are made and installed for these according to the design. The machine cuts the steel sheet. Every part of the car is cut. Workers run that machine. So, first the body of the car is cut.

Then this structure goes to the weld shop. There the box or outer shell of the car box is prepared by welding together all its pieces.

Now it is ready for all its components to be put in.

From the weld shop this box goes to the paint shop. The giant tanks out there have a basic colour called white paint. Machines immerse these boxes in these tanks and the entire steel is covered with white paint at the bottom. Due to this there is no danger of rusting in the car. This is called ED [electro deposition] or electric coated paint.

After the paint is applied, the paint is dried by heating the box in a *tandoor*. The baking is important, otherwise you may have to wait many days for the paint to dry!

After this the assembly line starts. It is called a line but it is not linear, it is a big zigzag thing, goes up and down. Sometimes the car will go up so that you can put stuff in it from below. Sometimes you are standing in a pit and the car is running on the line above you. Sometimes it will be moving in front of you and you will run to put stuff in it.

Every worker has an area of work and everyone has to complete his work within the stipulated time. The hardest work is done on the assembly line itself. Heavy parts have to be lifted and fitted in a box moving at a fast pace. Engine mounts are installed. Engines are put in. Seats, steering—everything is fitted here. This is where the box becomes a car.

There are many stations on this line.

From start to finish the box moves in 46 seconds. Every station gets 46 seconds. To make a car in 46 seconds means that, at the same time, different types of work on a vehicle are done simultaneously at different stages. That means if you have a line of 200 cars, then 200 cars are being worked upon at different points and each point gets its 46 seconds. When it comes to parts, a worker may get only 5 seconds on one part and 7 seconds for another because he has to apply the same things in nine cars within those 46 seconds. In this way, hundreds of vehicles are prepared in a day. In some sense, it is fascinating. The worker cannot see the whole process, he only sees the little part he is doing.

Actually, it takes much more time to make the car than 45 seconds if you count the time spent in the manufacture of each component. But yes, putting it all together takes 45 seconds!

The car that leaves from the assembly line then goes directly to the Vehicles Inspection (VI) section where it is checked for quality. They check to see if everything is installed properly or not.

I learnt all this much later. For one whole year I just kept on putting pistons. Then I moved to Honda. I worked in Honda for about three months.

At this time there was an exam in Maruti. They were recruiting trainees for their Manesar factory. I also took the test. It was a one-and-a-half-hour test. Only theory; I passed. I was called for the interview in which they asked me my caste, about how many members there were in my family and about the family's financial condition. Maybe they want to assess just how badly you need the job. I was made a trainee.

I became a trainee on 14 November 2007. My salary was Rs 3,200 per month. It was almost half the salary I got at Honda. I was hoping to become a permanent worker at the end of three years of training; and then life would be good.

At that time there was only one assembly line there. It now has three assembly lines. There are now four lines in Gurgaon.

In Manesar I started installing the driver's seat and the steering column. In a day, I used to install 550 to 580 seats and columns. I got 46 seconds to install them in a car. I had to physically lift the seat which weighed around eighteen kilograms and slide it inside the car. After this, the tightening gun had to be lifted and [the nuts] torqued. Then the column that is under the steering wheel would be put in. During this the car would keep moving and I would work moving along with it. Sometimes I would be standing in a pit and the car would be above me. To mark the completion of the work, I would put a mark on it and run towards another vehicle which would now be entering my area.

I used to do this work continuously, running back and forth like this. Initially, I found it difficult to do things like lifting the seat, sliding it, bending to position the steering column, turning it very quickly. Later, I got used to them.

I was finally made permanent in 2009. My salary went up to Rs 8,200. This was not a lot. But I got many facilities. I got bonus.

Now I got ten casual leaves. I got twelve holidays like Independence Day, Holi, Eid, etc., that we got anyway. Now, for every twenty days of work, one day's extra leave started to be available, which you could accumulate up to a total of 240 days. Earned leave.

You could also take money in lieu of these holidays. Apart from this, we also got the facility of production performance reward. It is known as incentive. This used to add up to Rs 8,000 per month. So the salary, counting incentive, became Rs 16,200. That was not bad even though it was not very good. It was just okay.

I soon realized that there was a problem in this. Actually, it is like splitting the salary in two parts. If you take a single leave, Rs 2,000 is deducted from this incentive! Similarly, other fines are imposed. They are all of huge amounts. So, notionally your salary is 16,000, but every month you will get less, and some months you may lose the entire incentive and get only 8,200. Some month you may make 10,000.

Sometimes a vehicle would break down for some reason even before the parts were installed. That car would be rejected, the parts meant for it would become surplus, and such parts would accumulate.

The company used to stamp them and sell them as spare parts.

When such spare parts came out of our stock, we also got some extra money for it. But to earn this we had to work on these parts to give them a finished look, etc. This rarely happened though.

These were the conditions in which we worked and these were the conditions that forced us to begin our struggle to register our union. The previous union under Sonu Gujjar was never registered; and it had already been crushed. Sonu had been forced to leave.

The changes in the production process have other consequences too for workers working in the auto industry. The workers working in the smaller factories or workshops have no protection when they are injured at work. According to Safe-in-India Foundation (SII), Maruti Suzuki and Honda suppliers remain the largest contributors to accidents in Gurgaon. The Foundation also found that, in Haryana, factory inspections have decreased over the years leaving the workers more and more vulnerable. Workers in the supply chain, especially migrant labour are vulnerable to all kinds of accidents. Many lose fingers, hands; some have suffered worse.

The 2021 Safe-in-India report titled 'Crushed' states that 80 per cent of the injured workers met with accidents in the supply chains of some of the largest auto sector brands; 70 per cent of those injured lost their hands/fingers; and on average 1.97 fingers were lost to a crush injury.

It also found that those injured were from vulnerable sections of the population: 92 per cent were migrant workers; 81 per cent were educated only up to grade 10; 71 per cent earned less than Rs 10,000 a month (of which many got no overtime pay despite working approximately twelve-hour shifts); and 70 per cent were on contract. There appeared to be a direct correlation between how bad the injury was and the salary and educational level of the worker: the lower the salary and education, the worse the injury.

Maruti Suzuki, Hero and Honda suppliers were the largest contributors to accidents: in Gurgaon (93 per cent) and Faridabad (75 per cent). Suppliers of Bajaj, Eicher, JCB, Tata Motors, TVS, Yamaha were also significant contributors in Gurgaon, Faridabad, Rudrapur and Neemrana.

The pain and injuries that the workers suffered on a regular basis was reflected in the interviews SII conducted with workers from the Maruti Suzuki factory as well as vendor companies.

Ram Niwas

One of the 546 workers dismissed from the factory, he is fighting his case before the labour court. Interviewed in the premises of the District Court, Gurgaon on 26 February 2020.

Don't ask me how bad the working conditions in Maruti were, they are indescribable.

Injuries were common. Once I got a deep gash in my forehead; my right eyebrow was cut in the middle. I was working on the instrument panel. Things like the steering column are installed in it. Something was coming in my direction. I could not see it in time to avoid it and it hit my forehead. I did not even notice the injury. The worker next to me saw blood oozing out; he even told me that I was hurt. But I was engaged in work; he was also working. There was no time to listen to anyone. So I paid no attention to him and continued working. Then blood dripped onto my hands as I was trying to fit some instrument and I had to get away and go to the dispensary. The doctor in the factory clinic cleaned the brow. He put three stitches. The doctor asked me to go home but I went back to work. These things kept happening.

There were terrible accidents in our vendor companies too. Once in a factory, a die fell on a worker. He was flattened out. It happened in the press shop. The die is the thing that gives a vehicle its shape. It is very heavy. He died on the spot. Just like that. One minute he was working, the next he was dead on the floor under the heavy die. He was a contract labourer. No case was registered and nothing happened. The matter was suppressed. We did not have a union then.

In another vendor company, a worker got stuck in a conveyor belt. Had they cut that belt, he would have survived. But the belt was very expensive, it cost perhaps twenty lakhs. The management refused to cut it. The workers kept asking them to cut the belt to save him. He could have been saved. But this was not done. The worker died. Then they had to cut the belt to remove his dead body. I am not sure of this, perhaps they did not have to...I do not remember. The point is human life has no value. The life of a worker has no value at all. In that case, I think, his family was given some five lakhs.

Then the people of the Honda union went there and began asking about the accident. It was a terrible incident. Many people had reached the factory to find out the truth. An FIR was lodged against eighteen such people who went there to talk to workers. These people had gone inside the factory for enquiries. That was treated as illegal entry, trespass.

But no case was filed against the supervisor who was there. There was no case against the manager either for not cutting a belt to save a worker's life.

There have also been cases where a worker has been deliberately killed. A bouncer shot a worker in a plant. He died. This happened in 2009. That time a lawyer here, Rajendra Pathak, began asking around about it. A case was filed against him. The lawyer spent a few days in jail!

In such an environment, a union is necessary even for the safety of the worker.

Four

Japanese Style Management, Indian Resistance

Which side are you on?
Which side are you on?

Don't scab for the bosses
Don't listen to their lies
Us poor folk haven't got a chance
Unless we organize

—Florence Reece (1900–1986),
who belonged to a coal miner family in the USA

The Indian economy has been liberalized since 1991. This has meant relentless privatization, de-regulation, downsizing, and outsourcing, which have all led to massive unemployment; the number of permanent workers in factories and public sector enterprises has come down drastically.

It is important to point out that the project report of the company in 1982 envisaged production of only one lakh vehicles on a manpower base of 4,000. This target was reached in 1988 when a new incentive scheme was introduced. In 1995, the production level had gone up to two lakh cars and in 1999–2000, it had crossed four lakh units. Worker productivity was only thirty-eight cars per worker in 1988; in 1995, it had risen to seventy-seven cars per worker per year, and in 1999–2000, it had reached nearly 107 cars per worker per annum.* In 1995, the old incentive scheme was withdrawn; the new productivity cum profit-based scheme introduced that year lapsed in 1999–2000 and it was over the incentive scheme that Maruti workers launched a major agitation.

During this time 'production had increased by 400 per cent though employment had increased only by about 65 per cent' (Sen 2011, p. 193) compared to 1992.

The trade union movement faced many challenges and these challenges were even more formidable because foreign transnational companies in the auto sector insisted that their investment plans could be implemented only if the Haryana government gave its full support to ensure independent unions were eradicated.† That is why it is all the more remarkable that the workers of Maruti Suzuki were able to form unions and organize such militant struggles.

The trade union movement has traditionally not concerned itself with the unorganized workers in the informal sector. It is now faced with an even bigger challenge given the greater number of contract workers and casual workers.

In the case of the automobile industry, the production process itself makes the task of organizing workers, spread out into so many factories, vendor shops and workshops, ever more difficult. The traditional trade union movement has not been able to evolve new strategies and effective ways to protect workers. But with years of experience it does continue to provide some support to the new generation of workers struggling for their rights.

---

* These figures are from a Centre for Workers' Management report quoted in 'Hard Drive', PUDR, 2001.

† See 'Forging Solidarity', *Economic & Political Weekly*, vol. 49, no. 8 (22 February 2014).

There are broadly four kinds of trade unions involved in the Maruti Suzuki workers' struggles.

The first are the national federations affiliated to the various political parties such as the INTUC, affiliated to the Indian National Congress, the AITUC, affiliated to the Communist Party of India, the CITU (Centre of Indian Trade Unions), affiliated to the Communist Party of India (Marxist), and the HMS affiliated to the Socialists.

These trade unions have all been involved to varying degrees even though the unions formed by the workers in the Maruti Suzuki factories did not have formal affiliations to any of these.

The second kind of union is what the workers call '*jebi*' or pocket union, or scab union. The oldest union in the Maruti factory in Gurgaon was the Maruti Udyog Kamgar Union or the MUKU. It has been referred to as such by the workers. But even MUKU showed solidarity with the Manesar workers when it opposed the move by the management to de-recognize the independent trade union at Manesar in the aftermath of the 18 July 2012 violence.

Which brings us to the third kind of trade union involved in the Maruti Suzuki workers' struggles. These are independent unions or rank-and-file unions, formed by the workers in the factory without affiliation to any political party or trade union confederation—like the Maruti Udyog Employee Union (MUEU), which led the strike in 2000; the Maruti Suzuki Employees Union (MSEU; it was never registered), which led the strikes in 2011; and the Maruti Suzuki Workers' Union (MSWU), which led the agitation in 2012.

'Given the specificities of the union in India,' remark the authors of one report analysing the emergence of the MSEU in 2011, 'it is not surprising that the first time that an autonomous defensive organization is created and decided by the workers themselves it should take the form of what might be called a "rank-and-file union" or "base union", that is to say one which is outside of any link with the pre-existing union apparatus of whatever sort. The will to immediately control all actions, a certain refusal of delegation, first of all pushes the workers to constitute a good, honest union. The definite inexperience, the lack of reference to some of the struggles of the past for the new generations of workers naturally opens the way to base unionism.' ('Workers Autonomy Strikes in India', 2012)

These observations are borne out by the interviews in this book of members from among the leadership of all three unions mentioned above—the MUEU, MSEU and the MSWU.

More recently, around 2014, four of such rank-and-file unions came together to form the Maruti Suzuki Mazdoor Sangh.

The New Trade Union Initiative (NTUI) is the fourth kind of union. It was founded in 2001 when several independent trade unions in the organized and unorganized sector came together under a single banner. They provided various kinds of support to the Maruti Suzuki workers, including financial, and helped link it to international trade union movements as well.

The NTUI has decided to constitute itself formally into a federation and seek the status of a national trade union federation. The organization says that it is independent of all party affiliations. This kind of organization has been referred to as social movement unionism.

In addition, there were independent but small organizations which provided solidarity and support to the Maruti Suzuki workers such as the Inqlabi Mazdoor Kendra. Though they are independent, they are generally influenced by left ideology.

Apart from the trade unions, several organizations have been representing a specific section of workers, mainly those belonging to the Scheduled Castes. In the Gurgaon Maruti factory, for example, an SC-ST employees association raised issues of postings and promotions. These organizations of course played a bigger role when the Maruti plant was still a public sector enterprise.

The workers and their leaders were aware how dangerous identity politics could be to the unity of workers and did not emphasize caste or communal issues in their struggle.

There is a high percentage of Dalits in the trade union leadership. They say that they do face prejudice and discrimination in their daily lives but it is tough to lay a finger on specific examples. As Mangeram told us during the interview: '*Vaise to kuch bigaad nahi sakte lekin kalam ki maar to maarte hi hain.*' (They can't do much openly but they can give you a bad report.) What he meant was that the management can prevent timely promotions or awards for performances by manipulating the annual confidential reports of the Dalit workers.

While Dalits have largely protected themselves against blatant forms of discrimination, those who stand up to harassment and protest are made to pay a heavy price irrespective of caste.

In a way, the incident of 18 July 2012 was sparked off by the casteist remark made by a supervisor to a Dalit worker and an activist in the trade union, Jiya Lal. Jiya Lal maintained that he had not reacted to the casteist slur, which he faced almost on a daily basis. What made him angry was the use of expletives by the supervisor referring to his sister and mother. The result was not only the suspension of Jiya Lal but the termination of 2,500 workers, 546 of whom were permanent workers.

Modern Times

Like Jitendra Kumar in the previous chapter, several workers of Maruti Suzuki compared the conditions within their factory to the factory shown in Chaplin's *Modern Times*.

By 2003, Maruti Udyog Limited was fully privatized with the Government of India selling the controlling interest to Suzuki. What did that mean for the workers? It meant that the Japanese work culture had successfully converted the young men into efficient machines.

Someone has calculated* that a worker in the Maruti Suzuki engine shop does the following eighteen tasks every two minutes:

1. Lifting the block (weighing about thirty kilograms) or crank shaft
2. Placing the bolts (of which four out of the sixteen have to be placed manually by the worker)
3. Checking all the sixteen bolts
4. Tightening all the bolts, torquing them
5. Turning the block back
6. Putting a pin on the crank shaft
7. Placing the stopper
8. Placing the flywheel (which weighs eight kilograms) on top of the pin while centrally orienting it
9. Pressing the bearing after aligning the flywheel
10. Fixing six bolts
11. Torquing the six bolts
12. Marking all the bolts as checked
13. Placing the clutch and the pressure plate on the flywheel
14. Aligning the plate and torquing again

* See 'Hard Drive', PUDR, 2001.

15. Placing the block straight once again
16. Removing the centre and stopper
17. Removing one bolt
18. Lifting the block with the help of the crane and placing it on

The workers had many grievances by 2000 and they were ready to organize themselves to fight for better working conditions. They were not happy with the existing trade union backed by the INTUC and which had been supported by V. Krishnamurthy. The union did not have elections and office bearers were chosen through a voice vote.

The management was determined not to allow a strong trade union to emerge in the Maruti Suzuki plant. And they had the full backing of the State government which had assured Maruti Suzuki of an 'investment-friendly environment', which meant creating a quiescent labour force through a pliant labour department that would not implement labour laws and an overactive police force at the disposal of capital to crush labour protest.

The registration of a trade union is done under the labour laws and is done by the State labour department. But the recognition depends on the sweet will of the management. In 1993, for example, a trade union close to the Hind Mazdoor Sangh (HMS) had been formed, but the Maruti Suzuki management did not recognize it.

The registration of a union protects the leaders from prosecution to some extent. But in reality it does little to protect them from being suspended, dismissed or forced to take voluntary retirement. Labour laws have protected workers from arbitrary actions of the management by forbidding the retrenchment of workers without permission of the State labour department. However, in the case of Maruti, the State government fully backed all decisions of the management including the sacking of over 500 workers in 2012.

The first agitation against the Maruti management was led by the MUEU, which was an independent union but which worked closely with the AITUC. The new leader that emerged in late 1980s was Mathew Abraham. The workers loved him because he was honest and told them everything the management told him. He would hold gate meetings and even managers would stop to listen to him speak.

The first issue that this union took up was the attempt by the management to cap the incentives. The agitation focused on the fact that labour intensification was accompanied by a cutback in productivity bonuses. The workers were deprived of monetary compensation for a higher workload.

Mathew Abraham

Elected President in 1987 of the Maruti Udyog Employees Union, the only registered union functioning in the company since 1984; suspended in April 1988; elected general secretary in November 1988 and served as such till 1989; became general secretary again in 1994 and continued till November 2001; suspended in 1996 for calling a strike.

He led Maruti's first long strike in 2000 and was sacked; he raised the issue of transfer of technology from Suzuki to Maruti.

Interviewed on 28 February 2020 at his brother's home in Dwarka, New Delhi.

I am a resident of Kerala. Actually, I wanted to be a priest. I am a Catholic and I went to Montfort School. Montfort Brothers have been working in India for over a 100 years. A good number of these Brothers hail from Kerala. There I studied till class 8. Perhaps the Brothers felt that I was not fit to be a priest; I did not have a calling. So they suggested that I should go to study elsewhere. I enrolled in another school and till class 12 I studied in Tamil medium. Then I went to Kerala and got a diploma in engineering.

Since I studied in Kerala and Tamil Nadu I can write and speak both Malayalam and Tamil; I also know English and now having lived in North India, I have learnt Hindi.

For two years I was working in Jodhpur with the Border Roads [Organisation]. Then one day I noticed an advertisement in the newspaper for jobs in the Maruti company. I applied. This was in 1986. At the time I had barely heard the name of Maruti and I did not know much about the company.

I got a job in Maruti and started working the same year. I joined as technician Grade IV in the assembly shop. I thought I would have a cushy job. I had gone to Maruti because I wanted to stay and work in one place not move around continually like I had to in the Border Roads.

When I started working there the form of production was not what it is today. At that time a complete knock-down (CKD) kit used to come from Japan. Boxes would be opened and parts would be put together: the car would be ready. Well, not literally, but you get the drift, I think. There was a paint shop. There was also a welding shop. This press shop was built later. There was also a conveyor belt. But everything was in the early stages.

There were also a couple of robots in the paint shop. Those robots sensed a car, picked it up, rotated it up and down and turned it left and right and painted the car. They used electrostatic painting. What it meant was the car would come out of the water and paint would stick to it. To tell the truth, I had never even seen all this before. It felt like a miracle.

My job was great. I had gone to Maruti because I wanted to

stay and work in one place and not move around continually. However, I regretted it very soon. I had never worked so much in my life.

At that time the market for Maruti was being established. There was heavy booking of its cars. People had to wait for months to buy it. Realizing its potential Suzuki then bought another 16 per cent of the shares.

In 1987, a press shop and a machine shop were being built. R.C. Bhargava held a high position in the company and he said that we do not have enough money to invest in all this. He asked Suzuki to invest and he also convinced the government that Suzuki is interested in investing.* Then Suzuki bought 14 per cent more shares in Maruti. Gradually, its share went up to 40 per cent.

R.C. Bhargava was an IAS officer and was set to retire in 1992. Before the date of retirement, he got Suzuki's stake increased to nearly 50 per cent. However, all this happened much later. There were some CBI cases against him also.†

In the joint venture agreement signed between Suzuki and Maruti, it had been decided that both the companies would take turns alternately to appoint the chairman and managing director. When it was Suzuki's turn to appoint the chairman the Government of India would choose the MD. The next time the Indian government would choose the chairman and Suzuki the MD.

Till Maruti was a Government of India undertaking, it

---

* Suzuki was not interested in investing and the government had enough money. According to Mathew, by convincing Suzuki to invest, Bhargava enabled it to buy more shares. And therefore he had to convince the government too, to let Suzuki invest.

† The allegations against R.C. Bhargava have been enumerated in the judgement in *Union of India (UoI) vs R.C. Bhargava* on 23 June 1998 (1999 95 CompCas 394 CLB).

was in the public sector and the government made all these appointments.

Krishnamurthy was the first head of the company and he left Maruti in 1987 and went back to BHEL. He was very unhappy with Suzuki.

Now, under the terms of the agreement, Suzuki chose to appoint the MD not the chairman. By mutual agreement, Bhargava was made MD. The government did not appoint a full time chairman. The secretary of the Ministry of Heavy Industry used to go to the board meetings. He was not the chairman but he had to work as one. [K.] Karunakaran was the Minister of Heavy Industry.

That was the time when a serious tussle took place between the Government of India and Suzuki. Suzuki, as part of the agreement to invest in Maruti, had agreed to transfer technology to India so that eventually everything would be made here in India. The gear box technology was to be transferred and there was some delay in it. Some proposal on this issue was to be presented in the board meeting.

Karunakaran called a meeting and told all the government directors on the board to vote against this proposal.

There were two directors. One of them was Jagdish Khattar. They voted in favour of the proposal. They did it in their own interest because R.C. Bhargava, who was the MD, was a Suzuki man and they wanted to remain loyal to him. The government removed both Khattar and Kumar from the post of directors but Bhargava made them executive directors. Executive directors cannot attend board meetings.

I was then working in assembly. The assembly line is the largest division of the factory, and in 1986, very few things were made here. See, it was a joint venture. But one of its partners, Suzuki, made a lot of things in its own country and we used to buy them. Like mechano-plastic bumpers, batteries, tires. We bought all this, imported them. Before 1986, even tires came from Japan. The government wanted things to be made here.

I have noticed a strange thing in the Japanese system. They had no drawings. We are taught that every part, every tool, has a design and there is a drawing of that design. The part is made on the basis of that drawing, and must meet its specifications. This happens in the Russian system too. But Suzuki did not have any drawing.

They gave the part they wanted made to the vendor as a sample and asked them to make it. Then they would check to see if it was like the sample or not. This was very strange.

I was finding it tough to work in assembly. I had worked a lot in the Border Roads Organisation in two years. That used to be tiring work. In Maruti it seemed to me that in one day I worked as much as I had worked in two years in the Roads Organisation. I worked all the time. The management also observes who can work how much and how fast. The more work you do, the more quickly you work, the more you have to work because more work is piled on you. I was tired all the time. I wanted to quit and go back to my parent organization. By then six months had gone by and I was sent to work in the sub-assembly.

The sub-assembly is where parts are put together. All parts made of smaller parts, they are joined and given their final shape and these are then taken to the assembly line to be fitted in vehicles. I was making shockers and brakes and putting them on the assembly line.

At that time Krishnamurthy became the chairman. He was very close to Mrs Gandhi. She was very fond of him; he had worked in BHEL, where INTUC had a union. Many people from BHEL had joined Maruti. As soon as Krishnamurthy joined Maruti he got K.K. Datta [a member of INTUC and who had been with him in BHEL] to form a union affiliated to INTUC at Maruti.

Workers had many problems. Gurgaon hardly had any public transport then and it was difficult to get to the factory from home. The work was killing. The canteen was run indifferently. The union did nothing at all. Union office bearers thought they could get away by doing nothing because they had the blessings of Krishnamurthy, the chairman. All they did was enjoy themselves.

Top HMS leaders used to come to the gate and hold meetings but they could not form the union. All this had happened before I joined. By the time I joined, Indiraji had been assassinated. I heard about all this in the factory. Some workers had joined HMS but they could not get their union registered. The INTUC-affiliated union had been registered in Delhi and they got their registration transferred to Haryana. They used to say that there was no need to go to faraway Chandigarh if they could get their work done in Delhi, and of course they could!

All this was going on when ten supporters of HMS were suspended and the matter was raised in the union. Supporters of HMS protested vociferously that the union did not care about them. The management then proposed a meeting in which an impromptu election was held; all the old BHEL office bearers were removed and new workers were elected to the various posts.

But HMS could ensure that very few people attended this meeting because most of the people were with HMS even though their union was not registered. So now the management insisted that workers form an independent union. All union activity thus ended.

One day when I reached the factory late, I was not allowed to go in. For half the day I wandered about the area because I had nothing else to do. Some HMS people saw me, came to me and started talking to me. They thought that I was a supporter of the HMS. One of them offered to talk to the manager and let me join duty. We went in, spoke to the manager and I was allowed to work. After that I began to meet this guy.

In the meantime elections to the union were announced and the HMS leaders, who had been suspended, also joined the INTUC. This led to a lot of dissatisfaction. The people I had begun making friends with planned to contest elections and had joined INTUC. They began to get threats from other HMS supporters who said that because they had joined INTUC they would be beaten up. There was this one Sikh man who on hearing this became very emotional and started crying. I felt very bad, and only to console him, I said, forget everyone else, I will contest the election! There were around fifty people standing there and none of them knew me. Things quietened down but I soon realized that people were now pointing towards me in the canteen and many would walk up to me to ask me not to fight the elections.

I began to feel uneasy. I had had no intention to contest and I did not know why people were asking me to stay away from contesting. When people began asking me to not get involved I became very angry. My awareness of unions was really low. I did not even know how to fill in forms for elections and what documents were required. By then I had been picked up and sent to a very hard work station.

A manager then called me and asked me whether I was a communist. He thought that because I belong to Kerala I must be a communist. Now, I have a habit that I answer accusations in the affirmative. If you have the temerity to assume something about me I will not take the trouble to deny it. So, when he asked me if I was a communist, I retorted with some asperity that yes, I was. He asked me, 'Will you contest elections?'

I got very angry. Whoever I met would tell me to not contest. A stubbornness began to grow inside me. I became adamant and decided that I would definitely contest. Thanks to all these discussions I had become quite well known. Even popular. When the time for elections came, Darshan Singh, the same man who had started crying, took me aside and filled the form for me for the post of president. Since no one was ready to contest for the post of general secretary, he became a candidate. Darshan belonged to Parwanu. He had come from the Eicher factory and was also in CITU. The elections were being held for an independent union, where HMS had the support of 90 per cent of the people. Two more candidates entered the fray for president. Votes got divided. I won, Darshan lost. Sombir Singh from Hind Mazdoor Sabha was elected general secretary.

In spite of not wanting to I had joined the union and become its president. I was terrified when I was elected. I offered to resign but Darshan held me back and said that he would come over to my house to talk. Then some twenty people came to my house. They said it was not good to run away and I should stay put.

After this a general body meeting was held and a fight broke out in it. The HMS group said that everyone would have to follow whatever order they issued, because they had made many sacrifices. They had also brought a leader of HMS from outside, from another factory, to the meeting. They said that the union would affiliate itself with the HMS. The workers got very angry and they beat up all the HMS leaders.

This fight continued and after about eight months the entire elected body was dismissed and an ad hoc body was formed in its place. When we went to register the union, the trade union Registrar said that such an ad hoc body could not be registered.

Then in 1987, things changed. Perhaps Devi Lal ji had become chief minister in Haryana and Sushma Swaraj was the Minister of Food and Civil Supplies. I had gone to the Chief Minister to seek help with registration and he gave a letter to me addressed to Sushma Swaraj. I went to meet Sushmaji. She called the Labour Commissioner and told him to help me. When I went to him he accepted our ad hoc body, got the union registered but imposed some conditions. They were good conditions. One was that we would hold elections soon and the union would not again indulge in violence and have ad hoc bodies in future. The name of the union was Maruti Udyog Employees Union, MUEU.

Now the management had no choice, they also had to accept us as the representatives of workers. Our talks on wage settlement started.

In those days, about 75,000 vehicles were made annually. This number had to be increased. An incentive scheme was launched. Production had increased, there were few complaints. Vendors were also being set up. The number of dealers was going up. But there was no adequate infrastructure. The ad hoc body already started dealing with all these issues even before the union was registered.

In 1989, the factory had a total of around 3,000 workers and 1,10,000 vehicles were being made a year. By then the time had come to implement the incentive scheme.

INTUC did not have enough support to get the incentive scheme implemented despite the fact that they were involved in the discussions with the management and had got all the details worked out. They could not because people were not ready to listen to them.

Then we entered the picture and negotiated with the management and we got a scheme of incentives based only on production implemented. The management even called it the Productivity Incentive Scheme. This caused a great deal of friction later so we must understand this plan.

The number of vehicles that were to be manufactured in a day was fixed. Now, for every car made over and above this target each worker was to get Rs 5 as incentive. This was the rate paid to the direct worker on the assembly line. Those who played an indirect role were to get 85 per cent of the incentive. All such rates were fixed for every department related to production.

In those days the total salary of the worker was Rs 1,250 a month and the incentive was to be added to his salary. There was no ceiling limit to the amount of incentive. It could go up as much as it could or as much as the worker worked. Of course, the worker cannot make more than a certain number of extra cars but there was no cap on the amount.

The one who works directly on the assembly line to make a car was to get 100 per cent of the incentive, the one who works on the conveyor belt 115 per cent and the one who works indirectly, like in marketing, or on the sub-assembly, would have 85 per cent of the incentive.

This percentage is a percentage of the salary. Bhargava was also involved in this entire discussion. So now this scheme came into force.

When we had made the incentive scheme, we made a mistake. We got it implemented for only three years and then we were to review it. R.C. Bhargava too made a mistake. He didn't think that we would get so much extra work done. Bhargava had not capped the amount. When Bhargava saw how much more work was being done he felt that too much incentive had to be paid out. Now he threw up his hands and began to say that they would not be able to pay so much, that the amount of incentive was getting to be bigger than the salary.

Then they started keeping apprentices, who did not get incentives. But now workers started benefiting because their workload, especially the harder work, was reduced a little. They made apprentices do a lot of the heavy work. This was followed by some further investment and the assembly line was extended. The incentive scheme was also not revised.

Let me tell you an interesting anecdote about working with Bhargava. Elections to the union were being held at the end of 1988. One day, we were protesting at the gate, raising slogans, when R.C. Bhargava's car arrived at the gate. On seeing his car, people got highly enthused and began to shout even louder. Bhargava got out of the car and said that 'these leaders are misleading you'. He actually stood there and started making a speech. We heard him. When he finished I said to him that now that you have been heard, listen to what we have to say. 'You have spoken, now I speak, you listen,' I told him. He kept standing.

Those days my Hindi was not so good. I began to speak, 'Despite what you have said we are not misleading anyone, we are fighting for the rights of everyone...' The word for 'despite' in Hindi is *baavjood*. But I got totally confused and instead of *baavjood* I said '*bhenchod*'! I didn't even understand what I had said. People roared in laughter. I must say Bhargava took it very well. He did not mind. He simply smiled faintly and left.

In my view, R.C. Bhargava is a broker. He benefited Suzuki a lot.

~

According to the constitution of our union, elections were to be held every year. They were held in 1988 but I did not contest them. Till 1994, I did not contest. However, in 1994, old friends started pressing me to contest. They came home, they used to call, repeatedly asking me to contest the elections. They harassed me no end. Just to get rid of this constant pressure I agreed. That one decision changed everything in my life. It changed the whole direction of my life. I contested and I won. I became general secretary.

That was the time when the salary revision was due. Once again there had to be an agreement with the management on wages and everything else. The management simply would not open negotiations.

Meanwhile, there was a countrywide general strike in 1994–95 and we also participated in it. We did not work for one day. I and many union office bearers were promptly suspended. There was an uproar of protest at this.

One day suddenly Osamu Suzuki himself came to the factory. R.C. Bhargava had brought him along in his car. It was four o'clock in the evening, when the shift used to change. Many workers were at the gate and they began to raise slogans. Very loudly. Bhargava was driving the car. Seeing the restive crowd, he had to stop. We actually physically lifted the car they were in and then we brought it down, parted in the middle and allowed them to go in. It shocked them. We had made our point. We did no harm to them.

I was there, but I had already been suspended and I could not go inside. Bhargava called me in and said, 'Drive away that crowd or I will call the police.' He was very angry. I told him that if it was a threat, I would not ask the workers to clear out and I asked him to go ahead and call the police! Then I told him that if he asked me nicely, requested me, I would see what

I could do. Then his tone softened a bit. Suzuki had by then been shown out of the back door.

I came out and told everyone that it was time to go home.

The management was not even talking about our wage settlement. The issue of incentives had also become contentious. There was a proposal to change it.

One day in 1996, Bhargava called me to the company's headquarters in Connaught Place. I went there with all the files related to incentives, salary, etc. I thought we were finally about to open negotiations on these issues.

They seemed to have some different plans. They began to offer me lots of money. They asked me to take fifty lakh rupees and leave the company. They also said that they would open a workshop for me in Hyderabad and get it registered. They wanted me to resign. They said they would accept my resignation only after the workshop became functional.

Bhaskarudu had already told me that this was the decision of the board, and that I should accept it. He was in the top management and was privy to such decisions.

That day I asked Bhargava what would happen if I did not accept his offer. What would he do?

Bhargava looked into my eyes and said, 'I will terminate you.'

I picked up the files and was leaving but from the door of the room I went back to him and told him, 'Today, you are the MD and I am an employee. When you fire me tomorrow, I will not be an employee any more. You will still be the MD. Then I'll teach you a lesson on the road.'

From there I went straight to A.B. Bardhan and I handed over the entire responsibility of dealing with the matter to Gurudas Dasgupta.* We used to read a lot about Dasgupta in

---

* A.B. Bardhan (1924–2016) was a trade union leader and the former general secretary of the Communist Party of India. Gurudas Dasgupta (1936–2019) was a leader of the AITUC; elected as its general secretary in 2001.

the newspapers. He was a sharp leader but he made you do a lot of running around. He would constantly make you do things.

In two days, Gurudas Dasgupta cowed down Bhargava!

Dasgupta called Bhargava to Vithal Bhai Patel House, where MPs had small quarters, made him sit down on the floor on a *durrie* and explained to him that it is not good to commit excesses, it is good to talk to the union, good to make a compromise. I don't know what all he said but Bhargava understood that it wouldn't be good if he did not talk to us and reach a compromise.

In those days, it was forbidden to hold a meeting at Maruti's gate. The management had got a stay order. Gurudas Dasgupta wanted to hold a meeting there and I told him about the stay order. He said the police would not refuse him permission. Dasgupta came to the gate. There was always a posse of police there. The SHO was there too. He walked up to Dasgupta and told him about the stay order.

Dasgupta was amazing! He said, 'Nobody can stop me!' and went ahead with the speech he had come to make. The SHO simply stood there watching.

Dasgupta had also explained the matter to the minister, [Murasoli] Maran, who asked Bhargava why he would not revoke my suspension. Then Maran too called a meeting. Deve Gowda was the prime minister then. Can you imagine, even Deve Gowda attended the meeting?

Bhargava, the Secretary in the Ministry of Industries, Maran and Gurudas Dasgupta, we were all in that meeting. The Prime Minister himself was present. Deve Gowda asked Bhargava, 'Why don't you take back the charge sheet you have given to Mathew?' Bhargava said, 'He makes speeches at the gate. He says that Indian culture is better than Japanese culture. He says that the Indian way of working is better. How can he be allowed to work in that factory? The factory has to be run in the way the Japanese want, in the Japanese way.'

Having heard this Deve Gowda got very angry. He said, 'I will not tolerate all this. These people should be inside the factory in fifteen days.'

That was an order from the highest functionary in the government of India. Bhargava had no choice.

So the Maruti company set up an enquiry! A firm of lawyers, Bhasin and Bhasin, was given the responsibility of investigating all that I had done. Its lawyers would come to the factory every afternoon after court hours and hold the enquiry meeting till eight o'clock in the night. Every single day they asked me the same things, the same silly questions. They were dragging their feet.

I began to drag the process of cross examination out of sheer anger at the process. I started putting unnecessary questions to anyone who testified. The chief security officer was a retired army officer. So I asked him if the name he had given us was his real name! In this way, I too started harassing them by asking stupid questions the way they had been doing with me.

One day Bhargava called me and asked why I was not allowing the enquiry to be finished quickly. 'Why do you ask irrelevant questions?' he asked me. I said, 'I will ask whatever I want to and whatever comes to my mind.' Bhargava then said to me, 'I will tell those who are fond of you about this.' I said do what you want to. So he said, 'I will fire you from the job.'

My health was not good those days. I had a stone in my kidney and had had it surgically removed. A stent had also been inserted. I used to pass blood in my urine. During this investigation, more blood started coming out in the urine. A friend of mine, who was from Kerala, had come to visit me and one day he accompanied me to the inquiry. I requested them to postpone the hearing for one day because I had been passing a lot of blood. They said, no, it is not allowed, and that I should cooperate in the investigation. I asked them to come with me to the bathroom and see for themselves how unwell I was. They said that was not their job. I said I'll pee in a bottle right here and you will see that I'm not lying. They said that cannot be done.

All this was being typed up by a secretary. They always do that, record everything that is said in the investigation. I asked to go see the doctor in the factory dispensary because I had a stomach ache. Eventually, they agreed and said, go to the doctor and get back in four minutes.

I went, the doctor gave me a pill, I had just put it in my mouth when the security guy shouted that four minutes were up! I spat out the pill, went inside, picked up a potted plant and was about to hit someone on the head when I came to my senses and put the pot down.

Now they began to tremble. The lawyer's trembling was clearly visible. Security people arrived. I said, I will knife everyone. I was very angry and a lot of abuses were flying from both sides. The security in-charge prepared a report on this whole incident saying that I had threatened everyone and asked me to sign it. I was not about to do so.

They adjourned the hearing till the next day. I picked up the file and told the lawyer, 'This is your last inquiry,' and I left.

You see, this is their tactic. They drive you crazy. Then you do something that you really don't want to do, that you never wanted to do.

Anyway, the next day, I was not allowed inside. No one had come to hold the inquiry that day. I needed proof that I had come. I wrote a note saying that I had come and wanted the security person at the gate to receive it. He refused. I told him,

'Now I will slap you, you will complain, and that will be my proof that I came. So let me give you a tight slap.' He silently received my note.

It is not good to do all this, but it has to be done because no one listens to you even if you are the union leader in that company. I am telling you all this because there is a need to understand to the extent to which the worker can be, and is, harassed. It becomes difficult for him to keep his composure. He has to take every step very carefully and after much thought. Anger has to be controlled. Labour leaders have to be ready to face all kinds of situations at all times and have to think of ways to counter them.

That lawyer who was holding the inquiry filed a complaint against me that I had abused and threatened him. But nothing happened in that case either.

Then, after fifteen days, my suspension was withdrawn, I went back to work. This time a manager was made the inquiry officer. He conducted some hearings but that inquiry was stopped. Meanwhile, Bhaskarudu became the MD.

The change in the top management impacted the whole factory.

Bhaskarudu began to insist on technology transfer and the issue of gear box technology transfer became a major point of conflict. Bhaskarudu wanted gear boxes to be made in India and he wanted Suzuki to give us the technology. He also began questioning the imports of various parts from Japan.

A serious conflict began between Suzuki and the Government of India.

We had a United Front government in the centre and whenever we met the minister for heavy industry we used to tell him that we would support the Government of India, and that meant supporting the MD, Bhaskarudu.

Now there were wage negotiations and our salaries were raised. Bhargava felt that the wage increase happened because Bhaskarudu used to support me. It does not happen like that. These settlements are the result of collective bargaining. Khattar was also involved in the bargaining.

At that time a general manager of the Bhaskarudu lobby had gone to Japan. He resigned when he came back. I don't know why but I later heard from others that once when he was having a conversation with a Japanese manager, for a full forty-five minutes the Japanese manager talked about me, asking him about my financial condition. Apparently, the Japanese manager told him that they will suppress me, make me kneel to beg for mercy. This manager from India felt bad that a Japanese was saying this about another Indian and perhaps protested too. He felt very bad about it, is what I heard.

Our salaries had increased but there were many other outstanding issues. Many other demands had to be discussed. The issue of incentives was on top of the agenda. There was a proposal to change the scheme. There were elections in the country. Dasgupta lost the election and ceased to be a Member of Parliament. The Vajpayee government was formed.

Bhaskarudu was removed from the post of MD before the end of his term. Khattar became MD. In Haryana, O.P. Chautala became the chief minister. He used to recognize me and if he saw me anywhere while addressing a public meeting he used to call me on the stage too.

We began agitating again. We started with a tool-down, stopping work for an hour every day. Then we had a relay hunger strike at the gate. Nothing made the management budge. Then we started a fast unto death. The management got a stay order from the High Court. I was dragged away to the Civil Hospital on charges of attempted suicide. The doctor's plans to confine me to the hospital bed went awry so the doctor got very angry.

I and union president Dinesh Kumar were sent to Rohtak jail. I was once again the general secretary of the union. Although we could have got bail the magistrate refused, saying that he wanted to check the papers of the union's registry first.

Some 500 workers had gathered at the courthouse. They scuffled with the police. There was an uproar. We were sent to jail. The Bar Association of Gurgaon went on a one-day strike in our favour. Soon I got out of jail.

Again the same *dharna*, picketing and agitation started. The police came and told me that they had orders to shoot if anything went wrong. We got up and went to Udyog Bhawan. It was on 13 December and we stayed on there in the cold till 8 January 2001. Manohar Joshi was the then minister for heavy industry. They did not even talk to us.

Finally, an agreement was reached in January 2001. The management said that the union would have to give a bond of good conduct. By then some 100 union activists had been suspended and some fourteen had been dismissed. Those dismissed were not taken back although some suspensions were withdrawn.

We were exhausted. We had waged a long and hard struggle.

I had not been suspended, but our president Dinesh Kumar was. We had had relay hunger strikes and tool-downs and we now said, let us work without signing any good conduct bonds. We even filed a petition in the High Court but it was not admitted. We signed the terms of the agreement and got back to work.

The union elections had not been held in this chaos. The Registrar of Trade Unions sent us a notice to ask why the union's registration should not be cancelled. The reason for this notice was a rule they have. Section 15(j) of the Trade Unions

Act states that a union cannot spend more than 25 per cent of its income on any item. Meaning, if you want to spend 100 rupees then you have to deposit 400 rupees in the account. It was difficult to pay attention to all these details during so many agitations; the expenditures were high.

We soon announced elections and made a retired High Court judge our returning officer. The Registrar's office cancelled the registration of our union in December. The management put a lock on the union's office. Now there was no union and no elections were to be held.

An investigation began against suspended workers. I started accompanying them in the inquiry. The management then handed me a charge sheet accusing me of having caused a loss of crores to the company. They did not even complete the inquiry.

They dismissed me.

At that time the company brought in its first VRS [voluntary retirement scheme].

I had two children then. The elder was only five years old, the younger three years old. I did a variety of jobs. Nothing worked. I used to live in Gurgaon. I had bought a plot there at a low rate. I sold it. I lived on rent in Mahipalpur. My younger brother supported me a lot.

Now, my brother has got this flat in Delhi. He does not live here, I live in his flat. I do some construction work on contract now. After all, I am an engineer and that helps.

Mathew Abraham was served three charge sheets. The charges included making a statement asserting that Indian culture is better than Japanese culture!

Having crushed the Maruti Udyog Employees Union, the management promoted a union called the Maruti Udyog

Kamgar Union (MUKU) at the Gurgaon plant. It was set up by workers who had signed the good conduct undertaking. It was what the workers called a *jebi* union. The MUKU was registered in November 2001.

The Joint Labour Commissioner told the International Commission on Labour Rights that MUKU had been 'nurtured and developed by the management' ('Merchants of Menace', 2013). The Labour Commissioner also told them that the Maruti Suzuki management wanted an internal union with no outside influence from such federations like the AITUC.

The International Labour Commission points out that MUKU was in violation of international labour standards which require that workers' organizations must have total independence from employers in all activities.

But by 2010, MUKU underwent some changes. Genuine union leaders stood for elections and changed the character of the MUKU from being a scab union to becoming one which genuinely represented the workers' interests.

Rajesh Kumar

President of the Maruti Udyog Kamgar Union (MUKU). He was active in the 2000 strike led Mathew Abraham. Long after MUEU was de-registered, when MUKU had its first proper elections by secret ballot in 2010, he contested it. He lost. In 2014, he contested again and became president. He was interviewed on 1 March 2020 in the union office inside the Gurgaon factory.

I was born in 1973 and was only twenty years old when I joined Maruti as an apprentice in 1993. Maruti had by then become a famous car but I had no idea that there was such a car; even though I lived in Palam which was only about fifteen kilometres away from the factory.

We were very young. We could work hard, we could stay up nights. We had no problems lifting heavy parts, bending over 200 times an hour and doing other things also if necessary. In the beginning my hands hurt, my arms went numb, and I had constant pain in the back. For all this as an apprentice I got a stipend of Rs 610 a month, and if I did overtime, I made Rs 900 or even more. After finishing the 'A' shift, we used to sometimes work in the 'B' shift also. I got ten or fifteen rupees for working an extra shift. Yes, the whole shift, not an hour on the shift.

When I became a trainee in 1994, I began to earn a total of 1,900 to 2,000 rupees in this way. I was a trainee for two years and in 1996 I became a permanent worker. My salary was Rs 3,500 a month. It was still a public sector enterprise so I also got Dearness Allowance (DA), Housing Rent Allowance (HRA), Conveyance Allowance and a medical allowance.

In 2000, things started to change. At the time 60 per cent of my salary came from the incentives. I was a member of the Maruti Udyog Employees Union or the MUEU.

The change started around 1997.

I.K. Gujral (1919–2012) was the prime minister during 1997–98. When, in 1997, it was time for the GoI to choose the MD, he chose Bhaskarudu despite Suzuki objecting to his appointment. Bhaskarudu's relationship with Suzuki was not good.

The leader of our union then was Mathew Abraham. Mathew was in the good books of Bhaskarudu. Suzuki was annoyed that Bhargava had not been made MD.

Then things started getting really bad.

Bhaskarudu used to think that the company was importing too many things from Japan. Why can't we make some things ourselves, is what he wanted to know. Also, he began to ask why we had to get all the goods from Japan when many of these things were made by other countries and could be bought at cheaper rates.

He decided that he would buy things from wherever they cost less, wherever they were cheapest. He also began to insist on making a few components in the country. A conflict began on these issues in the top management. Efforts were made to remove Bhaskarudu.

The impact of this whole struggle began to be felt in the union as well. Later, Atal Bihari Vajpayee ji made good use of it. When Vajpayee's government was formed in 1998, he intervened in the ongoing battle with Suzuki over the appointment of Bhaskarudu. Bhaskarudu had to resign some four or five months before the completion of his term. Jagdish Khattar was made MD, who belonged to R.C. Bhargava's lobby.

At the same time Maruti divested some of its shares. These were sold to Suzuki and the shares of Suzuki increased. Maruti sold more shares to Suzuki later.

Before that the incentive plan that we had here was changed. In the original incentive scheme, if we produced more cars than the target, we got more money.

Soon workers began to produce so much that sometimes they got more than their salary as incentive. Initially, all the cars used to get sold very fast. Then an inventory began building up.

Then the management wanted to revise the incentive scheme. They said that the incentive would be given only if the cars are sold. They argued that the factory could make money only when it sells cars. Otherwise, how would it make profits? And if it made no profits it could not pay extra money as incentive. The union argued back to say that selling the cars was not their job. They worked hard and they deserved to be paid the incentive. That was the original scheme anyway.

By that time the Vajpayee government had been formed

at the centre, Om Prakash Chautala was the chief minister in Haryana, and the MD changed in the factory. Manohar Joshi was the Union minister for heavy industry.

Mathew and Khattar did not get along. Controversy started on the issue of this incentive in 1999. Workers started an agitation. One day the workers would wear black bands, on another they would raise slogans at the gate. There were tool-downs and slow-downs and other such forms of protest. Workers also refused to eat in the canteen. We were threatened with disciplinary action.

The management decided to teach Mathew a lesson. One day when we reached the factory, we saw that police barricades had been placed on the Kapashera border. We were in the company bus, yet our bus was stopped too. We got down and walked towards the factory. Police were stationed all around. We were very surprised. I could not understand what had happened, why there was so much security. When we were close to the gate we saw that the entire executive body of the union was standing there.

They told us that a 'Good Conduct Undertaking' had to be signed before we would be allowed in. They also told us that nobody *has* to sign it. I refused to sign like most of the workers. This face-off continued for three days.

We would walk from the barricade to the factory gate, not sign, not enter the factory. After this some people started signing it to go in but we sat on a *dharna*.

There was a Jwala Mill there that was closed. We sat on a *dharna* in front of the mill because there was no space near the gate.

Those workers who were still working inside the factory were not allowed to come out; they were forced to work inside to ensure the essential work of production was not disrupted.

They were forced to work inside the factory for three days. It was then that one worker died inside the factory.

There was a lot of panic. The post-mortem report said he had died of a heart attack. That scared our families too. This had happened when we were still sitting outside the Jwala Mill.

We were then driven away from there by the police so we went and sat in front of Udyog Bhawan in Delhi for three months.

Ramesh Dalal

An old worker and staunch supporter of Mathew Abraham; he inspired younger workers like Khushi Ram to join the trade union movement. Interviewed on 8 February 2020.

Our first strike took place in the year 2000. It was on the issue of incentives. The factory had a wonderful scheme of incentives. If you met your target and worked more than the set target you would get paid for it. Every day they would give us a target. We used to cross it and we would benefit by doing so. This scheme had been devised for three years. When we worked more than was required by the target set for the day the company saved a lot of money and the company distributed 65 per cent of the savings among workers and 35 per cent among managers.

Then the company said that they would revise the scheme. Managers spoke to the union but they could not come to an agreement. By that time Mathew Abraham had become the union head. He called a general body meeting of the union. It was decided that we would go on strike. That is how the first strike in Maruti took place that lasted a full one and a half months.

We worked up to the strike. Before that we did a lot of

things. First we decided that we shall not have tea. Then we stopped having meals in the canteen. We used to work on empty stomachs. Then we decided that we would work less and every day we stopped work for an hour. Then we began to stop working for two hours every day. It went up to four hours of tool-down every day. This was our agitation.

The management had put up a table outside the factory gate with good conduct forms on them. Jagdish Khattar was then the MD and he himself would be seated near that table. M.M. Singh and C.S. Raju were also there. Singh was then the in charge of the weld shop. Raju was another manager. These people then started calling our families in Maruti Kunj and began to threaten them, telling them to ask the Maruti employee in their family to sign the good conduct form or he would be in trouble. Then police gypsies began making the rounds of Maruti Kunj. In fact police gypsies took the workers who had joined duty to work and also brought them back. Their wives would come to the houses of those still on strike and talk to the wives to persuade the workers to give up the resistance to the good conduct forms. The wives of the workers who had joined duty would keep taunting our wives. The atmosphere was tense in the colony. Some people came to my house too and threatened my wife. She did not know what was going on and she got a bit scared too but when I explained the whole thing to her she stood by me firmly. In fact all the women of the families of striking workers banded together and resisted the threats and stood by us.

There are 916 flats in Maruti Kunj. The majority of the workers there were on strike and the ones who had chosen to work were few. The struggle seemed to spill over to the colony and both factions would raise slogans against each other all the time. The families were likewise divided in two factions.

Maruti had its head office in the LIC building in Delhi and 15,000 members of families of the workers held a protest demonstration there. There has never been such a large demonstration of families of striking workers. Except for some traitors everyone was with us.

Five

Karoshi: Death by Overwork

When I grow up, I want to be a doctor in science.
I will make a time-machine, like the one Doraemon has.
I will ride the time-machine, and go to the day before my father died.
And I will tell him, 'Don't go to work.'

—'My Dream', Fujita Hiroshi,
the seven-year-old son of a city worker,
who died of karo-suicide

Osamu Suzuki's utter indifference to the welfare of the workers is reflected in an oft quoted statement of his to R.C. Bhargava. He says that the reason why Japan emerged as the lowest-cost manufacturer of cars in the world was because, back home in Japan, they were veritably wringing water out of a dry towel. By comparison, the Indian towel was dripping!

In Toyota, they call this just that: *Kawaita zokin wo shiboru* (wringing drops from a dry towel).*

This metaphor illustrates the Japanese production method referred to as Kaizen, or 'continuous improvement', a regime of production to remove 'waste' by increasing work intensity and reducing 'idle' time.

---

* 'Wringing drops from a dry towel', *The Financial Express*, 28 April 2005 (https://www.financialexpress.com/archive/wringing-drops-from-a-dry-towel/132006/, last accessed 17 January 2023).

We initially thought the Japanese were perhaps indifferent to their employees in India, but they treat their own people with scarce respect. An American engineer who worked in a Toyota company writes how shocked he was by the punishing work ethic, unyielding deadlines, the widespread practice of unpaid overtime, the oppressive 'culture of rules' (Mehri 2005).

Stressful working conditions in Japan are so much a part of life that they have even led to the coining of words for some alarming phenomenon like *karoshi*, or death by overwork, and *karojisatsu*, suicide due to overwork and stress. The term *karoshi* was coined by a group of labour lawyers in 1988 when they established the National Defense Counsel for Victims of Karoshi and started the 'Karoshi Hotline' to provide consulting services and to draw attention to the problem. (Shibata 2012)

The Japanese government received 2,835 complaints of death from overwork, or *karoshi*, in 2020. Compensation was paid in some 800 cases, including a suicide case.*

Mathew Abraham had also complained about at least two workers who had died of sheer exhaustion and overwork. (See also 'Freewheelin' Capital', PUDR, 2007)

At least one journalist, Naren Karunakaran, writing in *The Economic Times*,† asked the question: Could it be that in the name of being efficient the Japanese are exporting the stress and trauma of work conditions back home in Japan to their overseas operations, in India, and elsewhere?

---

* 'Toyota apologizes to family of employee who committed suicide due to overwork', *HT Auto*, 2 February 2022 (https://auto.hindustantimes.com/auto/news/toyota-apologizes-to-family-of-employee-who-committed-suicide-due-to-overwork-41643695338022.html, last accessed 11 January 2023).

† 'After Honda & Maruti Suzuki, Toyota faces labour unrest in India; are Japanese cos insensitive?', *The Economic Times*, 27 March 2014 (https://economictimes.indiatimes.com/news/company/corporate-trends/after-honda-maruti-suzuki-toyota-faces-labour-unrest-in-india-are-japanese-cos-insensitive/articleshow/32746066.cms?from=mdr, last accessed 11 January 2023).

The Indian media has not gone into the causes of stress among the workers of Maruti Suzuki. Instead, they have taken the management's version at face value or their own political understanding has coloured their reporting and even led them to demonize the trade unions.

The accounts by union leaders reflect their maturity and also the deep sense of solidarity among themselves and their families.

Rajesh Kumar

I remember how we sat on a *dharna* outside Udyog Bhawan in the bitter cold. By that time I was married and had two children. One was only a few months old. But my family stood by me. They said, either all of you go in together or stay put; don't break ranks.

When we were on the *dharna* outside Udyog Bhawan, our families gave us a lot of support. Our families used to cook food and bring it for us. I have also read history and political science, but I had never read about such a struggle anywhere. I actually participated in it.

We did not get a salary for two months but our families did not complain at all. They supported us in every way. Despite a shortage of money, our families got together to make 150 *rotis* and bring them for us. Some would bring lots of *daal*.

We were not allowed to set up tents and we slept under the open sky. Some people brought us quilts from home or they rented them from tent suppliers. The quilts used to get wet with the dew by early morning and then we felt cold under them.

Sometimes it rained too. We used to sleep underneath such wet coverings. We could not even change clothes for two or three days at a time. Later, we managed to put up tarpaulin covers. The wind would be so strong that one day the tarpaulin flew away. Nature had also turned against us!

When the tarpaulin got blown away the pole it was tied to fell on someone's head. His head was injured. Two others were also injured.

We told each other stories and played cards. We actually had a good time. We laughed a lot. We played games. Once we formed a human chain to prevent people from entering Udyog Bhawan. Employees of the offices there came to meet us and heard about our problems.

People from the press came to meet us initially, for a few days. For the first few days they even published a little bit about us. After that they did not bother. No one came from the ruling party. Gurudas Dasgupta from AITUC used to come. And some people also came from INTUC. As far as I remember no one came from CITU and HMS.

After the settlement the management took action against many of us. Some got a warning letter, some got a suspension letter. I did not. A friend of mine also got it.

Many were intimidated in this way. Then they would appear before the management officials and get the letter withdrawn.

They had changed our departments so the speed of our work slowed down and Maruti showed losses.

The most interesting thing was our salary slip. We got the slips of three months stapled together. We were thrilled when we were handed these that they were paying us wages for the time we had been on strike. Then they showed us the calculation of what needed to be deducted because of the strike. That led to everything turning to zero! So we got nothing. We thanked our stars that we were lucky enough not to have to pay them!

After the strike in 2000, automation increased. Lots of huge machines came into the factory. The die machine is gigantic and it covers an entire football field. The die is the most important thing. Once you make the die it is useful for every vehicle. When they brought the die machine a crowd gathered to just look at it with amazement. The truck that brought it had 258 tyres. A team of six people had to help the truck to turn around!

The union elections were held. Perhaps Mathew again became the general secretary then. I can't remember who became the president. By then the situation was so bad that no one wanted to contest the elections because whoever got elected got a warning letter.

The management made a very strong case against Mathew. He lost his job.

Then came the VRS. Many were thrown out via the VRS. The union was also derecognized.

The strike in 2000 had started with a tool-down strike of two hours each shift in October for nine days. It brought the production down to 299 vehicles a day. Police was deployed in front of the factory and workers were not allowed into the factory unless they signed a good conduct undertaking stating they would not engage in strikes and agitations. Of the 4,800 unionized workers some 600 finally signed the undertaking.

The good conduct undertaking was later taken back by the company and the union accepted the changes in the incentive scheme.*

* It was a complicated scheme involving, among other things, linking incentives to sales, factoring in capital investment (e.g. improvements in technology) to calculate the incentive, etc. See 'Hard Drive', PUDR, 2001.

The struggle, however, did not end with this. The company introduced the voluntary retirement scheme which was opposed by Mathew's union, the MUEU. More than 2,000 workers were forced to take voluntary retirement and they were replaced by contract workers. Those workers who had signed the good conduct undertaking then set up the Maruti Udyog Kamgar Union, MUKU in the Gurgaon plant.

Ramesh Dalal

After the settlement we began to be harassed. First of all they changed our work stations. It takes time to get used to new work but they would insist on a high speed of work. We were given too much work. The targets were impossibly high.

Some workers were promoted to the level of supervisors. This was a new policy. People who had worked in production were to be promoted to supervisory tasks. These supervisors, who used to be workers like us, were haughty and exceptionally badly behaved. They never spoke nicely, bristling all the time.

The supervisors were now being rude to us, really rude. For the slightest of mistakes we were issued charge sheets. If we left one bolt unfixed, we got a charge sheet. Earlier, it never used to be like this. We would be gently shown our mistakes and they would be corrected. Supervisors are diploma holders, they are educated people and they used to be very well mannered. They used to be more forgiving. They gave us a chance to correct our mistakes. Now, they issued charge sheets for the most minor of mistakes.

The workload increased too much. People who worked with me had been transferred to other stations. This was done to separate friends from each other and break our unity. This went on for a year or so. Many workers, especially those who were more active in the union, were charge sheeted and some were dismissed after enquiry. Within a few months about fifteen leaders of the union were sacked.

Workers began to feel terrorized. They announced a VRS. I did not want to retire since by that time I was married and had two schoolgoing daughters and a son. [My son] is very fond of archery and is truly good at it. Now he is in his BA first year. But a lot of pressure was put on me to leave my job.

The head of HR at that time was one Talukdar. He had designed this VRS. He had a single policy, divide and rule. He would get people fighting with each other. Factions began to form. There was always tension on the shop floor. It was difficult to work with so many pulls and pressures.

They used many tactics to mount pressure on people like me. They would call me to the rest area. Someone would then come and start telling me how good a scheme it was, how much money I would get, what all I could do with the money. Workers till Level 6 were all in the union. Supervisors are at Level 7. They are not union members.

I was a supporter of the union and when all this began happening I yelled at them a couple of times. Once I even had a fight with someone trying to persuade me to take advantage of the VRS. And now, those people, those traitors, who had not sided with us, they too got thrown out! The management did not spare anyone.

Whenever there was a break or you went to the rest area someone would follow you and start persuading you to opt for VR or taunt you. Then they began to threaten. They said, what will you do if we dismiss you? Do you have enough staying power to fight this company in court? Go ahead, resist, get fired, and keep running to courts for years. All your savings will be gone. You will be reduced to penury. They will be rid of you, one way or another. So be sensible, take whatever you can get and leave with something in the bank. Then again, they would pull out a piece of paper and start writing down numbers. They did this to a lot of people, even those who worked in the store and not in production. Like one worker whose name I remember was Mahavir Yadav. He worked in the store. He too got pressured into opting for voluntary retirement.

My children were small. I discussed this in the family. I had to think of the future of my children too. I was still paying instalments towards the flat I had bought from the company. Eventually, I gave up and quit. They deducted the remaining amount I owed them for the flat. That is another story.

We had been given a loan for fifteen years for the flat. But when I took VR they not only deducted the remaining amount of the loan but also the interest that we would have paid in fifteen years. The calculations they had been showing us while persuading us did not have these details. Now our whole budget went haywire. But I could not have risked being dismissed. My family also said, just get what you can, no point working with so much stress and falling ill.

Till 2012 I lived in Maruti Kunj. Then I sold that flat. We had not been given the registry papers. It was not easy to sell it since it was not a freehold property. It could only be transferred to another's name in the cooperative society papers. But we could not have the sale deed registered. I made the sale through transfer of the property in the records of the group housing society. When it is tough to get the right papers prepared you also get much less than the market price. I managed to sell it somehow and bought this plot in Neelkanth Colony. There are three houses of us three brothers on the same plot. My daughters are now grown up. The elder has a BSc degree in Physics and is thinking of going abroad for her majors.

As for me, whatever had to happen has happened. After we left Maruti, conditions improved there. The management made a new union called MUKU. That was a pocket union of the management. Kuldeep Jangu became its president. He was my junior, very junior to me. I know him. He never got into any argument. I don't remember where he was during that long strike. Perhaps he was one of those who signed the good conduct form and went inside to work.

A lot has changed. When I came to live in Neelkanth Colony it was surrounded by farms. Now it is full of buildings, a congested colony.

Rajesh Kumar continues...

After having cleared the factory of most of the vociferous protestors the new scheme of incentives was implemented. Earlier our incentive had gone up from Rs 11,000 to Rs 12,000 in a month. It was cancelled.

In the new scheme the management imposed an upper limit on the incentive. That meant no matter how much work you do, no matter how well you do, you will get a maximum of Rs 5,000 a month as incentive. They also made a new rule that for a sudden absence from work for three days you lose the entire amount of the incentive. For one day's leave we lost Rs 1,500 and for two days of 'uninformed leave' we lost Rs 2,000, if I remember correctly. So, every leave you took had to be taken only with their permission.

The system of this leave is very complicated here. If a worker for some reason failed to come to the factory on one day then it was considered one and a half day's leave. Even if someone had died at home the worker had to inform, seek permission and only then go on leave. Such a sudden absence on a Saturday was counted as two and a half days' leave. See, Sunday is a holiday, the factory is closed, but it was counted as leave along with half the day of Monday even though the worker reported for work on Monday.

Those days they had manual card punching here. We had to push in a card in a slot at the gate. Sometimes it malfunctioned, or the card was not entered properly. You were marked absent even though you were working inside the factory. The supervisor has the name of every employee, his work station, shift, staff number, everything on a 'K' sheet. Despite this, if the card was not punched right it was considered an unplanned leave. This happened with many workers.

Also, we used to get a reliever who would relieve you from work if you needed a break. Earlier, that break was given for twenty minutes, then it was reduced to fifteen minutes. After the strike, for some time, the reliever, who works in your stead if you need to go to the bathroom, began coming for only five minutes. Then after some time we had no relievers.

The company also discontinued the bus service after the strike. Our transport allowance was Rs 50 a month. Which did not even cover a bus pass. To reach on time meant extraordinary effort and if you took an auto and it had a puncture on the way you were sure to lose a lot of money.

The working conditions then became horrible. The work was like physical and mental torture. Body ached. The mind was tense. The salary was not being raised.

Then a puppet union was formed. On 28 November 2000, MUKU was formed. No one wanted to become a member of MUKU. The management would summon MUKU office bearers and ask them why they were unable to persuade workers to become members. Then MUKU office bearers began to threaten workers with increased workload if they did not join.

MUKU also got our salaries raised. It was a nominal raise but we lost most of it because it was deducted for uninformed leave.

In those days MUKU elections meant gathering a bunch of workers near gate number 2 and selecting people with a voice vote. That was recorded on a video camera. This situation continued till 2010. Then we thought of joining MUKU and capturing it. But whatever we did we could not hold proper elections. Then something happened which changed everything.

It happened in July 2011.

Dalchand

A Dalit worker, active in the MUEU and also member of a Scheduled Caste Association which is not officially recognized. He was dismissed and is now reduced to selling vegetables in Maruti Kunj. Interviewed on 1 March 2020.

I am from Mathura in Uttar Pradesh but I went to the ITI in Palwal. I became an apprentice in 1987–88 and in January 1991 I got confirmed as a trainee and became a permanent worker. I was not an office bearer of the Maruti Udyog Employees Union. I was an ordinary member. Everybody is a union member. I didn't know much about such things. When we had that three-month-long strike I joined the strike too because I had to do what everyone else was doing.

After such a big struggle, a settlement was reached on 8 January and the lock-out was lifted on 12 January 2001. Many were fired after being given a charge sheet. It was a backdated charge sheet. No warning was given. They gave me a charge sheet accusing me of having raised slogans.

Then an investigation took place. I presented seven witnesses in my favour. Investigators said the testimony was false.

When we ended the strike and our *dharna* outside Udyog Bhawan and came back to work, we had so much more work to do that we had no time even to go to the toilet. There was nobody to relieve us even if we were desperate. Every worker had to handle the workload of four men. The supervisor used to speak so sternly that we were always tense and the mind used to be disturbed. The supervisors were people who had previously worked on the line. Still, they had no sympathy for us.

On top of all this we were moved from the old work stations where we were used to working to new stations on the assembly line. I had to get used to working at a new station and it took some time to adjust, adding to my stress.

~

They had given charge sheets to all of us, all the 165 workers. Apart from that they had fired close to 100 workers straight away. They had forgiven only fifteen people.

I was the first to approach the Scheduled Caste Commission and then about thirty-five SC workers followed my example. They had given me a charge sheet saying that my production was low. But that was not true and I had proof. I complained saying that the management was targeting SCs. They used to call me in the office and threaten me and tell me that they could fight me up to the Supreme Court. We were about 500 SC employees in Maruti and about 250 were in the SC Association.

I gave my address as care of the Maruti factory, so all the responses of SC Commission used to go to the MUL office and I never got a reply to my complaint.

Then I wrote again to the Commission saying I had been dismissed and my caste was a factor, and that the management was targeting us Dalits. Some thirty-five of us had been charged with false allegations claiming that we had stood around raising slogans and had not worked and fulfilled our targets.

Khattar, the MD of Maruti, was summoned to the Commission; he went only after being sent a notice that he would be arrested if he did not appear. The thirty-five of us waited outside.

Then we were called in and told that I would get the job back. I got a letter from one Yadav Enterprise offering me a job for less than 3,000 rupees and I refused. They must have been asked to give me a job. I told them that I was a government sector employee in Maruti and did not want a private job loading and unloading stuff.

I did not complain again to the SC Commission. What is the point?

In the VRS, after eight years of service, they were giving me only 1.63 lakh rupees. Of this, one lakh would have been deducted for the flat in Maruti Kunj. I would have got 63,000 only. So, I refused to take voluntary retirement.

In the meanwhile the investigation of the charge sheet issued to me started six months after it was given to me. That was their method of harassing you: issue a charge sheet, make some allegations, let the sword of an enquiry dangle above your head and make you work beyond your capacity and also suffer the rude behaviour of your supervisors. The stress was almost unbearable.

The enquiry lasted for three months. There would be hearings continually. They would question me, cross-question me, and then give me another date to appear again. In the end a final report of the enquiry was submitted and they threw me out.

I filed a case in the labour court. Seven more people had

been thrown out with me. All of us went to the labour court. One of these was a Shravan Kumar Gupta. I am telling you his name because his name figures in something that happened later.

We had all filed the case together. It was a common case and the lawyer was also the same. All eight of us collected the money and paid the lawyer. Each one of us gave Rs 50,000. The lawyer got a full four lakh rupees.

We had all been given the same charge sheet. The charges were the same.

The verdict came after seven or eight years.

Now just see what a funny thing happened. The labour court gave two decisions. The first decision was in the case of Shravan Kumar alone. He was reinstated. The decision went in favour of the worker.

A week later, the judge delivered the verdict against the remaining seven. We were not reinstated. We went to Chandigarh and appealed against the decision in the High Court.

The management also appealed against the decision in the case of Shravan Kumar in the High Court and got a stay order. So he too was not reinstated. Even after winning his case in the labour court he remained jobless.

Our appeal has not been heard till now. We are given a date. We go to Chandigarh. Stay in some *dharamshala*. The whole day we sit in the High Court. Then, just before our case is to come up, the judge goes away or some such thing happens. Our file is moved to the next date. We go back.

It has not been heard for eight years. Once we were very close to being heard. We thought the case would definitely be decided that day. The lawyer for the management was one Rajiv Raina. The judge asked him what it meant to give a back dated charge sheet. 'How can such a thing be done?' he asked Raina. The lawyer had no answer. He kept silent. And we were so happy! We were there. We thought we were about to win our appeal.

The next day was the date of hearing for the management's appeal in the case of Shravan Kumar. Perhaps the management was nervous. I don't know why but they suddenly sent a senior lawyer in his case, senior to Raina. This senior lawyer came and asked to be given a week's time because the case had just been given to him. Time was given to him. There has been no hearing since then. Shravan Kumar Gupta is still jobless like us.

All the other workers who were fired have also gone to court. All of us are in the same boat that is headed nowhere.

Now Maruti will go to the Supreme Court. That is what they used to threaten me with. They would say, '*Tumhari aukat kya hai hai ki tum Supreme Court tak lad loge.*' [What makes you think you'll hold out till the case goes to the Supreme Court.] I am sick of everything. I have three sons. Their future prospects were destroyed. Two had to be taken out of DPS and put in a government school. They passed with difficulty. They are unemployed now.

My wife does not have a job. I live here in Maruti Kunj. We own the flat and do not have to pay rent. That is the only relief.

I sell vegetables to make a living. I studied for so many years, learnt so much technical work. I am so skilled. I have years of experience in one of the most modern factories and I cannot find a job. What's the use? What is the worth of all that today? I am selling vegetables.

I tried very hard to find a job in many places. The management has long arms. They can reach very far. Perhaps everyone has been told not to hire us. After all, the vendor companies work for them. Nobody gives us work.

For eight years, we paid the instalments of the house we bought in this Kunj in Badshahpur. This was Maruti's second housing project.

I got no compensation, no severance pay—nothing—because I had been dismissed. The flat is ours but I still do not have all the papers. I had asked the management to deduct the amount I owed towards instalments from whatever they gave me when they settled my accounts after my dismissal. They did not.

We cannot pay the instalments. We don't have money to pay. We have not paid any instalment for seven years now. There is some penalty too. I perhaps owe 1.60 lakh rupees. I did not even take my provident fund. We will see later what happens.

This housing project is also a scam. We only have an allotment letter and a possession letter. Nothing else. Even those who had paid all the instalments did not get any other paper. I do not know what the legal status of my house is.

I remember that when I got the house I did not get a single penny of my salary for six months. Everything used to go towards instalments. The salary slips I got in those days had a list of deductions towards PF, transport, housing...and in the end, what they owed me was shown as zero! So we have also taken zero salary slips from this company. It is a great company!

Now, I live by selling vegetables and only one of my children goes to the Delhi Public School located inside the Maruti Kunj colony; I cannot afford to send the others to that school.

The union and the management signed a settlement on 8 January 2001. The company was forced to withdraw the good conduct undertaking. It was a victory for the workers.

But at what cost?

The company had dismissed eighty-two workers. They did not take back all of them; twenty-four workers lost their jobs. These dismissals were without an enquiry and many of the charges against the union leaders are laughable except that it is not at all funny to lose your job without any prospects for an alternative one.

The charges include: shouting '*Inqilab Zindabad*'. G.K. Walia, the treasurer of the union, was charge sheeted for slogan shouting, conducting meetings.

The company acted in a very vindictive manner. As we saw in the interviews with Rajesh Kumar and Ramesh Dalal, they wouldn't allow workers relievers to even go to the toilet. It sounds unbelievable that such a thing goes on in a modern, automated factory. The technology may be mind boggling but the brutality of multinational companies like Suzuki is equally unbelievable.

There are many reports that have documented these illegal and unethical practices, how they violate labour laws and even amount to criminal offences and human rights abuses. We do not wish to quote those reports at length here. A list of reports has been given in the bibliography for those who may want to look into the matter in further detail.

The description of the working conditions and the allegations made by the workers and their union leaders were confirmed by a senior manager who agreed to be interviewed on condition of anonymity. He had resigned. He told Anjali that his wife and mother were still very upset with the events at the factory and did not want him to speak of his days at Maruti Suzuki. If a manager was scared of sharing his name so many years after he had resigned, the fear that Suzuki instils in its workers must indeed be quite forbidding.

Sathya Narayanan (name changed)

A former manager in Maruti Gurgaon. Interviewed on 20 March 2020 at his home in south Delhi.

To understand what happened in Manesar, it is very important to understand this company and its management style and its history.

I used to be a manager in Maruti; worked there for twenty years. I started working in Maruti when it was still in the public sector, and I saw it move into the private sector. I must say that despite being in the public sector, it had elements of a private sector management from the beginning.

Before talking about [Awanish Dev and the events of 18 July 2012] it is important to understand a few things.

It will be good to understand the mindset of the business class. Whether he is an industrialist or a big businessman or a trader, or a Japanese company...all have a similar mindset. They all want a direct line of communication with the top guy in government.

Easy access to the prime minister is like the proverbial cherry on the cake. It is very important for the corporate class to have easy access to the highest level of functionaries of the government, especially when they are doing something in collaboration with the government, like running an undertaking with them or working on a project for them. To be able to have access to the PM whenever they want is their biggest achievement.

The fact that the prime minister would meet with Suzuki whenever they wanted was one of the key elements when it came to the company's decision to work with Maruti. Right from the time of Indira Gandhi they had access to the prime minister. When I was employed in Maruti, Narasimha Rao was the prime minister and Narasimha Rao was easily available to the senior executives of Maruti and Suzuki.

It is also important for us to understand what Maruti means for Suzuki; what Maruti meant for Suzuki when it agreed to enter into a collaboration with it. And after so many years of collaboration, what does Maruti mean to it now? What is the importance of Maruti for Suzuki? Let us first understand this.

It is well known that when the Maruti factory was set up, Suzuki invested very little money. For Suzuki, Maruti was its workshop in a foreign country. The purpose of that workshop abroad was to make Suzuki richer by making tidy profits. It should be clear that for Suzuki Maruti was just a workshop that made profits for it. It was nothing more than that. I want to underscore this point. It should be very clear to us.

For us, Maruti was a new kind of industry. For us, its importance was much greater. It meant a lot more to us. That is not how Suzuki saw it.

When Maruti started production, there was no one like them in the market. There was no competition or rivalry. The whole market was open to Maruti. There was simply no one else who was making passenger cars except Hindustan Motors [which manufactured the] Ambassador, and Fiat. They could not compete with Maruti.

Obviously, if Maruti made something cheaper they stood to capture the entire market. That is common sense.

However, there are a number of ways to make something cheaper. The methods adopted to reduce the expenditure inside the company can be very complicated and they need to be understood in detail.

One way to reduce expenditure is to reduce the expenditure on the workers. It may sound simple but it is not a simple matter of paying less wages to workers. They have to work within a particular legal environment. There are laws. There is a labour department. There are courts. There are all kinds of complications. When you hire workers as permanent workers, wages have to be increased from time to time. Some facilities have to be provided. Industrialists want to avoid all this as much as they can.

There are many other ways to reduce this cost.

One way to reduce the expenditure on wages is that the workers not be given permanent jobs, they should be given work on contract. There are many benefits to doing this. One, you can fire such workers whenever you want. Two, you do not have to increase the salary from time to time; you also do not have to spend much on facilities that the law says you must provide them.

If work is to be given on contract then there must be contractors who can bring as many workers as the company wants and when they want them. It is very important that there be contractors and those contractors must have a large number of workers lining up for jobs. Only then will they be able to provide as many workers as are required, including those with the required skills.

In the beginning, the number of contract workers was low; they were hired only for packing and unpacking. The work did not require much skill. Material that came from Japan had to be unpacked. Back in my time, one such contractor started work with 1,015 people. Let us assume his name was Phool Singh. This Phool Singh started by providing 1,015 workers on contract to Maruti. Today, 3,000 workers come to him for work. More importantly, he can find employment for so many people.

The value of a contractor to the company is very high. You cannot even imagine how important a contractor is to the company. In some senses the contractor is more important than the manager. Why is a contractor important? Because he can give bribes. A manager will not bribe executives; he will take a salary which will cost the company. The contractor adds value to the company. He does value addition. He brings workers and controls them.

Permanent employees are in a different category altogether. The company has to spend money on them; they are costly. An entire HR department has to be employed for them. That's why the contractor is more valuable to the companies. He saves money for the company. That makes the product cheaper.

In economics, it is said that goods are ready to be sold only when there is value addition. There is a need to understand the role of the contractor in value addition. It is not as if laws stop applying when workers are hired on contract. Actually, the laws in India are very good. The government also gives work to people on contract. The legal position in India is that almost all labour laws that apply to permanent workers also apply to contract workers.

Now, if all laws apply and minimum wage rates are also fixed, then what is the benefit to companies from contract labour?

Here you have to look at the work culture. One problem is that permanent workers do not want to work at all. In India this is a major problem. To be honest, at least in the public sector, permanent workers do not work. Yes, in the private sector, permanent workers have to work; they cannot shy away from work.

Even though Maruti was in the public sector, right from the beginning, it operated as a private company. There was a manager, Dr R.B. Deshpande, who used to be with us. He had a PhD from USA and he did not care for R.C. Bhargava at all. He thought that Bhargava *saheb* was doing the work of indigenization of the company at a very slow pace. Deshpande was an aeronautics engineer and he had the habit of working at a very high speed. He wanted technology transfer and he wanted things to be made in India and he wanted this done as fast as possible.

This indigenization and its speed were at the root of much controversy and tension in Maruti.

Let me jump to 2014. That year a Maruti factory was established in Gujarat. This factory belongs to Maruti Udyog Limited [*sic*].* That means it is the factory of an Indian company in which Suzuki had become a partner. That Indian company got land in Gujarat. The company had a board meeting in January 2014. Bhargava was the chairman at that time. He did something rather amazing. It has been alleged that Bhargava helped Suzuki rent the land that had been given to Maruti to set up their factory. What does Suzuki do now? It makes cars in the factory that it set up on the land given to Maruti, and then it sells the same cars to Maruti Udyog!

Now just remember one more fact. Suzuki is a shareholder in Maruti Udyog Limited. Therefore it is also a shareholder in the profits that MUL makes. Suzuki's share in the Maruti industry now stands at 60 per cent. So, proportionately, Suzuki takes 60 per cent of the profit that Maruti makes by selling cars.

First, Maruti got the land. It sold it to Suzuki. Then Suzuki set up a factory on it and made cars in it. Suzuki sells those cars to Maruti. Suzuki makes a profit in that deal. Then Maruti sells the cars in the market and makes a profit. Then Suzuki takes 60 per cent of that profit because it owns 60 per cent shares in Maruti. Double profits on same product!

This was the situation in 2014.

---

* The name of the company had changed to Maruti Suzuki India Limited by then.

Now, Maruti Udyog Limited has become a one hundred per cent subsidiary of Suzuki. So, Suzuki is no longer making vehicles there, Maruti Udyog Limited is making vehicles there. Maruti now pays rent to Suzuki for its factory on that land which was originally Maruti's land. So again, Suzuki is making profit twice. It gets rent for the factory in which cars are made and then when those cars are sold it makes a profit.

Why did all this happen only in January 2014? It happened then because laws were about to change which would not allow such deals.*

Now let's focus on another thing. By the time the Gujarat factory was made, Maruti Udyog Limited kept its money in Indian banks. At that time, the interest rate was around 8 per cent per annum. Now, don't forget, that 60 per cent of the income earned by them used to belong to the Suzuki Motor Corporation because it holds 60 per cent shares! In this way, a large part of the interest also went into Suzuki's account. Suzuki was raking in profits through multiple avenues from India in this way.

Now what did Suzuki do with its share of the money it earned here? Banks in Japan pay very low interest rates. It was not a profitable deal for Suzuki to keep its money in banks in Japan. Suzuki used to bring its money to India and deposit it in the banks here and earn money from the relatively higher interest rates here.

If you take stock of all these accounts, you will find that India has contributed 80 per cent of Suzuki's profits. This is the first instance of foreign investment in India in which a foreign company was making more profit than us. Nominally,

---

* He is referring to amendments to the rules concerning corporate governance in the equity listing agreement of the Securities and Exchange Board of India.

Suzuki was our partner, but we were making so much profit for it that it seems as if we were working it. As if Suzuki had given us a contract!

I got a job in Maruti in 1991. R.C. Bhargava had selected me for the job. My boss there, the general manager, was a very intelligent man. Let us not name him. He told me that there were two stakeholders in this company, two owners: Suzuki and Maruti. Maruti is the Government of India. Suzuki is a private company. The Government of India can change, it will change. But Suzuki will not change, it will remain the same. He said his loyalty would be to Suzuki because that is not going to change. Be loyal to whoever is permanent! That was his mantra. Straight and simple.

So now let's talk about the division of labour. Maruti has three factories. There are two types of workers in all three: permanent and contractual.

The Contract Labour (Regulation and Abolition) Act, 1970 does not permit contract labour to be engaged to do the type of work that is permanent. Similarly, the use of contract work is forbidden in the core areas, in work that is essential for the factory.

In this context, a case of Air India is of great importance. The Supreme Court ruled that there is a relationship between the contractor and the principal employer (Air India). Therefore, Air India's responsibility towards contract workers would have to be what its responsibility was towards other permanent employees and they would have to give regular employment to contract workers after a certain period of employment. After this, Air India stopped hiring contract workers. This is just the gist of the ruling.*

---

* See *Air India Statutory Corporation and Ors vs United Labour Union and Ors*, (1997) SCC (L and S) 1344.

Now, this was a double whammy for private companies. Not only would they have to have regular or permanent workers, if they got the work done on contract then those workers would also have to be regularized. This situation persisted for a long time. More recently, in the case of the Steel Authority, the Supreme Court reversed its old decision.

When Maruti was in the public sector, the first decision of the Supreme Court was in force. According to the first decision, it was necessary to regularize the contract workers. According to the latest decision, there is no need to regularize contract workers. Earlier, workers were not hired on contract or fewer were hired and their work periods were kept short. Now, after the decision of the SC was reversed, the trend of employment in factories has also been reversed. What has happened now is that contract labour has become widespread.

It needs to be remembered that Indira Gandhi had passed a law that said that establishments with over 100 workers need the government's permission to retrench workers.

If you need government permission for retrenchment the process becomes very complicated. Very few want to do this. But a voluntary retirement is not considered retrenchment. You cannot even call it retrenchment because the workers are quitting of their own volition!

How this consent is achieved is a different matter.

Then there is the problem of unions. Unions here in India do not discipline workers and they do not ensure workers come on time or work properly. I really do not know how managements got work done in establishments where such unions existed.

It was in this background that the Maruti factory was built. There was fear from the very beginning that if there are unions work would suffer; it would be difficult to get workers to work.

That's why the practice of giving rewards on production started in Maruti. It meant that if production targets were met on time workers would get cash rewards, incentives. That's why the workers used to work a lot in Maruti. Maruti's goal was clear. Profits were a priority for them and production is necessary to earn profits. To ensure that workers put in their full effort such a system of incentives was necessary.

Ordinary people do not fully understand what kind of work this work of production is. In fact, 70 per cent of the work in any production process is in the non-core area and 70 per cent of this work is done on contract. It is outsourced. In many places, 70 per cent of the work is contracted to other countries where wage rates are low. Like it is happening in India and in Bangladesh; we get contracts from abroad to make goods.

If you look carefully, you will notice that in any company engaged in manufacturing, there are several layers. One part is made in one country, another in another country and some in one's own country. Parts come from many such places and then they are given a final shape. It is not visible to everyone. In our language we call it 'de-layering'. You can outsource production of components to really small units on which labour laws may not apply. In this way a hierarchy of production is formed.

Often within the company, there is no difference in work but different individuals get different wages.* The facilities or perks are also different. Apart from that the salary facilities or extra money are different at different positions.

Earlier the system was different. Now people don't understand the old system in which the first to be employed was the last to go. The one who comes first gets promoted and

* This may seem incredible but it is a common practice now in the private sector, where salary structures can often be different and only favourites are selected and rewarded.

reaches the top. Why should you work harder and better if your promotion is assured? People laugh at the old system. We too had that system till some years back.

Jack Welch changed all this. He is a theorist of management... or capitalism. He said that promotion should only be given on the basis of work. You work hard, you will be rewarded and you will be promoted to the next rank. It is not necessary to promote everyone.

With no background in business management we had never heard of Jack Welch, so we looked him up. We were curious because his name came up several times. For instance, in the Foreword to V. Krishnamurthy's memoir, *At the Helm*, the former managing director is compared to Jack Welch. There may be differences between managers, but in the end they are all trained to put the interests of the company first, and often at the expense of the workers' welfare.

It turned out that Jack Welch was an American business executive, chemical engineer and writer. He was chairman and CEO of General Electric (GE) between 1981 and 2001.

When Welch retired from GE, he received a severance payment of $417 million, the largest such payment in business history up to that point. Jack Welch is celebrated as the greatest corporate leader of the twentieth century. When he first became CEO of General Electric in 1981 the company was worth $12 billion. Twenty years later, it was worth a total of $280 billion.

But if we go beyond first appearances, we see that his real achievement was finding ways of getting rid of workers for his corporation.

During the early 1980s he was dubbed 'Neutron Jack' (in reference to the neutron bomb) for eliminating employees. In

Jack: Straight From the Gut (2001), Welch claims that GE had 411,000 employees at the end of 1980, and 299,000 five years later; 37,000 of the 112,000 that were taken off the payroll were in businesses which GE sold off, while 81,000 were removed from ongoing operations.

Welch is remembered for his outsized personality and aggressive management style, which had a direct impact on American capitalism. What many accounts of his life leave out, however, is the impact he had on the working classes and how that country is more unequal and unfair for it today. He was clear about unions: they were a hurdle to maximizing profits. Incidentally, Welch came to power the same year that Ronald Reagan, in a highly controversial move, fired thousands of striking federal employees.

The Professional Air Traffic Controllers Organization, or PATCO, an American trade union of air traffic control workers formed in 1968, had called a strike in February 1981 for reduced working hours and a better retirement package, among other things. Within six months, US president Ronald Reagan fired 11,345 striking workers and barred them from working for the federal government ever again.

The direct causal relationship between this episode and the crushing of labour in other sectors, including private businesses, in America is widely noted and celebrated on the political right.

Sathya Narayanan continues...

Now let's understand the structure of the management at Maruti. Jobs in the management in Maruti range from L11 to L18. L means level. I started working at L11. Status quo [with respect to promotions within a stipulated time period] is maintained till L14, and after that, from L15, promotions depend on the services you provide to the company, meaning how you help it maximize profits.

The higher you go the fewer the number of posts. So, if there are 150 managers only fifty will reach the top.

In the old system, everyone was assured of a chance to move upwards so they could say no to a wrong practice. If they felt that something was wrong, they could speak up, they could protest, they could criticize a decision they disagreed with. Although their promotion could be affected in that system too, it could only be delayed and not stopped for very long.

In the new system, it has become necessary to work according to orders from above. If you criticize the directions you receive you may never get promoted. Your salary will not increase. You may not get many perks. Worst of all, you will not get enough authority to participate in decision making.

There are standing orders in the company that you will not reveal your salary to anyone. Between two DPMs [departmental managers] one could actually be getting a salary that is three times higher than the other. They got other perks too. Like very high allowances to rent a house. Some of them got new cars. That is a public acknowledgement of that particular DPM's services and public humiliation of others. This is not common in the corporate world. Salaries are not secret. Everyone knows who is supposed to get how much on which post.

It is distinctly possible that for the same work, two people may get two different salaries. How will you know when you cannot tell and cannot ask?

In effect, the salary has become privatized! I am talking about the time when Maruti was still a public sector company.

So, every manager aspires to the level where the company will publicly acknowledge his service by giving him a car or some perk and make everyone aware of how important he is to the company! The end result is that everyone supports every policy of the management, to be able to forge ahead. Even if someone thinks or feels that something is wrong, he does not oppose it.

Suzuki needs contract workers. A manager is needed to arrange this. There is a sort of alliance between the manager and the contractors and aspiring managers will do what Suzuki wants even if it is something unethical. The manager will do what Suzuki wants and the contractor will get the workers to do what the manager says. In this way a chain of yes-men is formed. It is called sycophancy or *chamchagiri* in common parlance.

There is also a kind of mentality in multinational corporations whereby people just want to move ahead within their narrow world. It's called a rat race. When managers reach Level 12 after three or four years of service, they get into this rat race. They have to reach the top come what may and any which way.

Then there is performance management. This is about your work, your role and your performance in the company. Jack Welch has written extensively on the subject.

According to his way of doing things, a junior who has done well should be promoted because he or she is doing amazing work. It is possible that this junior is handed over the keys to a gleaming new car. Now all the seniors have been insulted.

In such a situation, there is a lot of competition, there is rivalry, jealousy and much bickering. There is practically a stampede to get ahead of others. It is not good for work.

DPMs will worry that they may never reach the level of a DVM [divisional project manager]. There is frustration. The atmosphere becomes vitiated. That happened in Maruti too. To save the work environment from further deterioration, the post of deputy DVM was introduced. That was not enough. Then specialists were introduced into this hierarchy.

All kinds of changes were effected to make managers less envious of each other. But whatever they did, promotions were not guaranteed and the system of rewarding only those who pleased the owner continued—if you do what the owner wants you to do you will be rewarded. How long can you manage by simply introducing new ranks and posts if the system is built like this?

I was a misfit in this arrangement. If you are an employee, you are a servant, you have to listen to the master. That much is true and everyone understands it. But I felt very uncomfortable. I felt uneasy always following directions, but I could not place my finger on what was bothering me.

When I quit the job and was free, I realized that this system was not good; it was unjust and the whole corporate culture itself is distorted in some way. That is what had made me uneasy. That corporate culture is built on a simple basis of return on investment. A human being does not remain a human being. The human being becomes an investment in this system. They keep calculating how much the factory is spending on you, how much you cost the company, and also how much interest should be charged on it and what returns the company is getting on its investment, what profits they are making. They don't care about anything else, they don't care at all.

Twenty years I worked in Maruti. I thought I did a great job. But not once did I get an 'A' grade. I was allowed to feel that I am a great manager. I was admitted at Level 11 and I thought I would reach Level 18 but that didn't happen.

Let's talk about the big strike in 2000 that took place in Maruti in Gurgaon. It surprised everyone. They thought Maruti was such a good company. How could something like this happen in it? Not the people inside the company, but common people outside were surprised that this had happened in Maruti.

All the disturbances took place when Suzuki's share in the company increased. When the increase in Suzuki's shares began, Bhaskarudu was the managing director; he did not oppose it. Mathew did not object either.

Then what happens is that Suzuki gives a target to the plant and we have to increase production to meet the target. Suzuki does not allow any increase in the number of permanent workers. Production has to be increased without increasing the number of regular or permanent workers. That is a lot of pressure. The workload on everyone goes up a lot. When that happens, pressure increases, many things become unbalanced. You start leaning on your subordinates to make them work more.

I never succumbed to this pressure, never bowed to it. I always did the best I could, but I never went to unjust lengths. I myself recruited some 2,000 people in the company and signed their appointment letters. I never gave a job to anyone on the recommendation of someone influential and I never took a bribe. I was known as an honest, hardworking manager.

I can't do injustice. For me Suzuki is not the biggest thing in life, it was not. Promotion in that company was not the goal of my life. There were other things that were important in my life; those were my priorities.

Being a big thing in the company was not my priority. The company was not my life. But for Awanish Dev, Suzuki was the priority. The most important thing in his life was the company; the biggest thing for him was to reach the top, to be recognized as a skilled manager and to reach the highest level. This was Awanish's goal.

Companies usually don't like a person like me. Why are you surprised? That's the truth. What happens is that gradually the company stops sending important work to a person like me. As a professional, I have no opportunity to grow because I do nothing challenging. The company had blocked the way ahead for me. And what is a life without challenges?

I had certain ethical standards and I got punished for it. I should have left the job long ago but I had a family and some compulsions. I kept working in Maruti till 2000. As long as Bhaskarudu was there, I remained there. Then he left...

Mathew Abraham was also very strong. I must say that the workers' union saved my job. Having Mathew Abraham was very important. He protected my job. Unions are not just a headache, they are also very important. This should be known and it should also be accepted.

When Mathew was in the union, he got to know of almost everything that went on. One day, in the parking lot of the company, Mathew told me that I was going to be fired. But Mathew Abraham also accepted defeat. Eventually, [realizing that I was soon going to be fired anyway] I mustered the courage to leave.

At that time the company had a pocket union; it was like a lapdog of the company. You should know how much power a pocket union of workers wields in the company. Let me tell you about an incident to illustrate it.

There was this leader of the pocket union and I shall call him Jai. This Jai was always posted in the general shift. The general shift works from 9 am to 5 pm. The second union, whose leader was Mathew, was actually very strong, so there was a lot of opposition to this Jai being favoured in this way. Everyone started asking why Jai was not doing his share of the work. When there was a lot of opposition to this, the management had to bend. The manager of the department, because of this pressure, posted Jai in the night shift. Let us say the name of this manager was Das.

Obviously, Jai was very angry. Soon, one day, while Jai was working, Das went to the shop floor. Jai vented his anger on Das. He grabbed Das's collar and lifted him clean off the floor. Both of Das's feet were above the ground and he was dangling in the air. Jai was of strong build and this Das was no match for him.

Now Jai may have been a favourite of the management, but Das was a manager and such misbehaviour could not be condoned. Jai had humiliated a manger in front of everybody, including workers. Something had to be done. Action against Jai became necessary. A management meeting was held at 9 am and it was decided that Jai should be suspended. Whatever his position, he had to be suspended. Otherwise, how would there be discipline? But that meeting went on and no action was taken. At around 10.30, the people of the pocket union went to have tea with the senior managers. After this the decision of the management changed. It said that if Jai apologized to Das on the shop floor, where he had attacked him, the matter would be put to rest and Jai would not be suspended. Then, by the lunch break, the decision was changed once more. The management said that Jai could go to the house of Das and apologize to him there.

When I heard this I began to fear that, by the evening, the whole matter might be put into reverse gear. The management might ask Das to apologize to Jai!

Finally, after much deliberation, Jai was charge sheeted but nothing happened to him. Despite this incident, no action was actually taken against Jai.

Let me tell you about another incident. There was a person

named Nag in the company. He was found writing a letter to Prime Minister Deve Gowda full of complaints against the company. He was suspended on the same day at 5.28 pm. There was a lot of discussion about it and after much pressure the manager had to withdraw the order of suspension. Look at the difference between the two incidents.

A person was suspended just for writing a letter of complaint. But Jai had directly attacked the manager and even then no action was taken against him. Such incidents kept happening. There was no effective resistance to such practices.

This kind of work culture creates a lot of pressure. That pressure affects the whole working environment and sometimes it leads to big and unwanted results.

What happened in Manesar was horrific. But we must understand the reasons why there was such rage and such violence.

Six

The Rank-and-File Trade Unions

When the union's inspiration through the workers' blood shall run
There can be no power greater anywhere beneath the sun
Yet what force on earth is weaker than the feeble strength of one
But the union makes us strong
Solidarity forever
Solidarity forever
Solidarity forever

—Ralph Hosea Chaplin (1887–1961)

In 2007, when Maruti Suzuki built a shiny new plant at Manesar, the management recruited an army of contract workers, hired through contractors. The workers were all young, between the ages of eighteen and twenty-five from neighbouring villages.

In Plant A at Manesar, there were around 1,000 permanent workers, 800 apprentices who did identical work but were paid less, and 1,200 temporary workers taken on by contractors. So there were around 3,400 workers altogether. They earned much less than the workers in the Gurgaon plant, less than twenty kilometres away.

A new generation of workers had joined Manesar. They had grown up seeing the contrast between the opulent lifestyles of the people who lived in the gated colonies and did their shopping in the shopping malls, with the lifestyle of the workers, especially contract workers, living in rented rooms without adequate ventilation. And they were impatient with their working conditions. They had no political background or experience of working in the trade union movement. They had heard of Mathew Abraham's struggle, but by this time that union had been de-recognized, and Mathew and his team had been forced to take voluntary retirement.

A new leader arose from among them with high aspirations and the determination to improve their condition. His name was Sonu Gujjar. He named his union the Maruti Suzuki Employees Union and was determined to register it and to fight for the right to be adequately paid without being overworked.

The workers opted for an independent union, by which they meant independent of the larger federations. Sonu Gujjar's union had the characteristics of what is called a rank-and-file union or a base union: guided by a layer of rank-and-file, i.e. workplace-based, leadership that can organize in the workplace on a day-to-day basis. This layer, sometimes called a 'militant minority', is composed of militant shop floor leaders, capable of moving their peers into action.

During the first occupation of the factory in June 2011, when the management cut off the water supply, the family members of the workers and people in the surrounding villages organized the food supply for the workers inside the factory. As the news spread to other villages, who saw the workers as, in a sense, their sons, they too began contributing to the effort. Later, the management would seek to drive a wedge between the workers and the villagers, and then they would start hiring workers from other States.

Anjali tried hard to get Sonu Gujjar to give an interview but he was most reluctant even if his identity was not revealed.

Probably, he wanted to put all the controversies behind him, which had come up when he was forced to take voluntary retirement. But while he was president of his Maruti Suzuki Employees Union he had given interviews. From these and from media reports and descriptions given by workers, it seems Sonu was a shy, modest and diminutive man. He was a welder and he would tell the media that the Suzuki factory had turned workers into robots at the assembly line. One of the main demands of the workers at this time was the demand that the government register their union. But the labour department refused to register it.

Following the death of his father, Sonu Gujjar was compelled to discontinue his studies. After training in an ITI in Jhajjar, he took up work at the Manesar facility in July 2006. He showed no signs of being the agitator he would become in future. In fact, not only was his attendance over 98 per cent, he also won the best operator award and the managing director's trophy for best employee. Sonu Gujjar's resentment against the management began when he witnessed their indifference to the pain of the workers. He felt they treated them as robots. For instance, on one occasion, when a worker's mother died, he said they should observe two minutes of silence in her memory, but the management did not allow it. In an earlier instance, he had felt compelled to take up the cause of workers who got injured in an accident when they got no support from the management.*

The immediate inspiration for Sonu and his fellow workers was the strike at Honda Motorcycle & Scooter in Gurgaon. That happened in 2005. The strike was in support of the

* 'Maruti strike: Did the hero, Sonu Gujjar, sell them out?', *The Times of India*, 6 November 2011 (https://timesofindia.indiatimes.com/home/sunday-times/deep-focus/maruti-strike-did-the-hero-sonu-gujjar-sell-them-out/articleshow/10626278.cms, last accessed 17 January 2023).

demand to form an independent union. The workers wanted a union of their own and therefore all categories of workers—permanent, temporary, apprentice and contract workers—presented a joint front in support of that demand. After the settlement of the strike the permanent workers formed their union but the contract workers were not made members.

In the end, just some fifty contract workers were made permanent after three years. Contract workers were very angry. They argued that they worked as much and even more than permanent workers and felt that the latter only use them and then do not fight for their rights.

Workers in Maruti were aware of this resentment among the contract workers and sympathetic to their plight since many of the permanent workers had themselves been contract workers once. The unity between permanent and contract workers was thus forged right from the beginning of the struggles in the Maruti Suzuki factory; they stood together till the end. One trade union leader said he thought that the July 2012 incident was part of a conspiracy to break the unity between the permanent and contract workers.

Sonu Gujjar led the strikes in 2011 which paralysed the Maruti Suzuki plant at Manesar: the occupation of the factory from 4 to 16 June followed by the resistance from 18 June to 28 August; the strikes from 29 August to 30 September; and then finally the second occupation of the factory from 7 to 21 October. The strike in October was provoked by the management when they refused to allow contract workers to enter the factory. Work resumed on 22 October when the strike ended in four Suzuki plants—including the Manesar plant and two vendor companies as well as Suzuki Motorcycle—and the management accepted 1,100 contract workers; sixty-four suspended workers were reinstated. The union, however, was not recognized, and Sonu Gujjar was forced to leave the company.

It is important to remember that the strikes in Maruti Suzuki did not suddenly come up as isolated events. There had been a succession of strikes since 2009 in the automobile industry in India:

- Mahindra (Nashik, Maharashtra), May 2009 and March 2010;
- Sunbeam Auto (Gurgaon, Haryana), May 2009;
- Bosch Chassis (Pune, Maharashtra), July 2009;
- Honda Motorcycle (Manesar, Haryana), August 2009;
- Rico Auto (Gurgaon, Haryana), August 2009, accompanied by a one-day strike of the whole of the car industry in Gurgaon;
- Pricol (Coimbatore, Tamil Nadu), September 2009;
- Volvo (Hoskote, Karnataka), August 2010;
- MRF Tyres (Chennai, Tamil Nadu), October 2010 and June 2011;
- General Motors (Halol, Gujarat), March 2011;
- Bosch (Bangalore, Karnataka), September 2011;
- Dunlop (Hooghly, Bengal), October 2011;
- Caparo (Sriperumbudur, Tamil Nadu), December 2011;
- Dunlop (Ambattur, Tamil Nadu), February 2012;
- Hyundai (Chennai, Tamil Nadu) April and December 2011–January 2012; among others.

At the end of the strikes led by the Maruti Suzuki Employees Union the management forced Sonu Gujjar, Shiv Kumar and twenty-eight other union leaders to take voluntary retirement. But their strikes had mobilized an exceptional level of participation.

Sandeep Dhillon

Chief patron of the Maruti Suzuki Workers' Union; sentenced to life imprisonment. Interviewed on 6 January 2020 in Serhada village, the home of Suresh Dhull, while they were out on parole.

I have been working ever since I reached adulthood to earn my living. When I became an apprentice I was only eighteen and when I became a permanent worker I may have been twenty-two or twenty-three years old.

I passed out as a motor mechanic in October 2004 from the Kaithal ITI, got apprenticed in Maruti Gurgaon and worked for a year for Rs 3,000 and got my diploma. Then I went to work in the Honda factory. Those days the Honda factory that made cars used to be in Noida. I was a contract worker and I got Rs 5,000 to 6,000 a month depending on the number of days I worked; I was a casual worker. But it never crossed the 6,000 limit, I think.

After about a year of such work I quit in February 2006 and joined as a casual in the Honda motorcycle factory in Gurgaon. It was closer to home. After about six months, in June, I heard of trainees being hired in Maruti Manesar.

I had had a lot of experience by then so I thought I was overqualified to be a trainee. However, there was an opportunity to become a permanent worker in Maruti that was not available in Honda. I took the test, I was interviewed and got selected as a trainee.

On 7 June 2006 I joined as a trainee in Maruti Manesar. I had been appointed for three years. The first year I had a salary of Rs 3,000 and it was to increase to Rs 7,000 by the third. Then I became a permanent worker in 2009 and began to get Rs 14,000 a month.

This Manesar factory is called a Maruti factory but actually it was a 'Suzuki Automobile India Private Limited' factory. Maruti had not yet merged in it. It was a separate factory. In 2009, it merged with Maruti Gurgaon. By the time I became a permanent worker it had become 'Maruti Suzuki India Private Limited'. There used to be a separate company, Powertrain, that made engines for Maruti but in 2012 that also merged in the MSIL.

As an apprentice in Gurgaon Maruti I heard of the Maruti Udyog Kamgar Union or the MUKU. MUKU did not have any elections from the year 2000 to 2008; some thirty or forty workers used to be called for a meeting and they would select office bearers and that passed for elections. I had heard about it. When I joined at Manesar the same MUKU arrived there. They added four workers from Manesar to their executive and claimed to have become our representatives.

The HR people called me one day and told me that I had become a member of some standing committee and that from now on I was a representative of workers in the union. The management had already spoken to MUKU and five such representatives were to be inducted in it. However, there was provision for only four representatives. When I heard this I told the management that I wanted to leave and that the other four could continue in the committee. The four workers were: Dhananjay, Anil, Ramanpreet and Amit.

That was the time when workers were being made permanent. Depending on their date of joining one by one the workers were getting their appointment letters. A form for union membership was given along with the appointment letter and workers had to fill it in and sign it. At the time of payment of their salaries Rs 10 was deducted towards union fees and they were deemed members of MUKU. Nobody was given any choice.

In 2010, the first elections were held in MUKU. Kuldeep Jangu was elected president and he began to visit the Manesar factory too. Now workers in Manesar began to say that they wanted to have a union of their own. All our seniors also said the same thing because MUKU would never listen to us or raise our issues with the management.

In 2011, our seniors met leaders of AITUC and HMS to find out how a union is formed and registered. When they got to know the procedure they got the forms, filled them up and submitted them to the Registrar's office informing them that they had formed a union and it needed to be registered. This turned out to be the origin of all our troubles.

About three or four hundred workers had become members of the new union. We had decided to call it Maruti Suzuki Employees Union. We had chosen Sonu Gujjar as our president and Shiv Kumar as our general secretary. Both had gone to Chandigarh to submit the file.

On 4 June in 2011 the management began to get workers to sign some blank papers. The 'A' shift was working then and blank papers were placed before them and they were asked to sign.

When the 'B' shift workers began to arrive they too were asked to sign blank papers at the gate. The 'B' shift workers raised an objection. They began to discuss it among themselves. Sonu and Shiv had returned from Chandigarh that very day. They saw that everyone, apprentices, trainees and regular workers, all were being asked to sign some blank sheets. Sonu said nobody would sign. Some had already signed and those sheets had been sent to the HR department. Nothing could be done about them. But he snatched the papers that supervisors had in their hands and tore them up.

L.K. Jain was then the head of the manufacturing

department. He came to meet us, apologized on behalf of the management and said that what had been done was wrong. Sonu and Shiv asked him to return the papers that had already been signed but he refused to do that even though he had said that getting workers to sign blank papers was wrong.

That very moment a strike was declared. This happened on 4 June 2011. Till then the 'A' shift had not left the premises. The 'B' shift had not yet begun work. We all sat down on the shop floor and the strike began. This strike continued for thirteen days. Some thirty or thirty-two workers were suspended. Of course Sonu Gujjar and Shiv Kumar were suspended and so too were some other active members.

In the end, when there was a settlement, the suspension orders of many workers were withdrawn. But twelve workers remained suspended. These twelve workers had given a written statement that they had nothing to do with the union and even in future they would not be part of it. I think they needed the jobs desperately, that is why they did this. Then the management said that an enquiry committee would be set up and a third-party investigation of these twelve workers would be instituted, and only after a report was submitted by them would any further decisions be taken. Sonu Gujjar and Shiv Kumar signed this agreement accepting these conditions.

Then what happened was that the strike ended, work resumed, these workers were charge sheeted but no enquiry was made. For a long time the management kept postponing the investigation or third-party enquiry.

In July 2011, one Sunday, people began calling me to tell me that a wall of tin sheets was being set up around the factory. On Sundays the factory is closed and only the maintenance staff works there. I was surprised when I got several such calls asking me what it was that was happening in the factory that there was a need for such a wall.

I couldn't believe that something like this was happening. I thought there might be some sort of fencing being put up and people were mistaking it for a wall. Our factory was an open place, the perimeter walls were not high; you could see the wide expanse of land and buildings if you stood outside the gate—everything laid out in a well-designed plan. It used to be a pretty thing to look at.

When we left our homes for work on Monday many surprising things happened. Firstly, the company bus did not arrive. We somehow managed to get to the factory. The scene had changed there. Tall tin sheets surrounded the outer wall. Nobody could go in. Even we, who were workers, were not allowed in. We were told that the twelve who had been given charge sheets earlier had been sacked. Many others too had been dismissed. A total of forty workers had been thrown out. They included Ram Meher and others who were active in the union. We were told that we would be given a 'good conduct' letter and we could go in only after signing it. The letter was circulated too. It said that we promise not to raise any slogans, not to stop work or disturb anyone and other such things. We were told that not only would we have to sign it but we would be captured on video signing it and only then would we be allowed to enter.

All of us refused to sign it.

Praveen

A dismissed worker who was convicted (for the violence of 18 July 2012) but was released because he had already spent four years in jail before the conviction. He was interviewed in October 2019 in Khubaru village where he has opened a pizza shop. He has a franchise of the Dominik pizza chain.

Sonu got a file ready to submit to the union Registrar's office in Chandigarh. The papers in that file did not have my signatures. He may have thought that it would not be proper to ask me to join the union. Whatever the reason, I was not included in the union. The file was submitted to the office in Chandigarh.

The management had got a few workers to sign a statement that they were happy with MUKU and they did not want a new union in Manesar. The management submitted the statement to the Registrar.

I did not sign the statement. Not just that, I even asked people to not join this union of the management. The manager himself would call workers to his office and get them to sign the membership papers. He called me too. I fobbed him off with some excuse. I knew why he was asking me to meet him. I told him I will come later. He began to insist that I come immediately. Finally, I had to go to his office. He asked me to sign on the dotted line. I asked him what it was. He only repeated his instructions asking me to sign it. So I read it. It said clearly that I should sign if I consent. I refused to sign. The manager began to point out the number of people who had already signed and told me that I too should sign. I told him that I did not consent so I wouldn't sign. We began to argue. He tried to convince me that MUKU was a good option for workers.

I won't lie to you. For a moment I dithered. I thought of signing it. Then something pulled me back. I knew it was wrong; I thought it was wrong. We argued for a long time. It began to get ugly. In the end he asked me in a threatening tone whether I would sign it or not. I said no, one last time. He got angrier. He said he would teach me a lesson. I left the room. He may have thought that I would now tell others about what transpired in the room.

I don't know what happened after that, whether he said something to someone or word spread, but all of a sudden people stopped talking to me. Every day I had to meet and discuss things with at least six or seven people. All the cordiality vanished. They began to keep their distance. We still discussed work, we had to, but it was no longer friendly. Sometimes people would taunt me too. Someone would say, 'Their union will now get us air conditioners,' and other such things. I would respond by saying we were all workers and would remain workers, but it had no effect. There was a Pawan Kumar in our department. He wanted to be the president of the union that the management was setting up. He was very upset with people who had not joined the management union and even more upset with those who asked others to not become members of this pocket union.

One day I had a major argument with my manager. Those days I got a monthly salary of 16,000. I also got an incentive amount of Rs 8,000 a month. If I took leave for two days the money would be deducted. I did not like the system. One day I asked the manager how I should plan my monthly expenditure. Assuming that I would earn 16,000 only or according to the 24,000 that I expected to earn? I was never sure which month I would get the incentive and which month I would have to go without it. I was complaining that my salary fluctuated each month, because I took leave or was late or for some other reason. He said I should plan to spend only 8,000. I was surprised. Naturally, I asked him to explain why I should plan on spending only half the salary that I was sure to get. He said I should do so because, after all, before I became permanent, I got only 6,000 a month, and now I was getting more—so I should know how to live on less. This manager was at Level 9 and obviously had been on a lower level some time back. His salary may have been 60,000 a month. I asked him why he had tried to get promoted to a higher level and even now was trying to get to Level 10. He replied that humans always want to rise to higher levels. 'Our system is very transparent,' he said to me.

I don't think the system was transparent. Even if I had been working in a small enterprise I would have known how much I would get by the end of the month. Even if I had been a daily wager, making say Rs 300 a day, I would have known that if I had worked for thirty days I would get 9,000 for it. That would be a transparent system. Here I worked every single day and even then I had no guarantee that I would get the whole amount. Some months I would get it, some months I would get less. It all depended on the incentive amount. If you wish to plan for something, how will you? As far as attendance issues were concerned I would know how many days I had been absent and how much would be deducted from the incentive amount. But what does one do with this thing called quality? It is so subjective. Only at the end of the month would they tell me that I had failed the quality check on so many days and would have to forego some amount. The incentive is also an extra; it was never part of the salary. So one could not even complain against deductions. I must say, whoever devised this scheme was very clever. Hats off to him!

There was another thing that I disliked. There are some standing orders in the factory; certain instructions that you have to follow. One such instruction was that no employee would look at the salary slip of another employee or show his salary slip to anyone. The idea is to prevent anyone from finding out who was getting how much. Is this transparency? I have a feeling that nobody in Maruti ever asked how it was appropriate for workers to get different amounts in different months when they worked equally hard on all days.

Consider the rules about leave of absence. Whether you are getting married, or your mother dies, you can't take the day off. If you do, you lose a lot of money. The health facilities were pretty bad. There used to be one MBBS doctor in the dispensary. Well, he could have treated at least some everyday illnesses but he did not do even that. I had many such arguments with the manager.

When the first strike took place in 2011 I had had some such argument in my department. That is when the strike took place. It so happened that I was in the general shift, which is like a straight nine-to-five job. We sat down on the shop floor. We went hungry for two days. Nobody was listening to our grievances. We were only saying that we had a right to form our own union and we did not accept the management union as our representative. The management had imposed the Gurgaon union, Maruti Udyog Kamgar Union, as our union. Our second demand was to make temporary and contract workers permanent. We used to think that all these malpractices were the doing of the lower level management and that the upper level bosses were not even aware of what was going on in the factory.

The CEO of production was a senior manager, M.M. Singh. We were under the impression that he did not know all that went on inside the factory. Once he finds out, we thought, he will teach these low level managers a lesson they won't forget. We thought he would listen to our grievances. We realized only later that he actually knew everything. We then realized that everyone knew and no one was listening to us. Within two or three days they had thrown out all the eleven office bearers, the whole union body.

I witnessed Sonu Gujjar's talent at work during this strike. Some tin sheets had been put up outside the factory and we were behind them. He simply tore through the sheets and made an unforgettable speech. People were riveted. He spoke of the conditions in the factory and our struggle and resolve to seek justice. By the third day all our leaders had made so many speeches their throats were sore.

Then the media arrived. They had these pretty umbrellas and they danced around us flashing their cameras. The grounds outside the factory looked like a fair. A lot was going on. All big and small trade union leaders arrived, [from] INTUC, CITU, AITUC. What a crowd it was. All this happened on the fifth day. They made speeches telling us that we had the support of five lakh workers. We were very excited. We thought the media would report about this now, that Suzuki himself would get to know the real picture. He lived thousands of miles away and when he would hear of all that is being done he would change the entire management.

Nothing of the sort happened!

This strike continued. It ended on 16 or 17 June; I have forgotten the exact date. With it a lot of things were gone. The cordial work atmosphere changed. All the laughter went out of us. Earlier, even with the managers we used to feel some sort of kinship. That was lost. We used to argue, yes, but there used to be no hostility. Now there was. I used to even party with some of the managers. All that was over. Some dismissed workers were reinstated. In June and July work went on but there was great tension in the factory. In this period some workers were sacked, they were charged with indiscipline.

After a few days we heard that the office of the Registrar of trade unions in Chandigarh had rejected our application for the recognition of our union. Protests began again.

One day, on 28 or 29 August we found the factory gate locked.

Sandeep Dillon continues...

The second strike began there and then. This time the strike continued for twenty-eight days.

The company got some workers from Gurgaon and some more from other places. Some had even come from Himachal Pradesh. Some 100 or 150 of such workers were taken in from the back door of the factory. They tried to keep the factory working. But how could so few and inexperienced workers operate those machines? Some of them had no experience at all, the experienced ones were few. The plant could not work and production was not possible.

When we noticed that the gate at the back was being used for this purpose we began our *dharna* there. Some thirty or thirty-five workers had gone in, now they were stuck inside. They could not come out. We wouldn't let them come out. Some managers had gone in too, they were also stuck inside. I think a total of 100 people were inside. They included managers, shift in-charges, supervisors and people from the engineering department. The factory was effectively sealed—no one could go in, no one could get out. There was a canteen inside so they had no problems with regard to food and water.

Now the company got a measure of our strength.

Finally, after twenty-eight days a settlement was reached.

It was decided that in the case of those who had been terminated the termination orders would be converted to suspension orders, and an enquiry would be completed within a stipulated period. There were some thirty-five workers in this category. In return, workers had to sign the 'good conduct' undertaking. The strike was called off.

We arrived at the factory for the 'A' shift the next day and began signing the good conduct undertakings and started entering the factory. The union leaders were standing at the gate, outside. Inside, there were some bouncers. It seems that the management had identified some workers as troublemakers and when they entered the bouncers began to jostle them and rough them up a little. However, they chose to ignore it and work resumed. We then realized that they had changed our work stations. Everybody was moved elsewhere and the whole team coordination had been destroyed. Friends were separated so that there would be no chatting. It takes time to get used to new kinds of work. Also, a team is used to each other's speed and work in a rhythm. That had got disturbed. Naturally, production began to fall. The management then told the Labour Department that production had fallen and began to hold us responsible.

There was a lot of tension. The thirty-odd people who had been suspended were still sitting at the gate. One day I arrived at work for the 'B' shift. Union representatives asked me to go in and stop the work and talk to the management because nothing was moving with respect to the enquiry and other such things.

I went in, asked people to stop work and they stopped working. The moment that happened the canteen contractor came running to us with his bodyguards. He had employed his own bodyguards who all had guns. Bouncers had guns too. They all began to point their guns at us and generally make threatening gestures. Managers refused to listen to our complaints. We sat on the shop floor and work stopped.

The attitude of the management was not good. Whenever we arrived at a settlement they never honoured it and always threw a spanner in the works.

This time the management went to the High Court so that the court could order us to vacate the place.

This was going to take some time. In the meantime the

management cut the electricity and water supply. Workers were sitting inside. Without water. Without electricity. The management even locked the toilets. I don't know why but the tin sheets outside were also removed. The walls were not high so we would jump over the walls to use toilets outside and come back in. We faced a lot of trouble, we were hungry and thirsty. It was humid and hot but we never damaged anything inside the factory, we never soiled it.

The High Court ordered us to vacate the factory. The police arrived to enforce the order. We had been inside for a week now. The police entered the factory wearing helmets and armed with sticks as if they were going to some war front. The moment they entered and told us to leave, we got up and left. We had decided to obey the HC orders and we did. This time the management either terminated or suspended sixty workers.

We came out and sat outside, and after a week, another settlement was reached.

This time the management said that the thirty who had been suspended would not be reinstated. Then the management brought in a VRS and those thirty were shown the door. That meant instead of being terminated they could leave voluntarily and for that they were given some money too. The suspension orders of the rest were withdrawn and work resumed.

With this VRS the entire leadership of the union had been thrown out of the plant. All union office bearers had left. Even the second tier of the leadership, meaning those who had any experience of union activities, had been thrown out. They could have risen to being new leaders. They had all 'chosen' to leave.

I don't blame them. There was too much pressure on them. The management was obstinate. Whenever they reached a settlement the management never honoured it. They had suffered losses; they hadn't got their salaries. They had families. How much could they suffer? A worker works for his family.

How long can he go without wages? They did what they had to do. It seems that the VRS was also part of the settlement. An unwritten part. The leadership had never told us about this. We did not know these details. Later, we learnt that perhaps they had been told of the VRS at the time of the settlement and they had agreed. By the time we heard that a VRS had been brought in Sonu had stopped coming to the factory.

Then the management began to taunt us. 'Look what we can do,' was what they said. 'We can throw out your whole leadership,' they said to us. They were behaving as if their power was endless. Our union had never been registered and all of our office bearers had already been shown out the door.

Amarjeet Kaur

General Secretary, AITUC. Interviewed on 6 March 2020.

When the Communist Party of India, CPI, was in the central government in 1995–96, Indrajit Gupta was the home minister. At that time we could assure workers of job security and support and we did provide them that. In those days workers knew that they had supporters in the government and they felt secure; they felt that they had someone to lean on.

There were many big struggles in Maruti. There was a prolonged agitation in Maruti Gurgaon after which a VRS was implemented and many active workers were thrown out. At that time too we had supported the workers but the entire leadership of the union was thrown out. Hundreds were fired. After this, the management had formed its own pocket union.

When workers formed a union in Manesar, they did not join us. We did not ask them either. However, they used to consult us. We had told all our local leaders that we had to help them in every way even if they were not in our federation.

I am talking about the time when Sonu Gujjar was trying to get the union registered.

Sonu Gujjar fought three big battles but his style was one of springing surprises on everyone. He did not adopt a process of slowly and gradually intensifying the struggle. He would not go step by step. There is an entire procedure of advancing slowly. Like, first give a demand letter, talk to the management, then tie black bands, slow down work, talk to other unions, get them to issue statements in your support, get them to take some action like holding meetings, give a notice of a strike, and then, when nothing works, go on strike. In this way, step by step, the struggle is intensified and the pressure on the management also gradually increases.

What these people used to do is go on a flash strike. If something happened they would suddenly, there and then, stop working in the factory and sit down inside the factory. The union Sonu Gujjar formed was not registered and they were asked to leave under a VRS. Many were made to quit.

I remember that the workers were extremely disappointed. They felt that Sonu Gujjar and other leaders had sold out. I don't think that the leaders sold out. No way. Not every leader is strong. Not everyone can be strong. That union could not be formed. Sonu Gujjar just took his VRS and left.

Mohan (name changed)

A full-time trade union leader working with the Inqlabi Mazdoor Kendra. Interviewed several times between September 2019 and June 2020 and then in August 2021.

Okay, this is not my real name and for various reasons I would much rather not give it. But I will tell you what I know about the struggle in the Maruti Suzuki plants.

Where am I from?

How does it matter where I come from, I now live and work in Gurgaon... All right, I am from a small town in Uttar Pradesh and had been active in the student movement since my college days. My family had a culture of reading and writing. I used to read a lot and I grew up with a sense of fairness and justice. In those days there were many protests against the Dunkel proposals* and I also participated in them. Slowly, I began to feel that this was what I wanted to do. I did not want a regular job. I wanted to be associated with the struggle for justice.

I had seen the plight of the workers in my town. I wanted to work with labourers. When Inqlabi Mazdoor Kendra was formed in 2006 I joined it and started working with several trade unions. The organization took care of my basic expenses.

I also got a job as a worker in a factory for a few months so that I could personally experience what a worker goes through every day, at a social and psychological level.

For the first time in my life I discovered what it was like to work eight hours. By the end of the evening, I used to be absolutely exhausted. I'd be so tired that I couldn't even look out for vehicles while walking on the road. I used to take leave in between so they would deduct money from my salary. I did not get my full salary even for a single month. They used to

* Arthur Dunkel was the director-general of the General Agreement on Tariffs and Trade (GATT) between 1980 and 1993. Certain proposals he put forward, known as the Dunkel Draft, were accepted and became the foundation of the World Trade Organization. There were widespread protests against the Dunkel proposals in India because they was perceived to be an attack on India's economic sovereignty by pressurizing India to withdraw subsidies on agriculture, textiles and other sectors or forcing us to buy medicines from the countries which had patent rights to these medical products at exorbitant prices. It was felt that through the Dunkel proposals Indian markets might get flooded with imported goods and the small and handicraft industries might suffer as a result thereof.

hire workers only for six months, so when my six months were over I quit the job.

I went to Gurgaon in 2005 when the Honda workers began their agitation. The workers were lathi-charged at the district mini-secretariat in Gurgaon. When I arrived, the strike had already begun. The workers thought I had come to join the factory as a casual labourer and threatened to break my legs if I tried to break their strike!

I had attended one of the union meetings at the time. Many workers were complaining that no one was listening to them. I told them, 'Try blocking the highway, then they will listen to you!'

I came away, having said that. I had said it casually, without much thought, and then left. But it so happened that they went on a march from Manesar with the intention of blocking the highway. When the police tried to stop them they beat up the police. Apparently, they broke the hand of the DSP.

Then the police laid a trap for them. The police told the workers that they had organized a meeting with the management for a settlement. They asked the workers to come to the mini-secretariat for the talks. When the workers arrived the police surrounded the workers and thrashed them. That assault on workers was widely reported.

I felt very guilty after this incident. I felt that had I been there at that time, I could have guided them. I would have told them to never go to an enclosed space like the mini-secretariat with about 4,000 policemen. I feel bad I was not there.

Another thing that saddens me about the struggle of the Honda workers is that the permanent workers and contract workers fought together—they all fought against the police too—but only the permanent workers benefited from it; the contract workers did not get any benefit.

Nowadays, in general, in any company, only one-third of the workers are permanent and two-thirds are contract workers.

In 2011, I again met the workers of the Honda union. They told me that they were trying to help organize the workers of Maruti. At that time, there was a union in the Maruti factory of Gurgaon by the name of MUKU. Elections in MUKU had not been held in ten years, and even in Manesar there was only MUKU. Things at the Maruti factory in Manesar were so bad that their workers did not even know they were members of MUKU.

On May Day, I went with some friends to the Maruti factory in Gurgaon to distribute about 1,000 pamphlets. First of all, cops in mufti, intelligence people, came up to me and asked me who I was and what I was doing there. I said that I was an unemployed man and someone had given me Rs 250 to distribute those pamphlets. The funny thing is that not a single worker took a single pamphlet from me. Later, I realized that this was a reflection of the extent of their fear.

I found out the reason for this fear. What had happened was that in 2010 Kuldeep Jangu of the Maruti union had circulated a pamphlet. That pamphlet was distributed by a worker who was later fired from his job. This was the situation there; even the smallest protest was punished very harshly.

In June 2011, the conflict in Maruti's Manesar factory started intensifying. Workers wanted to form a union. One day, after the end of the morning shift, all the workers sat inside the factory. This is called a sit-in or 'occupy' strike. It was about 4 pm on 4 June when the workers refused to leave and the strike began, inside the factory. It turned out to be a different kind of strike. I also got news of this. I went there to find out more about it but I could not get in and I had no contact with any of the workers.

The next day, which was a Sunday, the Honda workers bought half a truckload of bananas for the striking workers of Maruti since they had had nothing to eat. When the workers were eating the bananas, I tried to talk to them and told them that I worked for a newspaper. Some of them took my phone number. Two workers told me that they had even gone to Chandigarh to get the union registered.

The management had started asking the workers to sign statements which said that they had nothing to do with the new union that was going to be formed. That is when twenty-five workers gathered and decided that they would go to the manager and ask why they were being made to sign such a statement. When they met the manager, he tore all the papers that had been signed and threw them in the bin. As soon as this happened, the whole atmosphere changed. The workers understood that if they could achieve this with only twenty-five workers getting together, who knew how much more they could accomplish if they all united.

On the other hand, the management also realized its mistake. Then the management gave them a 'good conduct bond' form and asked all of them to sign it before entering the factory. When this happened, more workers got together and approached the management and said that it was wrong to compel them to sign such a statement. They must have thought that this time too the management would throw away the forms, but that did not happen. The workers got very angry. They came out of the manager's office and thought: Why not sit down right there on the shop floor? Work stopped. All this had happened on 4 June.

The local leader of the Honda union had probably told them earlier that Honda's union was very strong and that it was supporting the workers of Maruti. That assurance of support of workers of Honda also made Maruti workers feel very strong.

These workers occupied the factory and sat inside for thirteen days. Workers of all three shifts remained inside; which includes some 1,000 permanent workers, 800 apprentices, 400 trainees—about 1,200 are temporary workers. Their mobile phones turned off as the batteries died. They could not recharge them. There was no electricity, nor did they have chargers. There was nothing to do. They did not even have cards to play with. But they stood firm...did not budge. They sat on strike for the right to form a union. This struggle was truly rare, very vibrant.

The workers told me later that while they sat inside the factory with nothing else to do, they discussed various issues, including the question of maintaining unity among the contract and permanent workers.

When I told the workers of Maruti that I worked in a newspaper, it was not entirely a lie. I used to write for a small newspaper called *Nagrik*. That day, on 5 June, I also called up some friends in Faridabad. There is Sher Singh ji in Faridabad who brings out a newspaper named *Mazdoor Sangharsh*. He is very well known and highly respected among workers. He had also come to Maruti Manesar and together we called workers from many companies to help the workers of Maruti who were on strike. We asked them to send some roasted *chana* or some other food stuff for them.

In the evening, at 6.30 or seven, I got a call from [one of the] two workers of Maruti in Manesar who had exchanged phone numbers with me. He said that a bus full of police had arrived. The worker asked me what they should do next. I said first talk to the union leader of Honda. He said that he couldn't get through, that their phones were switched off. At that time only fifty policemen had come and there were 3,000 workers inside the factory. I asked him to sit tight. It was late evening.

He called again at 10 pm. This time he said that many bouncers had also arrived. I told them that everyone should cover their faces with handkerchiefs and sit peacefully—not do anything that could be considered violent. Nothing happened till four in the morning. The strike continued.

Then one day he called again in the middle of the night to ask me to come with my photographer! I said I am getting there, don't panic. Now, I didn't have a camera. They were under the impression that I was a reporter for a very big newspaper! I spoke to a journalist from *Hindustan Times*. I said, '*Bhai, tu aaja.*' He came.

The strike lasted for thirteen days; from 4 to 17 June. The big unions like AITUC, CITU, HMS, INTUC and UTUC formed an action committee but did nothing. When it ended, eleven people were suspended. After the strike, when the settlement was reached, it was decided that allegations against workers would be investigated first and then they could be withdrawn. This investigation was to be domestic, meaning there was to be a departmental enquiry.

Workers began to feel that they had become quite powerful. They were impressed by me too because my advice had been helpful. One day some workers came to my room to meet me. They realized that I had a very small office, with one and a half people working in it. They felt that we do not have power. They felt very disappointed. After that the workers never responded to my calls.

I too was busy with other unions. Our style of work is different. In pro-establishment unions, and central trade unions the method of work is different. Over there, the leadership at the top decides what to do. We never do that. We seek everyone's opinion, discuss things and never impose our decisions. All decisions are made by consensus.

In June the application for the registration of the union of Maruti Manesar was rejected. We heard that the Registrar of Trade Unions had said that Maruti already had a union by the name of MUKU, so another union could not be formed. On this basis the file was rejected.

Then in August, the management suspended four workers. The workers were very angry. They argued that domestic or departmental enquiries cost them their jobs and they did not trust such enquiries. When this happened, once again I got a call from a worker. He said that the union body was about to hold a meeting and asked me to attend it. I had fever that day. Still, I did not want to miss this, so I went.

When I got there, some eight or ten people active in the union were engaged in a discussion and I came to know that, in another room, a worker of the New Trade Union Initiative (NTUI) was holding another meeting with some workers.

They would ask me which union they should join. People of several trade union federations had been in touch with them. They wanted to know which central trade union to join.

I advised them to fight their battles on their own. Why are you looking for a guide? I asked them. They said that they did not have an organization. I said form your own organization, I will help you. I also told them that if necessary they could take the help of all trade unions, but they should fight independently. We talked for over two hours. After that we had many such meetings. The inclination of the workers was to remain independent.

Then a slow-down started in Maruti. I told them that there was no point in having a slow-down; if you want to fight then have a big fight. I must tell you that I rarely spoke in meetings; I often didn't speak at all, preferring to listen to them. But when I did speak, I used to speak frankly and give clear opinions.

Soon after, on the evening of 29 August 2011, the police were deployed at the factory. It was a Sunday. I again got a call from a worker to find out why this was being done. I got in touch with some journalists to find out. I learnt that contract workers had been asked to talk to their respective contractors and the permanent workers were to be given a good conduct form to sign. Apprentices had been asked to stay away that day.

We had a meeting and decided to talk to Mathew Abraham. He had been a leader of Maruti Gurgaon workers...a well-known leader of the trade union in Gurgaon; he is very sober and highly intelligent. We called him. The president of the Honda union also came to meet us. Both advised the workers to sign the bond of good conduct and go inside.

Somehow I didn't like this advice; I could not agree to this acquiescence. I told the workers that if they considered signing a good conduct undertaking just a formality they should go ahead and sign it. But I warned them that by signing it they would be cutting off their own hands. I also said that whatever they decided to do should to be a collective decision.

Of course, the real question was how many people they could persuade not to sign the undertaking.

Kuldeep Jangu and Pawan Kumar (who was later given a life sentence), the elected leader of the Gurgaon union, had also come to this meeting. Kuldeep said that Manesar workers should stay on in MUKU; the president of MUKU could be from the Manesar factory and the general secretary from the Gurgaon factory. I told the workers that this was a chance to capture MUKU and they could do it if they wished to.

The new union workers felt that every person who gave them advice had some selfish motive and were not convinced.

Actually, there was no harm in trying out MUKU. It was decided that Jangu would go talk to the management and get the suspensions revoked; then it would be decided which union the workers wanted. Jangu went to talk to the management. When he came back, he said that the management had been willing earlier, but was now refusing to cancel the suspension orders.

It was clear to the workers that they had to fight. Representatives of the central trade unions were also in that meeting. Along with me some other people from our centre were also there. Everyone told them to go ahead and continue their fight. We pledged support to them unconditionally.

Meanwhile, the management of Maruti was trying to get workers from Belsonica (an auto parts supplier located in Manesar) to keep their plant operational but they refused. All of them took leave. Who would protect them if the striking workers of Maruti began to fight with them? they asked.

The HMS leaders asked the Maruti workers to discuss a settlement and they presented a proposal to them. But the proposal was not clear about the issue of making contract workers permanent; the Maruti workers refused to accept such a proposal. The HMS then withdrew its strike from fourteen factories which had been called in support of the Maruti workers. This was on 16 October 2011.

On 1 September, 3,000 workers from thirty-five unions from the Manesar-Gurgaon industrial belt expressed their solidarity in front of [Maruti's] Manesar factory.

This long strike went on in 2011 under the leadership of Sonu Gujjar. Talks were held with the management on 16 September for a settlement but they could not reach an agreement. Then the Powertrain workers ended their strike. How long could they remain on strike?

A thirteen-member committee had been formed to organize all common actions and its meetings were held regularly. There were representatives of all central unions in it. We were part of it too.

By then, I had become good friends with the workers and they began to think of me as one of their own. Many trade union leaders and student union leaders started visiting Manesar.

Several days later, the central trade unions, probably AITUC, helped them arrive at a settlement. In this, some workers were taken back but forty-four permanent workers remained suspended. And wages for the strike period were not given; Maruti Suzuki announced that they had suffered huge losses.

Along with this, the 'good conduct' undertaking was also to be signed; the lock-out was lifted as was the *dharna*.

On 3 October 2011, the factory opened. On the first day after the lock-out the management did not allow the 1,200 temporary workers to enter because they had participated in the demonstration and occupation.

Once again the workers stopped working inside and sat down. This was the second occupy strike.

Many unions went on strike in support of the Manesar workers. Then heavy security forces—12,000 were CRPF men, five or six thousand police personnel—were deployed at the factory.

The management went to the High Court and got orders to vacate the factory premises. There was a lot of discussion among the workers about whether they should or should not vacate the premises. All the central trade unions advised that violence was not good, that workers should vacate the factory. Eventually, the workers vacated the factory. They came out and sat down near the gate.

Finally, it was decided that thirty of those who had been suspended would be sacrificed at the altar of the cause. All the contract workers and permanent workers returned to work inside.

Sonu Gujjar was still trying to get his union registered. When they had gone to file the application before the Registrar's office, a leader of the Honda union had advised them to select three teams of office bearers so that if one team was rejected by the Registrar, they were prepared with another team. These were the thirty people that the management now paid under VRS to quit their jobs. All three teams were out.

It was not exactly a VRS, which is a scheme for an entire class of employees.

The Economic Times reported on the front page that Sonu had taken Rs 40 lakhs, but that was just to defame him.

The VRS caused havoc; different amounts would have been given to different people depending on their level of activity. Some people said that reports of threats to Sonu Gujjar were only rumours, that he got greedy and made a lot of money.

I think Sonu was forced to take money and leave. A defeatist mentality, fear and dismay may have been at the root of the settlement.

When Sonu Gujjar and his entire team were taken out, workers felt a severe sense of disappointment. They had fought bravely and lost; they were dismayed.

On 14 October, some 1,500 to 2,500 cops entered the Manesar factory and shut down the canteen, the water supply and toilets and forced the workers to move out of the factory and continue to strike outside.

Sonu Gujjar and his team continued to negotiate, and finally, on 22 October production began again; he and his team decided to take voluntary retirement and quit.

That is when people spread all kinds of rumours about him and his team. Some say each of them got Rs 40 lakhs; some say

Sonu got one crore for his VR. But those who know him say he had not sold out. They had no choice but to quit.

Along with the two leaders there were twenty-eight others in his team who were also forced to take voluntary retirement. Sonu has stated that all of them got Rs 16 lakhs each. That's it.

When asked by a journalist why he was not answering his phone, he said: 'That was my NCR number. I'm not so big that I can pay roaming charges to hear other people talk. It's not like nobody had my local number.' People say he has bought land but he tells them, 'In our village 1 *keela* [about 1 acre] of land is Rs 85 lakh.'*

Sonu still rides his old motorcycle in which he used to come to the factory. He said in an interview that the money he got from Maruti has gone towards repayment of loans; some has to be spent to buy medicines for his father; and Rs 5,000 per appearance goes to his lawyer, because five court cases are still pending against him for '*maar-pitai*' (violence) during the strike.

He has not found a job. He says no company would give him a job because they know he led the militant strikes in 2011.

Mohan continues...

The workers were distraught after the union leaders took VR. So our Inqlabi Mazdoor Kendra and Krantikari Naujawan Sabha together took out and distributed a pamphlet exhorting the workers to carry on their struggle even though thirty of their union leaders were gone.

* 'Sonu Gujjar, the man who led the strikes that paralysed Maruti's plants', *Business Standard*, 18 March 2017 (https://www.business-standard.com/article/companies/sonu-gujjar-the-man-who-led-the-strikes-that-paralysed-maruti-s-plants-112021100071_1.html, last accessed 11 January 2023).

Whenever the workers prepare to form a union or prepare for a strike there are always some workers in every department who are more active than others. They are made line coordinators. For instance, Jiya Lal was a line coordinator.

There were many line coordinators in every department. Actually, such people emerge on their own, there is no formal appointment by the union. They are the products of their time and their struggle. These are active people who inform co-workers about the activities and programmes and even take donations if they have to. There are people like this on every line, in every shift.

It was around this time that many workers reported hearing S.Y. Siddiqui, in charge of human resources, say that 'we have cleaned a lot of dirt but there is still a lot of garbage left; that too has to be cleaned out of the factory'. Siddiqui's meaning was clear. He meant that many trade unionists had been thrown out; there were many more left and now they would also have to be thrown out. Workers say that they heard him mention the figure of 300; he said some 300 more people needed to be thrown out.

By then the situation had changed for me. Almost everyone I knew well had left. People used to tell me that there was talk of making a union in Maruti Manesar and the workers were saying that this time there would be a 'fight to the finish' (*aar paar ki ladai*).

I really don't know who started this kind of talk. It is distinctly possible that the management itself put the idea in their heads that a fight to the finish would likely happen; and it caught on. It is possible that some enraged worker said it. Anyway, everyone began to use that phrase and it became common to say to each other that they would fight to the finish this time!

Once again a union body was formed, the file was prepared, and this time it also got registered. This time the management was also compelled to help in getting the union registered. The insistence of the workers on a union of their own had grown to such an extent and there was so much resentment against the management that, even though production did not stop or decrease, there was a lot of tension in the factory and the working environment was vitiated.

During the occupy strike workers talked about a lot of things and their class consciousness had grown. The workers chose to abandon collision till the time they could get the union registered.

The workers agreed that they would not join any trade union federation and they did not. The management was also happy to deal with an independent union because they thought it would be easier to make it fall in line.

The management may have been in a fix. After all, if unions were not allowed to be formed, how would they deal with the growing resentment?

After the strike ended, production went on in full swing. The workers were doing a great job. But now, coordinators of the union were handling all the work and enforcing discipline, because now the workers were not even willing to listen to the supervisors.

Everyone was still agitated. Every worker was also conscious of his rights, full of self-respect and also very angry with the management. There was a discontent within him; his faith in his leaders was somewhat shaken but he himself was always ready to fight for his rights. Now he considered the factory as his own, and did not cause any harm to the factory, or reduce the speed of production; he continued to work untiringly. Everything was going well despite the simmering tension underneath. The management was left with no option but to allow the union to be formed. They finally stopped objecting to union formation. Some managers even went to the Registrar's office in Chandigarh to ensure it was registered.

In this way the 'Maruti Suzuki Workers' Union' was formed. It also got registered. I was present when they hoisted their union flag and celebrated their flag day. The new union office bearers said that they were preparing a demand notice and that they would include a demand to make the contract labourers permanent.

This was the first time in my experience that the union was first made, registered and the charter of demands prepared later. I have forgotten the exact date...I got a call from the union. They said that they had prepared the charter of demands and wanted to consult me, seek my opinion. I asked them to consult their workers, but they said that they were consulting a lot of people and I was one of the people they wanted to run their charter by. So I went to meet them. All the office bearers were in the meeting, some eight or ten people.

Their very first demand was to make the contract workers permanent. I told them that the contract workers were not even members of the union and that they should rethink the demand. They said that contract workers had stood by them, had participated in all their struggles and they had to be made permanent.

I asked them if it was even possible. Would the company make so many contract workers permanent?

They said that the contract system had started in Maruti Gurgaon. 'Now we will start the end of such a practice. Maruti Manesar will be the first to stop employing contract workers in the main production work,' they said. 'We will make history. Once contract workers are made permanent in Maruti, this will happen everywhere!'

It is true that in 1997–98 contract labourers started getting into production work in Maruti Gurgaon. Before that they never used to do the main production work. Contract workers were always employed to do jobs of a temporary or continual nature like the work of loading, et cetera. They were not employed in work of a permanent nature. The law also forbade it. However, contract workers came into production work from Maruti Gurgaon. And then the same thing started happening everywhere.

I told them that they did not understand how big a fight this was, how much preparation it required. That it was not just a matter of a factory but a question of policy, of the processes of production in the entire country.

I advised them to place the demands for increasing the wages of contract labourers and trying to make some facilities available to them. 'Try to get them 20 per cent increment in wages like you do. If they do not have a canteen, get them access to your canteen. Start preparing for this big battle if you insist on ending the contract system in production,' I remember telling them. I thought, while they negotiated for these initial changes, they could initiate preparations for the bigger battle.

I think I could not explain this to them properly. Or they didn't understand what I was saying. There was a lack of communication. It must have been my fault. I perhaps did not press this point strongly enough. I did not think that they were serious and that they would actually fight for contract workers so seriously.

Actually, they were unable to comprehend the situation in the country and the international situation. All the office bearers were there in that meeting and all of them were talking about ending the contract system.

It is a fact that contract workers had stood by them during

three strikes. All of them had promised contract workers that they would raise their demands, fight for them. Contract workers are never hired back when the strike ends. They used to work together, they were friends with contract workers and many of them had themselves worked as contract workers at some time or other.

They had to keep the promise they had made to their friends. They had a very idealistic attitude. They could neither see the countrywide situation nor could they understand the international situation. They were romantic young souls and I failed to understand that they would actually go ahead with their ideas.

They gave the demand letter to the management.

The management always tries to create divisions among workers and it did just that. Rumours and whisper campaigns began. That's what I heard. The management made it known that they had once bought over one set of leaders and could buy more. I only heard all this because at this time I was not working with them.

Slowly, the tension began mounting. Workers had fought several hard battles. It was clear to them that the management was not lending an ear to their demands. Their very strong leaders had walked away out of fear or sold out. The frustration of that unfortunate turn of events had not yet blown over. They were encouraged to think that their leaders were trying to cut a deal with the management. There was enthusiasm for struggle but there was also fear that what had happened during Sonu's time might happen again. They basically began to doubt their leaders. It must have been an awful situation.

Praveen continues...

We needed another independent union. Once again, the same process began. Getting together workers. Choosing union office bearers. Filling in forms. Preparing a file to take to Chandigarh. In every department some fifteen people began to stake claim to leadership.

Finally, Ram Meher became president of the new union. The union had not been registered. There were to be no elections. We only chose whoever was ready and was thought to be suitable. Sarabjeet became the general secretary. Suresh Dhull was chosen as the treasurer.

These people used to go consult people from other factories and trade unions on how to prepare a file to submit to the Registrar's office. They did not talk to Sonu. The management had told us not to meet anyone from outside the factory. They had said that if we did not meet outsiders they would recognize us as representatives of workers. I had also considered becoming an office bearer but the situation was so messy I gave up the idea.

Eventually, after a lot of effort in March 2012, the union got registered—Maruti Suzuki Workers' Union. That was the name. The old union had never got registered. Its file had been rejected. This union had succeeded in getting registered. Despite this the management did not recognize us. The government recognized us as a union but the management refused to. The workers accepted us; the management wouldn't. They began to raise many objections. Some day they would object to our flag being raised, another day they would say that the union is not democratic, that it does not have representatives from all regions.

It is true that most of the office bearers of the union were from Kaithal district of Haryana. This led to serious infighting among office bearers and they got divided into two factions. One was the Sarabjeet faction and the other was the Ram Meher faction. They began to quarrel on such small issues that it began to seem as if the union would fail. The Sarabjeet faction was demanding a copy of the constitution of the union but the Ram Meher faction would not oblige. They argued and fought on such minor issues.

One day there was a showdown. There used to be a CRPF camp near Manesar. Now it doesn't exist. The Ram Meher faction asked the Sarabjeet faction to come meet them there. They said they would give them the constitution to read. When the Sarabjeet faction went there the Ram Meher faction beat them up badly. That is how they taught them what the union constitution said!

After that there was much bad blood. Nobody talked to anybody. There was no activity. Sonu Gujjar used to be very creative. He had some activity planned all the time. He kept people engaged. People were constantly doing something or the other. Here, these people were only fighting with each other.

The day one faction had thrashed the other faction I had gone to meet Mohan. He is a trade union activist. He lived in Gurgaon and he always advised anyone who went to him. His advice used to be sound. I liked him a lot. The next day I heard about the fight between the two factions. I felt very disappointed. Everything seemed to be going out of control.

One day Ram Vilas was suspended. The union [leadership] had prepared and given the management a charter of demands. The main demand was about increase in salaries. Union members were asking them to raise the issue of contract workers and demand that they be made permanent. Ram Vilas was saying this too. They wanted the first demand of the union to be that of making contract workers permanent. He was also a member of the executive, an office bearer of the union. There was a serious argument on this in the union which turned into a fight on this issue.

At that time the management suspended Ram Vilas. They may have found some reason or excuse. Perhaps the management wanted to take advantage of the fight inside the union. They may have expected union office bearers to come to blows. Whatever they may have hoped for, when Ram Vilas was suspended, the union demanded that the suspension be revoked. The management was just not paying heed. There was much back and forth. A crowd had gathered and arguments continued. The management turned a deaf ear to our appeals. That is when a worker remarked that if we beat up these managers they would be forced to listen to us. The management immediately withdrew the suspension notice.

What was the message that people got? That the managers are afraid of violence and they only listen to us when we resort to violence.

After this the workers began to behave very badly. There was tension all the time on the shop floor. Work continued but the atmosphere was tense all the time.

What happened on 18 July? To tell you the truth I don't know much.

Mohan continues...

In this taut situation that day dawned, 18 July 2012.

There are many indications that the incident that took place in Maruti Manesar that day was actually the handiwork of the management. That day proved to be a very sad one for workers. I was not there but I was talking to Maruti workers on phone. I also kept getting news about what was happening. People kept calling me.

A worker called me around 2.30 pm that there was a lot of tension in the company. I called up the union leaders to ask what had happened. I came to know about the issue involving Jiya Lal. I told them not to insist on the withdrawal of Jiya Lal's suspension order, that it could be handled another day, that everyone must leave the factory and go home. It is not a big issue, is what I said.

I remember telling the leaders that the management wanted the matter to escalate; that they shouldn't fall into its trap. I advised them to end the discussion before it got too heated. They said that if they did this then the workers would lose faith in them. They were very scared of losing the trust of the workers. Perhaps the conditions there were too dire.

Downstairs, agents provocateurs of the management had been saying that they needed to clean up the mess, and they were going to do so soon.

I told them many times not to turn it into a big issue, to drop the subject for a day or two. I told them that the suspension of a worker was not a question of life and death; it could be dealt with later.

But it must have become a kind of test for the leadership. I was trying to explain to them again and again that they should treat the matter of Jiya Lal's suspension as an everyday event and let matters cool down. But either they did not understand or they could not figure out any way of extricating themselves from the situation in which they were trapped without losing the trust of the workers.

That whole day the union leadership tried to get the suspension order withdrawn. It was a trivial matter. The conflict could have ended in a minute. Revoking a suspension order is not a big deal for the management. But the management was adamant. Its stubborn attitude meant that it was wishing for some major disturbance to take place. It is not possible that the management was not aware of the increasing anger among workers. They had already seen how angry the workers were. In fact, it is their anger that had forced it to allow the union to be formed and registered.

Another indication that the management wanted the situation to get worse is the way they handled the quarrel that Jiya Lal had with Majhi. Why did they hand over the suspension letter to Jiya Lal the same afternoon?

Usually, these things are done very differently. What normally happens is that when the worker finishes his shift and leaves the factory he is given a letter of suspension at the gate. Or when he comes to work the next day, he is not allowed inside the gate and is told that he has been suspended and can also be given the order there. Or he is not allowed in and the letter is sent home. An ordinary worker never takes his suspension order from the hands of a manager. That is simply not done. Why did the management want to hand him his suspension order on that day in the middle of his shift? Why did they have to call him away from his work station to give him the suspension order? The union leaders said they would themselves enforce discipline and were even ready to accept the suspension if only the supervisor would also be suspended pending enquiry.

Obviously, the management wanted something bad to happen. There is no point in saying that the management could not have known that such a big accident would happen, a fire would start, someone would die.

Labour department officials had arrived. The management was not even amenable to the suggestions of labour officers whose attitude was positive and who were pleading on behalf of the workers. They had also told the management that in future the union would act against any worker who misbehaves, or at least not protest if they took action. But, they told them, let us bring down tension levels today. The management did not heed them even after the labour officers had prepared a document to that effect and got the union leaders to sign it.

The role of the obstinacy of the management should not be ignored. Clearly, there was something wrong in their intentions. Perhaps the management thought that the enraged workers would beat up their leaders. They wanted that to happen. Otherwise, there was no point in being so stubborn.

It is not as if the management was unaware of what very angry workers had done in other factories. In Gurgaon itself, just a few months back, in March, there had been large-scale violence in two factories. The management could not have been unaware of this. Despite knowing all this, the management gave so much importance to a minor incident.

The workers displayed great patience. They kept on working. And all the while the resentment against the management and its deceitful attitude kept growing.

That evening, I was sitting with the head of another union in Udyog Vihar when he got a call that Maruti Manesar had caught fire. He told me about the fire. I immediately called up one of the union leaders. He took the call but there was so much noise that nothing could be heard. I could not hear a word.

After that all the phones were switched off.

I don't know what happened inside the factory that day. Perhaps no one will know what happened there that day, who started the fire in which Awanish Dev died. He was a good man. Workers considered him a sympathizer. It is difficult to believe that workers could have raised a hand against him.

The agents of the management would also be roaming

around, throwing a sentence here and another there, mocking the workers or taunting them. It all must have boiled over then.

There were cameras everywhere in that factory. We don't know who broke the cameras. Assuming that someone in the crowd of workers broke the cameras I still can't understand how all cameras got broken. How many cameras could the workers break? There were too many cameras there. It is possible that some people in the management broke them or got them smashed. After all, the HR people were there. There were bouncers standing around too. The camera sees everything. The cameras must have seen, recorded what the management was doing, what everyone was doing.

The CCTV footage was never found.

The server was near the gate, outside that building. A burnt server was then presented in the court by the police. Anurag Hooda, who was the lawyer of these workers, asked for the footage many times in court, but it was not made available.

Where is the footage?

Altogether 546 people were fired from their jobs. The entire union body was imprisoned. Even those who were later acquitted by the court were not given back their jobs. This is a direct effect of that day and the horrible incident that took place.

The event had even bigger consequences that are not clearly visible. Whatever happens in any big industry affects everyone. But Maruti's reputation, and its place in the industrial scene, is different and highly important.

From Gurgaon to Dharuhera, and even in Faridabad, there is a whole network of people making goods for it in many small and medium establishments. More than one million people are indirectly dependent on Maruti for their source of livelihood. Count their families and this number will go up fourfold or more. Street vendors in front of the vendors' factories depend on the workers for their living. They sell tea and cigarettes and *gutka*. There are so many works associated with a big industry. People drive autos for them, carry goods, supply packaging material for big and small parts.

It was worse for contract workers. Earlier, even contract workers used to get work regularly in Maruti for five to eight years with short breaks in between or through different contractors. The rates may not have been good but at least employment was certain.

Now, Maruti does not hire contract workers through any contractor. It directly takes people on contract and throws them out after six months. They still do the work of production but they are taken on directly by the company.

Maruti has also begun training workers now. Many are taken on as trainees under the Pradhan Mantri Kaushal Vikas Yojana, and the company gives them diplomas once they finish the course. The company has itself become an ITI!

Maruti is the market leader in the car market, and what happens to it affects not only all the companies but the entire working class. Whatever happens in it has far reaching implications. The tricks of the management worked in Maruti though it did sustain some losses. The factory remained closed for a month or a month and a half. But then it opened and started making profits as usual. It was the workers who suffered.

It is true that it was a major setback for the struggle of the working class. However, class struggle is part of the structure of the industry; it never stops.

It is because of Maruti that occupy strikes have now begun in many places. People take inspiration from this struggle. They have begun to understand what kind of tricks managements can resort to. They learn from it. They have respect for the union in Maruti that led such a brave struggle.

New office bearers were elected to the union. Now the pay scale of workers in Maruti Manesar has improved. They continue to help their jailed comrades and their families financially. They have vowed to never abandon them. This is also the success of the struggle, a product of class consciousness.

The vitality and the exemplary spirit of unity in Maruti Manesar is greatly admired among the working class. The union leaders are in prison but they know that they are not alone; the entire working class stands behind them.

After the 2011 strike, the Maruti Suzuki management was forced to increase the duration of the tea break from seven and a half minutes to fifteen minutes; to decrease the speed of the assembly line and thereby increase the time it takes to produce a new unit to 60 seconds; to provide transport for workers who had so far not been provided with it; to employ more workers to provide for relievers; and to allow the contract workers two days off every three months. One reliever per eight to ten workers is a norm, allowing the workers to take toilet breaks or drink water. But this went hand in hand with deepening the internal segmentation of workers and informalization of the work. In other words, the number of permanent workers was drastically cut down and the workload was transferred to temporary workers. (Amit and Nayanjyoti, 2018).

Seven

This Is a Class War

The law oppresses us and tricks us,
The wage slave system drains our blood;
The rich are free from obligation,
The laws the poor delude.
Too long we've languished in subjection,
Equality has other laws;
'No rights,' says she, 'without their duties,
No claims on equals without cause.'

—The Internationale, Eugène Pottier,
Paris, June 1871

The Suzuki factory in Manesar in Haryana was established in 2007 to produce an additional 550,000 cars or 1,152 cars a day on two shifts of eight hours each.

Within four years of its establishment, in 2011, workers organized strikes three times: a thirteen-day strike in June, followed by another strike for thirty-three days in August and then a fourteen-day strike in October. And then came the events of 18 July 2012.

The company's response to the workers' demands was to invite the Brahmakumaris to organize sessions with the workers in which the workers could talk to them about their problems ('Workers Autonomy Strikes in India', 2012). This response to the workers' demands and grievances is not unique to Maruti Suzuki. The involvement of this 'spiritual'-industrial complex—which includes the Brahmakumaris and individuals like Radha Soami Panth—in industrial management in Gurgaon is widespread.

The Brahmakumaris were first invited to deal with industrial unrest by Denso, a Japanese equipment manufacturer for the car industry. It invited them after a strike in February 2010 at its factory in Gautam Buddh Nagar in Uttar Pradesh. *The Economic Times* reported that 'the company, which has been struggling to handle workplace conflicts, has introduced sessions on spirituality by the Brahmakumaris for all of its 18,000 employees. Celebrity Brahmakumari Shivani will conduct the sessions on spiritual well being'. The report published on 12 September 2014 quoted Shivani claiming that she would 'keep emotions in place'.

However, others did not see the problem as one of a spiritual vacuum. Maruti Suzuki India (MSI) Chairman R.C. Bhargava said at the company's 30th Annual General Meeting that in his understanding 'the Manesar labour problem is essentially a political issue and not a problem which involves any significant demand from the workers'. He said that since it was a political problem, 'its resolution will be based on Maruti's established principles for industrial relations'.*

So, on the one hand, the management was using spiritual gurus to 'help strengthen a workplace culture that restores the workers' pride and dignity', and on the other they denied the fact that the workers had any grievances at all and refused to negotiate with them on their charter of demands.

---

* 'Manesar plant problem is political issue: Maruti Suzuki', *The Hindu*, 8 September 2011 (https://www.thehindu.com/business/companies//article60499761.ece/amp/, last accessed 11 January 2023).

What were these demands?

The Maruti Suzuki Workers' Union's charter of demands was well thought out even though the more experienced older trade union leaders warned them that it was far too ambitious; especially their demand that contract workers be given the same salaries and perks as permanent workers since both did the same work.

This was their charter of demands:*

1. Basic salary—at least Rs 25,000 per month.
2. All contract workers be designated as permanent.
3. Dearness allowance—Rs 10,000 per month.
4. HRA—60 per cent of Basic salary and DA.
5. Laundry allowance—Rs 3,000 a month.
6. Child education allowance of Rs 8,000 a month.
7. Transport allowance of Rs 10,000 per month.
8. City compensatory allowance at 40 per cent of Basic salary.
9. Home loan amounting to ten years' Basic salary and DA at a concessional rate.
10. Car loan amounting ex-factory cost, with immediate delivery of car.
11. Gift to all workers at every car launch.

The leaders of the Maruti Suzuki Workers' Union showed the charter of demands to Mathew Abraham but did not pay heed to his warning. However, they did have respect for his advice on conducting their affairs.

Sarabjeet Singh, the general secretary of the MSWU, serving life imprisonment, made particular mention, when Anjali interviewed him, of the advice Mathew Abraham gave the new generation of trade union leaders:

* See Verma 2014.

'...Mathew Abraham was well known in the area; he was in the old Gurgaon Maruti factory and he is very experienced. We needed guidance. To this day I have not forgotten what he told us and I will never forget. Mathew said, "To this day I have never slapped anyone. Be logical, keep your arguments strong. The management will break."

'He was right. We all agreed and we never got physical with anyone. Yes, we had long arguments; we could argue endlessly. But we never got violent.'

Mathew Abraham

When the workers got the new union registered in Manesar, they talked to me. We had only one meeting. Ram Meher, Sandeep, all of them came to meet me. They wanted to show me the charter of demands they had prepared. At first I refused. I don't want to get involved in any union work any more. I don't even have the time for it. However, later I agreed so they came to see me.

I was surprised by the charter they had prepared. They seemed to have high expectations. They were asking for two lakhs as salaries.

I told them that trade unions don't work like this. 'If you think you can get that much then what is the need of a trade union? Go straight to the managers and demand and get it.' They said that the management had asked for a written demand letter. Of course it did. I explained to them that the management was asking for it all in writing only to expose the absurdity of your demands and to ridicule you. I told them to work out the basis of the raise they were demanding in detail, and then prepare a detailed demand letter. I told them that they had to have a logical basis on which to place their arguments.

Otherwise, how would they negotiate? If they had a solid basis for their demands they could argue. Otherwise, it would be their demand versus the management's refusal.

Then I told them to get the demand letter typed and come to me. I offered to make corrections in it. They were in no mood to listen. They never came back to me.

Actually, they were all young and inexperienced. They were enthusiastic and but their expectations were unreal. They did not seem realistic to me.

That day when the violence happened in Manesar I had called them. There was a lot of noise and we could not hear each other. After that the phones got switched off and remained switched off.

The management is also at fault in this. There, in Manesar, all the managers were new. I think perhaps no old or experienced manager was posted in Manesar. They did not allow the union that was formed earlier to be registered and then they brought in a VRS and got rid of all of the union activists. That was not a good thing to do. The workers were very, very angry; understandably angry.

What happened was very bad for everyone. For workers it was the worst.

The union had started negotiating with the management but one demand in their charter of demands became a sticking point—the regularization of the contract workers. On 18 July 2012, when the leaders of the newly registered Maruti Suzuki Workers' Union came to the factory around 11 am, they were expecting to continue negotiations around the charter.

Instead, they found themselves negotiating over the suspension of a worker, Jiya Lal, who was active in the union.

Even that was not an unusual occurrence; certainly nothing that could possibly lead to the violence which occurred later that evening.

Everyone we interviewed remembers that 18 July 2012 started off like any other day in Plant A at the Suzuki factory in Manesar.

In a way, the whole thing started with a minor altercation between Jiya Lal and the supervisor. It was nothing unusual and Jiya Lal certainly had no premonition that it would lead to him being arrested, tortured and ultimately being sentenced to life imprisonment.

A permanent worker had this to say about Jiya Lal: 'This company got a man like Jiya Lal branded as a serious criminal. I knew him very well. He was very soft spoken. They got him declared such a big criminal, got him imprisoned for life. He was totally innocent. He was gentle, he would listen to everyone. He seldom spoke. He weighed just fifty kilograms and was so small to look at. This company has done him a great injustice.'

When Anjali contacted Jiya Lal, he was out on parole, dying of cancer. He spoke with a slight stammer; he was soft spoken but his voice was clear and firm. He wanted his story told.

Jiya Lal

A Dalit worker active in the Maruti Suzuki Workers' Union as a line coordinator. He was sentenced to life imprisonment. Anjali interviewed him when he was out on parole during the lockdown over the phone on 3, 4 and 5 September 2020. He died of cancer on 4 June 2021.*

---

* A line coordinator, as was briefly touched upon in the interview with Mohan above, is an activist worker who is the link between the union and the workers in the assembly line, hence *line* coordinator. There would be several line coordinators from different work stations.

I am Jiya Lal. Nowadays I live in prison. Bhondsi Jail, that is my address.

A long time ago I used to live in Jind, in my village, Dhakalgaon, where my home is, where my brother is and now even my wife. We are very poor people. We belong to the working class; we worked hard to buy our food.

I studied in my village. I went to the school in Dhakalgaon. After that I joined the ITI in Narwana. I trained as a fitter. Narwana is forty-two kilometres from Jind. I worked very hard, truly hard, thinking I would get a job in a factory and my life would improve; I would have a job, bring home a salary every month, and we would live comfortably—there would be no worries.

Now my name has got into the papers. A lot of people have heard of me. But this is not a happy thing to have happened. The thing is, I did no wrong, but I will always remain in prison. That is how I feel. What is the point of wondering how it all happened? But I feel terrible.

When I joined as an apprentice in the Gurgaon Maruti factory in November 2004 little did I know that all this would happen. That very year I had finished my course and almost immediately taken up a job. I was so happy when I became an apprentice. When my apprenticeship was over I joined Honda. I went to work in the Honda factory in which they make the Activa scooter. That too is in Manesar IMT [Industrial Model Township]. There I worked for six months. Then I went to work in Sona Steering. For a little bit of money I was going from one factory to another. I used to make ends meet. I could not get any permanent job. I used to be anxious all the time about the next job, wondering whether I'd be able to get another job when this temporary one was over. But I always found one.

Those who worked with me...they would tell me where a job was available. Contractors also tell you about new job openings. They employ you for six months on contract. Then they fire you. After some days you get the same job again. I worked in three companies, nowhere was there any chance of regularization.

I started working for Maruti Manesar in 2007 on 13 April. I had worked for a while in Maruti Gurgaon. I had been an apprentice there. Now I went to Manesar. Here I had hopes of being made a regular worker. I rented a room in Gurgaon. The company had a bus to fetch us and all of us used to take the bus to reach the factory at 6 am. I had to get up very early. We truly worked very hard.

Once a truck collided with the bus. The bus turned over. An ambulance arrived after a while and ferried us all to the Sheetla Mata Hospital. I was hurt near the waist. A lot of my co-workers got discharged that very day but I spent three days in hospital. Some flesh had got torn inside the left side of my waist. Not outside. I was in hospital for three days, then I was discharged and given some tablets to take. I stayed home for a week. Now, after twelve years, it seems that that piece of flesh which had got torn off has travelled to my back and got stuck in my backbone. Now I have got cancer.

I have always been a healthy man. You know how people are always getting sick, with a stomach ache, or something or the other? I never got even a stomach ache, or fever or any other illness. I never fell ill. Once in prison I got a stomach ache. Very slight. Two injections and I was absolutely fine again. I did not have to take any pills. Now that I have fallen ill, I have got such a serious disease. Its treatment is so tough, and who knows whether it can be treated or not. Besides, I am a prisoner too.

I was so happy to have joined Maruti. I had been a

temporary worker in Honda; on contract. I got only 4,500 rupees in a month. I worked there for six months. Then I joined Sona Steering. Again, on contract. I got 4,900 rupees a month. Tell me. How can you live on such a meagre sum? I had to pay rent for the room too. Four people share a room. When they were hiring trainees in Maruti Manesar I joined as a trainee. But the wages there were very low, even lower than what I was making as a contract worker. Despite that I joined as a trainee thinking I would eventually become permanent and then all would be well.

I had to complete three years of training, then they would make us permanent. That was the deal. We were hired as trainees but we got no training. We did all the work that a regular worker does. We did all the work but they called us trainees and paid us less.

In 2009, I got married. Even then I was a trainee. I had fallen short of attendance. I had had to take leave because of the accident too. I wasn't in perfect shape. What do you think the management did? It extended my training period by six months. So, I became a regular worker only in 2011. I had taken up this ill paying job only because there was a chance of being regularized here. Finally, I had become a permanent worker. Now my salary went up. I can't tell you how happy I was.

The work atmosphere in Maruti was fine. Nobody used filthy language, no abuses. There was no casteism among workers. Sometimes when we got into an argument someone would of course taunt us with a casteist slur. We would also tolerate it. We are used to it. That supervisor, Majhi, he too was not a bad man. He was not abusive, he used to talk nicely to us. That day when this incident took place, this terrible incident took place, because of which I am in prison, it was a Wednesday. I remember every single detail of that day.

I had taken leave on Monday. On Tuesday I went to the factory, worked my shift and came home. Everything was normal. The next day, on Wednesday, this disaster happened. That day I was in the 'A' shift. The first shift, in which you have to reach the factory early in the morning. You leave so early in the morning that all you do is have a cup of tea. You don't feel like eating anything so early. You may snack on a couple of biscuits with your tea. That is all. Then you get down to work. It is truly hard work. You soon begin to feel hungry. The first break is at 8.30 am for tea. By that time you are ravenous. This break is of exactly seven and a half minutes. Not one second less or more. It is so exact. A buzzer goes off. Within those seven and a half minutes you have to gobble what you get, use the bathroom, stretch your limbs. The food is good. There is no time to enjoy it though. Everyone is just running around.

That day in the break I picked up a *samosa*, got my tea and headed towards the bathroom. That is how you have to do it; you have to eat while on your way to the bathroom. Another worker was with me. We were both walking to the bathroom when the supervisor came up to us. He began to say something to me. I said that we will talk when I get back. Now tell me, a man has woken up at four in the morning, worked hard and now he has got a small break to eat something—why should he discuss work in this break? You should give him some time to breathe easy.

I did not say all this. I am only telling you. To him I only said, 'Brother, we shall talk later.' Majhi said, 'No, we have to talk now.'

I said that if it was work related I would only discuss it after I got back. I had very little time. I had to have my breakfast, visit the bathroom, get back to my station and be ready to work. When all this was done, then we could talk. He kept quiet.

I thought it was just one of those things that happen in the factory every day, and it was over. Such arguments were routine.

When I got back I saw that the supervisor had posted someone else in my place. I went to Majhi to talk about this.

I said, 'Listen, did I say anything bad to you that you did this to me? If there was something you wished to discuss with me pertaining to work we could have talked later.'

He suddenly exploded in anger. He said, 'Go do what you can. You *dhed*, you *chamar*. I will get you thrown out of the company.' I did not react to his casteist slurs. I only asked him why he would get me thrown out. Majhi said again, 'I will get you sacked from the company, you *dhed*, you *chamar*.' Even then I did not react to the casteist abuse. Then he used the sister-related abuse. I cannot tolerate anyone abusing my mother or sister. So I caught hold of his collar.

We were both screaming in anger. Others heard it too, and when I caught hold of his collar someone rushed to separate us. He separated Majhi and me, and ran back to work. He couldn't be away from his work station for more than a few seconds.

Majhi left. It seems he went upstairs to complain against me.

I am telling you that I did not slap him. I am willing to accept what I did. I accept that he used the sister-related abuse so I grabbed him by the collar. This much happened. Then I too went to my station and began working.

At 11.30 I told the union about it. Ram Meher, Ajmer and Ram Vilas from the union came to the factory at 11.30 am. That is the time they normally came to the factory. So, when they arrived I informed them. They said, 'No problems, keep working. We will sort this out.' I kept working. Around 12.30 I noticed that police had arrived at the factory.

I kept working. For a long time nothing happened. The

head of the department in our factory is known in short as 'DPM'. Around 2 pm in the afternoon I got a call from the DPM to say that I should come down to the fire brigade office. The fire brigade office is behind the main gate. When you enter the factory from the main gate and turn left then you will find this office behind the security guard's room.

When I reached the fire brigade office, I saw that some five people from the HR department were sitting there. There was nobody from the union. I did not have the courage to go into the office when I saw so many managers gathered there. I turned back and after putting some distance between the office and me, I called Ram Meher. He was the president of our union. He asked me to come to the union office so I headed there. All union office bearers were there. Ram Meher, Sarabjeet, Amarjeet, all of them—some eleven or twelve people. When I told them all that had happened they said let us all go to the fire brigade office.

They all went with me to the fire brigade office. When we went in, someone from HR asked, 'Who among you is Jiya Lal?' I said, 'I am.' Then that manager took a sheet of paper and was handing it to me but Ram Meher took it instead. He read the paper and said, 'If you are going to suspend him then suspend Majhi too. Whatever the argument was it happened between the two.' That is how I go to know that that sheet of paper was actually my suspension order. Ram Meher returned the sheet. I left after that. By the time all this happened the shift was about to end. However, I went back to my station and put in the few minutes of work left.

The 'A' shift ends at 2.45 pm. It ended. Ram Meher had asked me to come to the union office after work. So I went there. I sat there for a long time. The union president and other office bearers were not there. I heard that they had gone for a meeting to the HR office upstairs. I kept sitting in the union office for a long while.

When it was about 6 pm I left the office. I came out of the factory and had tea at a kiosk outside. There is a kiosk outside the gate. A lot of people stop for tea there. Even at that time there were some six or seven people having tea there. I don't know who all they were. I don't know whether they were workers from our factory or not. I had my tea. Then I left. I don't know when the fire broke out, who did it, how it happened—I don't know anything. Around noon or 1 pm all CCTV cameras had been turned off. I did not know even that. I got to know in court that at 1 pm CCTV cameras had been switched off. I did not know it then.

I have two children, both sons. One is nine years old and one is only a year and three months old. We are poor people. We have one and a half *keela* [roughly one and a half acre] land, meaning it is just a little more than nine *kanals*. I have a younger brother. I have a sister too; she is married. I am the oldest. My father too had a problem in his backbone. When I was a child he had come under a tractor. It was a bad accident. He was a labourer. He used to carry loads. He did it in the village. Our family is one of labourers. My brother is the only one to have studied up to MA. But has he got any decent job? No. He is working the land. He too has a son. My wife is not educated either. She too has no job. She can do farm work. She does all the work in the house. She has to care for the children too. I live in prison. And now I am also dependent on her.

When I joined as a trainee in Maruti my salary had gone down considerably from when I was a contract worker. However, I had hopes of being regularized someday, of a better salary when I would be regularized. I thought then we would all live comfortably. In 2011, when I did get regularized, I began to get 18,000 rupees a month. Everybody was very happy. I too thought our fortunes had changed; now we would live in comfort, not fall short of good things. I could not get that salary for long though. I had to go to prison.

Ram Meher

President of the Maruti Suzuki Workers' Union; sentenced to life imprisonment. He belongs to a family of small farmers in Guliyana in Kaithal district of Haryana. Interviewed on 6 January 2020 in Serhada village in Kaithal at the home of Suresh Dhull when the two, along with Sandeep Dhillon, were out on parole.

There is a village called Guliyana in Kaithal district of Haryana. I belong to that village. We have a bit of land but our family is not economically strong. We were farmers, we still farm our land. Nobody in my family has ever been part of any struggle. We were ordinary farmers, we never participated in any struggle. Even among my distant relatives nobody was part of any union or association or participated in any agitation.

When I got a job in Maruti I thought everything would change in the family. It was only when I started working that I realized just how hard and long they made you work without even paying you enough. They did not even pay our full wages. Sometimes they would deduct money for some leave we had taken, at other times the incentive we got would be reduced for one reason or another. We wanted justice. That is why we formed a union. Earlier, Sonu Gujjar had made a union.

Only when I joined the factory did I begin to think of fighting for my rights, for justice. They make you do too much work and pay you very little. When I was a trainee in 2007, I got only 3,200 rupees a month. I had to do the work expected of a regular worker. I could not leave the work station even for a sip of water or to urinate. Then we boys began to talk to each other and thought we should protest.

On 18 July [2012], when we arrived at the factory we got to know that during the tea break Jiya Lal had had some argument with his supervisor. Jiya Lal was the sort of man who hardly ever raised his voice. He was not the type to pick fights. But that day he too must have got angry.

We learnt that during the tea break the supervisor tried to pass on some instructions to him and he refused to pay heed. When he got back after the break he realized that the work line had already started moving. The break is of seven and a half minutes. The line only starts moving after that. That day the supervisor may have started it a bit early, perhaps only after six minutes or even five minutes. Jiya Lal asked him why he had done it. Majhi, who was the supervisor, apparently said, 'Don't play the leader with me. I will teach you a lesson, get you sacked.' This threat of 'I will get you sacked' was a common one on the shop floor; supervisors said this to everyone for the slightest reason. Jiya Lal was also abused because of his caste. That could have angered him. You would naturally get angry if someone abused you in those terms.

Jiya Lal was suspended. We never took the stand that workers are allowed to be rude and abusive. We only made the demand that either both should be suspended or Jiya Lal's suspension be taken back. This is what we said. It was not a big deal. Such fights do take place on the shop floor. These things happen. It could have been handled very easily.

When we heard about Jiya Lal's suspension we had gone to discuss it with the management. That day we were discussing only this issue of Jiya Lal.

We were in the meeting with Vikram Khazanchi, Birendra

Prasad, Vikram Sarin and C.S. Raju—all managers.* Awanish Dev was not in the meeting. He was outside in the hall. Actually, Awanish Dev had resigned but these people were not releasing him. He knew us very well. We got along very well. He was a good friend of ours. Had we had that meeting with him he would have agreed to take back the suspension order. But he was not in the meeting.

The administrative block is above the assembly shop, on the first floor. Above the shop floor is this big hall in which a large number of managers have their seats. There are a few rooms too on one side. We were sitting in a room discussing the issue. The workers did not gather together either outside in the hall or anywhere else for that matter. Work continued normally, like it did every day. The crowd gathered only after the 'A' shift was over and some people stayed back. By then the 'B' shift workers had come in and had begun working. The crowd had not prevented anyone from working or hindered work.

Yes, it is true that I had told Ram Vilas to ask some people to stay back. When there is a small crowd there is pressure on the management. The whole day we had held meetings. We had broken for lunch and then we had continued with the meetings.

It is not true that I had made a speech that day saying that today we are going to have an '*aar paar ki ladai*' [fight to the finish]. It is not at all true. There was no occasion for a speech that day. We had only left the meeting for lunch. From there we had gone with Jiya Lal to the fire brigade office. There Jiya Lal was given his suspension letter which I had taken. He is

* According to the FIR, Maruti officials C.S. Raju, Vikram Khazanchi, Vikram Verma, Vikram Sarin, P.K. Roy, Birendra Prasad, A.K. Gour, Salil Bihari and Awanish Kumar Dev were present in the meeting along with labour officer Dinesh Kumar and labour inspector Chandra Pal.

right, I took that letter. After that we had not addressed any workers' assembly in the HR building. Nothing of the sort happened that day.

I, Sarabjeet, Sandeep and Pawan Dahiya were in the meeting inside a room and we never got out of the room. How would we know what was happening outside? There was tension. I was getting phone calls too. Ram Vilas and others too were getting calls from union office bearers to find out what was happening. They told us the workers were very upset, that many had stayed back. We knew that there was tension. No speeches were being made outside.

I honestly do not know who started this talk of fighting to the finish. But the phrase was being thrown around since after the 2011 strike. A lot of boys used to say that this time we would fight to the finish. Who knows what is meant by this '*aar paar*' or 'finish'. It may mean something for me and something else for you. People can make it mean whatever they choose to.

We don't even know why the management had called the police. By five in the evening the police had arrived on the shop floor.

We tried for a long time but the management did not listen to us, so we called the labour officer. Labour inspector Chandra Pal and labour officer Dinesh Kumar came to the factory. They too started negotiating with the management from our side. At one point, Chandra Pal got us to write an application to say that we would do what the labour officer asks us to do. He even got us to sign it. This must have been around five or quarter past five in the afternoon.

He said, 'Just wait, let me talk to the management and I will get back to you and we will resolve this issue.' He left the room and we kept sitting there. After about twenty minutes he got back and said that the management was not agreeing to it. That application we had written was not given back to us either. It would have been really useful to us in court. Had we got it we could have proved that we were willing to settle the issue, that it was the management that had been adamant. We did not get it back. We had signed and handed it over to Chandra Pal. We don't know want happened to it.

When he got back to say that the management was inflexible, we decided to try to talk to them once again. The meeting began once again, at around 6 pm. The management was stand-offish. Their attitude was one of 'I don't want to listen to you'.

By then some disturbances had begun. Things began to be broken. Who knows who was doing what. Everyone was wearing the uniform of the company. We saw many six-feet-tall men around. There were bouncers too. They were thrashing people. Scuffles broke out. We thought we should leave now and take up the matter the next day. By 6.15 pm we had left the factory.

We later heard that there was a fire in the factory too. We were not there.

Sarabjeet Singh

General secretary, Maruti Suzuki Worker's Union; sentenced to life imprisonment. Interviewed over telephone on 10 February 2021.

[On the events of 18 July 2012:]

We wanted contract workers to be made permanent. Negotiations had begun. Every day we would have meetings but nothing ever came of them.

This began to make workers wonder why we were so ineffective. They kept asking us why it was taking so long. One day, Ram Meher told the workers that he wanted to resign, and that we should hold elections to the union. A new team could be better at the job. It is not true that the workers doubted their intentions or thought that they were trying to cut a deal with the management, but they just could not understand why no settlement appeared possible after months of negotiations. Ram Meher and Sandeep were a little disappointed and wanted to quit. It happens, when negotiations continue fruitlessly. I talked to them and pointed out that we had a new union, little experience—we shouldn't get disappointed so soon. It wouldn't look good if office bearers resigned so soon after the union had been registered with such great difficulty. How long could the management not bend? They were persuaded to continue.

That day, on 18 July, the same thing was going to happen, another meeting and no results. That is what we thought. Early in the morning, Jiya Lal had had an argument with Majhi, a supervisor. Jiya Lal was suspended. So now we had another demand to place on the table: revoke the suspension of Jiya Lal or suspend Majhi along with him.

That day I was on leave. I used to be in the general shift. We all were in the general shift. The tussle continued. The management wouldn't budge. I was called to the factory. I wish I hadn't gone. Had I not gone perhaps the horrible tragedy would not have happened, perhaps they would have been forced to suspend negotiations because of the absence of the general secretary of the union. However, I went to the factory at around 2.30 pm, when they called me, our union comrades.

By then a lot of arguments had already taken place. Earlier, they had been talking to Awanish Dev. He had also proposed putting off the talks till the next day. That is what he said again when I went to the factory, and even I wanted to do so. But the situation was very tense, and there was too much pressure from the workers on us, so I too did not insist on it and said that whatever could be done tomorrow could be done today; we should conclude at least the issue of Jiya Lal. So we agreed to do so after a short break.

There is a big hall upstairs on the first floor that can hold a hundred people. There is a small room adjacent to it. The meeting in the evening was being held in that small room and Awanish Dev was not in it. He was outside in the hall. C.S. Raju and Vikram Khazanchi and one Prasad were with us in the room. They were not agreeing to our request. Raju and Khazanchi were constantly getting calls on their phones. And they in turn were calling Awanish and telling him that they were facing problems because of him. '*Inka badhta jaa raha hai,*' they told him on the phone, perhaps trying to tell him that pressure from our side was increasing. They were insisting on an enquiry. We said, let there be an enquiry, but be even handed—either revoke Jiya Lal's suspension or suspend both him and Majhi.

We had decided that this time we would not strike work. Strikes tend to break once they drag on for long. But there was increasing pressure on us too and the workers were asking us to assert ourselves. I and Ram Meher were also getting calls continually to find out why we were unable to get this small thing done. The 'A' shift ended. The workers of the 'A' shift had not left the factory. The workers of the 'B' shift had entered and were working. Some people came upstairs and stood outside the hall. I don't know who all were there because we were inside the room. Bouncers had arrived too. The police had arrived and they were inside the factory, not outside. Not inside the room but downstairs. There was a big crowd outside the room.

We never raised a hand against anyone. We did not hit any officer. Awanish was not even inside the room. There was no question of getting violent with him. We were friendly. Only about ten days earlier he had been discharged from the Max Hospital after some surgery. We had gone to meet him there.

It is also not true that someone from upstairs had screamed that these people were beating up union leaders. It is true that the management did not get violent with us either or hit anyone of us. They were prepared for violence, they were ready for it. That much is true, because they had organized bouncers, they had called the police. They may have not anticipated that such a big tragedy would take place.

Nobody called from upstairs to say that union leaders were being beaten up. But yes, someone did say very loudly, 'These people are not agreeing' (*Yah log to maan hi nahin rahe*)—meaning that the management was not agreeing to our proposal. It is also possible that some bouncer had called out saying, 'These people are not agreeing'...that is, the workers are not agreeing. I don't know who said that and what it meant; who was accusing whom of not agreeing. However, someone did say that and said it loudly. Who was it? A bouncer, some policeman, some worker? I can't say. This was going on in the HR building. It is possible that some people got enraged when they heard this. Someone may have said something to one of the bouncers or the bouncers said something...and then they got into a brawl. Sandeep, Dhanraj, Amarjeet, I, Ram Meher, we were all in the small room. We did not touch anyone. That much I know for sure.

When we came downstairs we saw that some bouncers were beating people up. The police was with them, on their side. The police was also asking workers who stood around to leave. They were chasing the workers away. They were not intervening in the fights that bouncers were having, restraining the bouncers or asking them to leave.

Yes, we could have postponed the discussion for the next day, but we also knew that the management was under tremendous pressure that day. We wanted to push our demands because it is not every day that the management seems so tense and under pressure. They should have accepted the demand concerning Jiya Lal. At least that much they could have and should have done. Had they revoked the suspension or suspended both him and Majhi and ordered an enquiry the tension would have been relieved considerably. But they were obstinate. We were agreeing to an enquiry. What was the problem in revoking a suspension or the suspension of both till the enquiry was held? But the management was so rigid and unbending!

It is true that they did not beat us and we did not beat them. But there was violence. However, all of us who are in prison, we did not get violent at all. It is also true that some managers got hurt. P.K. Roy was badly injured. Awanish was very seriously injured.

I don't know how the place caught fire. The fire broke out in the HR department building. Work continued till seven in the evening. We had all left the place. It caught fire after that. I want to know what the fire brigade was doing when the fire broke out. They had everything in place to deal with fires. They had alarms and smoke alarms and hoses and everything. And the one day it was needed it did not work!

Ram Meher, Suresh [Dhull], they all live in Jind.* The police began to go to their houses and harass their families. Once one of their family members called some twenty-five-odd villagers to complain how the police was harassing them. The villagers then held a *panchayat*. Ravindra Tomar (ACP) appeared before the *panchayat*. Rajbir Singh, the IO of the case, also appeared

* They live in Kaithal.

before the *panchayat*. There, in that *panchayat*, these two police officers held water in their cupped hands and swore that if *these* people (if we) surrendered, the police would not beat or torture them, not give them any trouble. They did not keep their word.

We all surrendered on 1 August in the Sector 10 police station of Gurgaon. We had surrendered, but they wrote us up as arrested. I have learnt that it is highly risky to surrender without knowing the consequences. You should have a good lawyer before you surrender. But we had no one to protect us and the police thrashed us badly. They hang you from the ceiling and hit you on the soles. Some people could endure it. They beat you in such a way that your bones don't break. Some people cannot tolerate such torture. They suffer all their lives. Sohan was hung up and beaten to a pulp. His hands hurt even now. Jiya Lal got cancer. Ajmer got brain tumour.

Sandeep Dhillon

Nowadays, I live in Bhondsi prison. It was built for 2,000 people and there are 2,800 people in it.

In the prison I work as an electrician. I also work as an attendant at the STD booth inside the prison. It is an official booth. There are three such booths that look like computer screens. Every prisoner has to give two numbers they want to call and they are fed and saved in the machine. They can call only one of those two numbers. Calls are metered and after the allotted time they get disconnected. There is always a long line of people waiting to make a call.

There is a lot of technology being used nowadays. Relatives of prisoners can transfer money online in the accounts of prisoners. Earlier, it used to be tough to get money. Where would prisoners keep the cash? It got stolen. Employees also took a part of it as bribes. Now it is better. You have an account and you pay online for anything you get from the prison canteen. The canteen sells things like soap, toothpaste and other necessities.

Still, it is a prison. We get forty-two days of parole for farm work, twenty-eight days when we have to get children admitted to schools. We also get a furlough.

You want to know what happened on 18 July 2012 in Manesar.

I have to begin from the time we got our union registered; the union we registered after Sonu Gujjar was made to take VR.

It is important to emphasize that as far as unity goes, the unity of workers at Maruti was unequalled. Our unity was cited as an example. All unions talked about us. Whichever central trade union they were affiliated to they all consulted us about our strong bonds and our unparalleled unity.

We consulted Sonu [Gujjar] on what we should do next. The old application for a union was of no use. We chose the president and general secretary and all other office bearers and once again we went and handed the file to the Registrar's office seeking registration.

We had submitted our file to the Registrar's office on 27 October 2011. Our office bearers were: Ram Meher, President; Sarabjeet, General Secretary; Sandeep (me), Chief Patron; Suresh Dhull, Treasurer. There were executive members too. We, all twelve of us, went to Chandigarh.

Jaswanti Ahlawat was the Registrar then. She kept postponing the registration on one pretext or another.

M.M. Singh, a manager, who was very knowledgeable about labour law and unions, and S.Y. Siddiqui of HR would meet us off and on. Siddiqui was the head of Maruti industries. They were both in the top management. They used to keep reassuring us, telling us not to worry, that our union would be recognized.

And finally it was recognized. On 23 February 2012, the Maruti Suzuki Workers' Union got registered. Our registration number was 1923.

We got that certificate from Chandigarh and gave a copy of it to the head of the HR department. That is the procedure, that we have to give them a copy so that they know that we have been recognized as a union and they acknowledge it with a letter of receipt with their stamp on it to say that they have been informed about the formation of this union and in future they will consult the representatives of this union.

On 1 March we celebrated the flag raising day of the union. We talked to the management and got an hour off in the morning and we raised our flag near the gate. We had got a small room as an office. We all got together. We ate sweets. Then we went in to work. Production continued. All was well. We were all enthused.

Then we prepared a charter of demands. First of all, we wanted contract workers to be made permanent. At the time there were 1,500 contract workers there. We demanded that all of them be made permanent.

For three years, our salaries had not been revised. We demanded that workers be paid on par with whatever the Pay Commission had recommended for central government workers. After all, we did not work less than them. We worked as hard if not more, but we were getting paid less. We wanted our basic pay to be Rs 14,000 and DA and other allowances to be calculated on that basis.

We also wanted that the health care facilities we got be upgraded. Those days IFFCO Tokio used to insure us. The upper limit of the insurance claim used to be rather low. They paid only when we got admitted to a hospital and even for that they had fixed limits for different things like room rent and tests. We wanted it to be flexible so that, if necessary, we could choose a room or ward with a lower rent and use the money saved for a test that was expensive. This was not permissible under our insurance policy. We also wanted to be able to choose some more expensive or bigger hospitals if necessary. What we had realized was that the upper limit of payable claims was low and even that was divided into very rigid slots. Those IFFCO Tokio people were really bad; they used to harass us a lot for claims. Even unmarried people could not get their parents added on as dependants in their family policy.

The arrangement in Maruti Gurgaon was very different and much better. They had a panel system. They had given employees names of some hospitals that were on its panel and employees could go to any of them. They had a choice. They got cashless treatment in those hospitals. We wanted a similar system. Why should there be two health care systems in two factories of the same industry?

We also wanted the company bus service to be reinstated. It had been discontinued. Earlier they used to fetch people from a radius of fifty kilometres and we wanted the radius to be increased to 100 kilometres.

All our demands were justified. There was nothing illegitimate in them. There was nothing we had demanded that could be called too much. We said: we have three plants—Gurgaon, Manesar and Powertrain—and all of them are under the management of Suzuki and each one has its own union; the management should bring together two or three representatives from each union and organize the same facilities for everyone with their consent. We can then have a common agreement. What is the problem? That is what we said.

We asked them why they would not consent to such a

common plan that we could all agree upon. We said this in our meetings with the management.

Some of our needs were different too. No buses are required in Gurgaon. They have local transport. We don't have any in Manesar. For three years our wages had not been raised. Every three years the company makes a wage agreement with the union. In it, arrears of the past year are paid. In the current year we get the revised wage rate. And the increase in the third year is already decided. Then another agreement for three years is made again. Three figures are mentioned and everyone signs accepting them. Now, we had fallen behind by three years. There had been no agreement at all for three years. So it was time now for a fresh agreement and we would have got the arrears for three years.

The management proposed a wage raise of only Rs 8,000 in total for six years. In the current year they offered Rs 4,000 including the annual raises of the past three years which meant an annual increase of approximately Rs 1,000 per month for the last three years as well as the current year... So we would have got Rs 18,000 as monthly salary in 2012, and in the future the same rate was to be applied for three years. In the third year, that is, in 2015, the monthly salary of a permanent worker would therefore be Rs 22,000.

The management was represented by Vikram Khazanchi, Awanish Dev and C.S. Raju. Khazanchi was the head of manufacturing. Awanish and Raju were from the HR department. Vikram Sarin was also part of the negotiation team from the Manesar plant. He was DDVM in the manufacturing department. I, Ram Meher and Suresh Dhull represented the union.

We refused their offer.

Negotiations continued.

Workers began to build pressure on us.

Every week we would have meetings and the stalemate would continue. Workers would keep asking us why a settlement was getting delayed. As far as production was concerned it continued without a hitch.

There was no rude behaviour. No misbehaviour. No suspensions. No threats. Only the meetings would take place and there would be no outcome.

In the Gurgaon factory they were about to reach a settlement. They had concluded their meetings. The management wanted a settlement in all three plants at the same time.

Production work was going perfectly. Perhaps the management was waiting for us to slip up or do something unacceptable. They were perhaps waiting for us to make a mistake so that they could suspend someone and then compel us to agree to the settlement they had decided on.

One day there was a fault in the electrical line. A blower stopped working in the assembly line. For three days it did not work. It was the month of June and extremely hot. This is a very big blower and it throws cool air. When there is a problem in the assembly line it is immediately repaired. It is given top priority. Nothing is ever allowed to go wrong or stay unfixed in the assembly line. For three days the blower remained unrepaired. That was surprising and it was in the extreme hot weather. People continued working in that unbearable heat. We raised the issue many times but nothing happened.

We asked why the repairs were delayed this time while assembly line faults were corrected immediately. No response. There were long arguments but nothing was done to fix the blower. One day when the arguments became too heated they suspended Ram Meher and Ram Vilas. Ram Vilas was a member of our executive committee.

I then went to meet the managers, Khazanchi and Awanish Dev and Raju. I met all three. I asked them to revoke the suspension. They agreed and withdrew the suspension order. That very night the blower was repaired. Everything then became normal. Work and negotiations resumed. Without any outcome, of course.

Many days passed. Then came 18 July 2012. It was just another day, another day at work. We had a meeting with the managers, we reiterated our demands and they said the same thing. There was no settlement. The workers as usual asked us what happened and we told them we were trying, still negotiating.

The workers wanted to know when they could get the revised wages. For them it was a big, big question. But our efforts were bearing no fruit. And we expected the same thing to happen that day too. We would put forth our arguments and that would be that. It was like any other day. Just another day.

That morning a supervisor on the assembly line, Majhi, had a spat with Jiya Lal. This must have happened around eight in the morning or perhaps 8.30. We were all in the general shift, which means a nine-to-five shift.

We got to know of the fight the moment we entered the plant. I personally went to Majhi and talked to him and got the matter resolved. He said Jiya Lal and he were like brothers, such things happen even among brothers—let us forget what happened. Work continued uninterrupted.

Around 12.30 pm, HR manager Awanish Dev called me for a meeting. He told me that a worker had misbehaved with an engineer. Supervisors have an engineering diploma and are called engineers there. I told him about my discussion with Majhi and how it had all been resolved and I assured him that I would talk to Majhi again. However, by then Majhi had been sent off on leave. We started talking about other issues too. Soon, it was time for lunch.

Awanish said we should have our lunch and continue with our discussion later. I told him that I wanted to meet Majhi. I also told him that if he wished to take action he should take it against both of them and that I was not suggesting that he should not act against a worker. If a worker is in the wrong he should face action, but in this case there should be action against both or no action against any of them.

I have a feeling that Awanish Dev did not want to suspend him. The HR was not in favour of such action. They wanted to resolve the issue by talking to all the concerned people. But the manufacturing people began to argue that if they tolerated such misbehaviour with a supervisor today who knew what might happen tomorrow. Many such incidents could take place. It had to be suppressed. Action had to be taken.

Jiya Lal had called Ram Meher.

Ram Meher told him do not take the suspension letter. That he should refuse to take it. He refused.

After lunch we began our meeting with the management again. This time the attitude of the HR was a little better. They wanted to resolve the issue. But the manufacturing people began to assert themselves. They began to say that such incidents would repeat and would increase in intensity and that these people must be taught a lesson.

I said, let us discuss this tomorrow. Let us leave it here today.

In the meanwhile, we had already called the Labour Department. The labour inspector and labour officer both had arrived at the plant. They also joined the meeting and they too were asking the management to go easy on the worker. The labour officer told us that he would persuade the management.

We wrote down a letter of assurance which said that, in future, if any worker misbehaved, the union too would take action against such a worker. I and Ram Meher signed it and we gave it to the labour officer.

However, Vikram Khazanchi refused to sign it.

The resolution got scuttled. We then said that they should give a week's leave to Jiya Lal like they had sent off Majhi on leave. We said that it was not clear yet who was at fault, so we should hold an enquiry and decide what to do after it.

The management refused point blank. They did not agree to even withdraw his suspension.

This began to create mistrust between us, the union and the workers. There was too much tension. We began to get calls from workers asking us how the suspension of Ram Vilas and Ram Meher had been withdrawn the same day and why we were unable to persuade the management to do the same in the case of Jiya Lal—a worker. They felt we had been forceful in the earlier case because it was a case related to union office bearers, unlike this time when it was an ordinary worker's case. They thought that we were letting the matter drag, that we were disinterested. They began to doubt us.

We began getting one message after another asking us why we were not able to handle the matter. Pressure was mounting on us. Had we asked the workers to wait for a few days they would have been very angry with us. They were already angry with the prolonged negotiations on the wage issue. We did not want this issue to become too big. We asked the management to call Majhi back to the plant so that we could talk to him. The management just would not budge. The negotiations continued endlessly.

It was about 3 pm now. The 'A' shift had finished work. The police had already been called and were inside the plant.* Group 4 security guards were already there. Some 150 bouncers had also come in. There used to be bouncers in the factory all the time. Ever since the strike of 2011 had ended they had vanished, but now, all of a sudden they had reappeared. The management was preparing for something big. Heated arguments were taking place. But that day our demand was a very small one: revoke the suspension of a worker. Nothing big. Either suspend both or do not suspend Jiya Lal. It was a simple and small demand.

The 'A' shift ended. Workers were restive. We had gone downstairs only once, for lunch, and had spent the whole day upstairs in the meeting. Workers downstairs were getting very uneasy. Restless. All this must have got recorded on the CCTV too. The CCTV there is an amazingly good one. You could not only see what was happening in all the three plants you could even see workers in Suzuki in Japan working in their plant. The Japanese could watch us at work. All CCTVs of the three plants and Japan are interconnected.†

Downstairs, some workers got into an argument with the police. This police force was headed by ACP Ravindra Tomar. Amazingly, this same Tomar was subsequently made the head of the SIT. Look at the irony!

The 'A' shift ended. The 'B' shift had entered the plant. The police asked the 'A' shift to get out.

We were still upstairs and tempers were running high downstairs. We were not there to control the situation. The police even thrashed Amarjeet, one of our union leaders.

The 'B' shift had started working. As the tension began to rise the 'B' shift stopped working. There were thousands of

* They had entered the plant but were not yet at the shop floor.

† This could not be established and it may not be true.

people inside the factory at the time. Around 500 workers had come upstairs and were standing outside the room where we were talking to the management.

We don't know how it all began, who beat whom. We had been negotiating for so many weeks now, we had never raised a hand or got physical with anyone. We did not beat anyone. We were in the factory till 7 pm. When we left the fire had not broken out. We were friendly with Awanish Dev; we used to go to his house. We knew his wife. We have had lunch at his house with his family and we would never have harmed him. He was also soft towards us; he wanted to resolve the issue. He was our friend.

Awanish had already resigned from the factory. The company had not yet accepted his resignation. They apparently said that they had spent a lot of money on training him and he would have to pay that amount if he wanted to leave. This amount ran into crores. Perhaps it was twenty or twenty-five crores. It may have been only a crore or a crore and a half. I don't know. But we had heard that that was the reason they were not letting him go. He did not have that kind of money so he continued working.

We knew his wife too. Whenever we went to his house she used to welcome us and was very nice to us. When the press people went to meet her soon after the incident that day, she said she couldn't believe that the people whom she knew so well had killed Awanish. She too could not believe that we had done it. It was reported in the papers.

The fact is that we were not in his room when the ruckus broke out. There were thousands of people there. Nobody could figure out who was where. The police was chasing everyone. They were asking people to get out of the factory.

We don't know who started the fire, how the place caught fire. We don't even know when it happened.

In the court they have claimed that people were standing on the stairs and were preventing the management from leaving. This did not happen. Had that happened how would the others have left? After all, the other managers did get out. All the other employees got out. They all left, did they not? Why did anyone not get Awanish Dev out or try to pull him out? Their whole department was on the first floor. Why did they not try to save him? We were not there but other managers were there. Had workers been blocking the stairs would they not have died too? Were they standing on the stairs to get burnt alive? No workers got burnt. They were not there, that is why. We had left. Or we would also have got burnt. That did not happen. Only Awanish Dev died.

When we left the factory it was twelve minutes past seven in the evening. The CCTV camera shows this clearly. The police showed us this recording in the police station. I don't know where the recording vanished afterwards. It was never produced in court.

When the police took us into custody they beat us really badly. They tied my hands behind my back and beat me. They hung us from the ceiling and beat us on the soles of our feet. They tortured us a lot. They abused us all the time in the filthiest of language using mother and sister swear words.

Then they showed us the CCTV footage and told us that they had all the evidence. In that footage we saw that when we walked out of the factory gate it was twelve minutes past seven.

Till then there was no fire in the factory. The flames became visible after four minutes, at sixteen minutes past seven.

We don't know what happened and how. There were just too many people there, too big a crowd. We had got out of the room in which the meeting was taking place to calm the workers down.

Frankly, I think the report that the police filed initially was the right one. The police was inside. It had seen what had happened. They were eyewitnesses. And they knew who had done what. In the beginning they had written what they saw. Nowhere in that report did it say that we set fire to the factory.

K.T.S. Tulsi threw away that first report. He was the government lawyer. He prepared a new challan and in it said that we stood on the stairs and did not let people escape. He got this new challan made in a hotel room.

And now I am in jail. I am not even married. Now I'll never get married. My life will be spent in jail.

Manish

I have already told you my story, at least a part of it. As I said, this is not my real name. Let me tell you want happened on 18 July 2012: I think it was a management conspiracy.

In fact, from the very beginning there were two factions in the management. One faction was of S.Y. Siddiqui and the other was of Awanish Dev. Awanish Dev was in favour of the union. He wanted an independent union to be formed and also wanted to have good relations with the workers and their union. He had helped us register the union.

On the other side was Siddiqui who was completely against it.

The union had been talking to the management about raises in salaries and about other facilities like transport for a long time. On that day too such a meeting was taking place on the mezzanine floor.

Awanish was there when Jiya Lal was suspended at 10.30 or eleven in the morning. We told him to take back the suspension. He was the general manager of HR. He too said that he would take it back. He suggested discussing the matter after lunch. We didn't see him after lunch. I wish he was with us that day, at that time. All this would not have happened.

Awanish Dev was a subordinate of C.S. Raju. Raju was the boss.

It seems to me that the management deliberately allowed the matter to gain a lot of weight. Perhaps the management wanted something big to happen or wanted to do something explosive. It may have planned something but did not realize that it could get out of hand. And they did not anticipate that it would end with something as tragic as the death of a manager. They would not have wanted to kill Awanish or have wanted him dead. But the accident happened.

Perhaps the management wanted someone to get beaten up. Perhaps they thought that if nobody got thrashed they wouldn't be able to crush the union. They let it boil over, they kept provoking the workers. That is what they may have planned—some little violence. They may not have thought that someone would actually die. Or maybe his death was also part of the same conspiracy. What can we say? What proof do we have?

We all liked Awanish Dev very much. He used to be on our side, speak on our behalf. I wish he was not dead.

Sathya Narayanan

Now to the events that led to the 18 July events in Manesar.

The violence that took place there is very unfortunate, but merely repeating that makes little sense. We must see where the root of such violence is.

One mistake made in Manesar was that Jats were hired to work in it. I am not against Jats. But it has to be understood that many communities have their own nature. The collective nature of Jats is somewhat different. They are hard-working but they lack patience. If a Jat thinks something is wrong he will fight back. Still, hiring Jats may not have been that big a mistake.

The second mistake was that the management wanted the union to become a part of MUKU, which was not only completely unethical it was also illegal.

Whatever work you do, you must remain within the boundaries of the law, whether you like it or not. If you do not like the law, you can campaign to change the law, you can petition the higher courts, but you should not violate the law. This applies to everyone and every manager knows this.

The management of Manesar prevented the workers of Manesar from registering a union. This is not a minor mistake. This is a violation of the law. It is completely illegal. In our country, workers have the right to form unions and the management was trying to prevent them from exercising their right. They were working against the law.

Awanish Dev was also part of it. He was an integral part of the same management which was depriving the workers of their rights. Everyone says that he was sympathetic towards the workers. Then why did he tolerate it when the management did not allow the workers to register their union?

For two years, on one pretext or the other, the management did not allow the union to be formed. What was Awanish Dev doing then? He may have sympathized with the workers, but was it just lip service? He was general manager of HR and where did he stand?

We have been taught in theory, in management studies, that even if you do not like the union, you have to work with them, interacting with them constantly, bargaining and using persuasion. You don't have to like the union but you have to work with them. This is the legal system in the country and you must obey the law. These are rights granted by the Constitution of the country and they have to be respected. All managers know this.

As far as preventing the formation and registration of unions is concerned, everyone was complicit—not just the management but also the State government. Officials who are supposed to register the union evaded their duty.

The issue became so serious that, in the year 2012, it was raised in Parliament. The Labour Minister, in his statement on the floor of the House, asked how the State government could obstruct the registration of a union. It had been prevented for two years on one pretext or another.

However, the persistence of the workers paid off. The matter had reached the Parliament and it was finally possible to get their union registered.

The young men who joined the Maruti Suzuki factory in Manesar were not political and did not understand class struggle; all they wanted was to work hard and make money to support their families. But their experience of working at the factory and their fight for justice showed them that their struggles were not merely disputes between workers and management; they were, taken together, a class war. Praveen, the dismissed worker who was convicted but later released, asserts this explicitly in his interview.

Praveen

I am from Khubaru village in Sonipat district of Haryana. My father was also a labourer. We are a family of masons. We are known as Khatis. We are OBCs [Other Backward Class].

I did a fitter's course from the Gannaur ITI from 2002 to 2004. The fees were nominal. They hardly taught us anything. They taught us theory but nothing practical. They just showed us some tools so that we could recognize what is what when we saw them. But yes, we had to be present from nine in the morning to five in the afternoon. The only thing we learnt there was how to stay put in one place from nine in the morning to five in the afternoon. In school we spent some five hours only. So I learnt this discipline before I started working at the factory.

Someone I knew in the neighbouring village was a permanent worker in Maruti. He took my documents and submitted them to the company. Two days later I got a call and I got selected.

I joined the Maruti Gurgaon factory as an apprentice in 2005. For one year I was an apprentice. From day one I hated the job. They made me work too hard. I was supposedly an apprentice but I had to do all the work of a regular employee. They just exhaust a worker by the end of the day.

I was given the work of loading cylinder heads on the engine. There is a crane that brings between 350 and 400 cylinder heads and dumps them before you. These were engines of the Swift car. Lifting the cylinder heads and placing them on the engine is heavy work. The cylinder heads are really heavy.* Apprentices are made to do all such arduous work like lifting heavy weights. I used to be very strong and could easily lift heavy things.

Till then production had not begun in Manesar. We were

* They in fact weigh around twenty to thirty kilograms each.

apprentices and worked as subordinates to permanent workers. They did the light work and made us do all the heavy work.

The stipend those days used to be only 2,800 rupees. The very first month they deducted Rs 800 from my stipend. This began happening to me every month. Sometimes they said I had no manners, that I was poorly behaved. Sometimes they said I was late for work. Strangely, I was even accused of being absent when I would be working there. I don't know how it used to happen but I would put in a day's work and realize that I had been marked absent. All manner of unusual things have happened to me. There are big scandals in that factory. Everything there is big. Machines are huge. Work is very heavy. Penalties are big. Everything in that place is very big.

Then you have the politics between permanent and temporary workers. Permanent workers don't like to work. So they make the temporary workers put in all the hard labour. They also keep provoking temporary workers to complain about things and then fights happen.

I can't even begin to tell you how bad the working conditions were. I had to get there at six in the morning. I went without breakfast. What could I do? Who would give me breakfast in the morning? All of us had the same life, we all rushed to the factory on empty stomachs.

The lunch system was even worse. We got half an hour for it. Now, you have worked since sunrise and this is the first big meal of the day. You need to relax, sit down and enjoy your meal. There we had no such luxury. Lunch break meant hurrying from one place to another and rushing back. First, get rid of all the safety gear, take off the helmet, the mask and gloves and whatever else one has to wear for work, run to the washroom, then make a 500-metre dash to the canteen, get in a queue, pile up your plate and shovel it in your stomach like it is a dustbin. The moment you finish stuffing yourself you have to rush back, use the washroom, wear the helmet, mask, gloves and whatever else and be ready to serve the machine. We never got a minute to relax.

As for living arrangements, I used to share a room with three others in Gurgaon. I spent 500 from my stipend on rent. I would get back from the factory dead tired and would have to cook the evening meal.

I began to feel awful. I would think to myself: if they want to deduct money from my stipend, let them do so; I cannot work like this. But how long can you not go to work? I had to be there on time on most days.

My apprenticeship ended on 31 March 2007. A friend of mine filled out an application for me and submitted it to the factory. I was called for an interview. I had to wait around five hours to be called in. Guess what they asked me in the interview? They asked me what my elder brother does. They wanted to know how many days I had been absent. They had my record, they have every worker's record. They know, but they ask. Then they told me I could go. I left. I went home to the village. What a relief it was. I had no intention of working in that factory.

However, I had to find a job. In the family everyone began commenting that I was not doing enough to find some employment. My grandfather knew someone in Gujarat and he told him that I had passed out of an ITI and found no job. His friend told him to send me to Gujarat and said he would find me a job there. My grandfather agreed. I did not want to go so far, I did not want to leave my village. The only way to avoid going there was to find some work here.

In those days interviews were being held in Maruti Gurgaon for employment in Maruti Manesar. I had appeared for one interview and flunked it. They say that once you fail an interview in Maruti you cannot appear for another for at least six months. Well, I know it is not true. I went there a few days later and sat outside the room in which interviews were being conducted. They came out and made an announcement that those who had appeared earlier for an interview and not been selected had better leave because they would not be interviewed at all. I kept sitting there.

I have a habit of never listening to anybody the first time. I never pay heed. So when they said leave, I did not. They called me in. This time I gave them the answers they wanted to hear. This way I appeared in two interviews at Maruti a few weeks apart! This time I got selected. It was the second time Maruti was employing me. This time I was a trainee in the Manesar factory. I told the family that I had found work. It is true that I had landed a job but I was so reluctant to work there I simply did not join. People began to whisper in the village that I may have lied, for who does not go to work after finding a job in these days of high unemployment. They began to insinuate that I had not been selected and that I was lazy.

Tired of such barbs I finally joined the factory on 25 August and discovered that production had not yet begun. The production line was being set up. There was not even a canteen there. Everything was in flux so they let me join even at that late date. There were a lot of Japanese there at the time. Some local workers too were learning the Japanese language.

I was sent to the press shop. I had never seen such machines. They were gigantic. The sheets of metal they cut were enormous. I am a fast learner. When they gave us a written test about those machines I scored as high as the supervisors did who are senior workers and are promoted to that level after working on such machines for years. After that they tested our knowledge some ten or fifteen times and every time I used to score as much as the supervisors did.

All this was very well but my problem was different. Nobody was willing to induct me in their team. I would spend some time with workers in the repairs department, some days in some other department. Everywhere there were workers who had worked together for three or four years and they all got along well; they did not want a newcomer.

Finally, I was given the work of production planning. There used to be a supervisor and me in the shift. We worked as a team. This time the work was not heavy and it was not even too much work. They needed some 1,200 parts for a car. We had to plan the number of cars to be made and accordingly calculate the number of each part we needed to stock. It was not tough.

In the beginning the manager and supervisor taught me how to calculate all this and being quick on the uptake I soon began to do it on my own. Gradually, the workload increased as production began to increase. All the shift in-charges used to report to me and I used to report to the head of the department. Everything was fine. People began to say that I had landed a cushy job.

For three years all seemed well. I became permanent in 2009 and after that too, till 2011, work continued normally. The going seemed good. That is when I heard that a union was going to be formed. I worked out of an office. Kuldeep Jangu used to come there and hold meetings. He was doing it on behalf of the management.

Sonu Gujjar was a worker in the weld shop. I would meet him every day. He would say '*Ram, Ram*' to me, address me as *saheb*. '*Ram, Ram, Saheb,*' he used to say. He was a nice man. He never tolerated any foul language or if anyone said anything that was not right. I heard that Sonu too was trying to make a union.

There was another man in the supply department and his work too was light. He would keep saying that we would make a union of our own. He used to say that he felt pained to see how hard workers were made to work and how pitiable their condition was. He would often say he could not understand why the management would not give them time to use the loo or drink some water. Perhaps they did not give them enough time to drink water because that would mean visiting the toilet and that meant a loss in production. All this was so inhuman.

What happened on 18 July? To tell you the truth I don't know much. Those days my attention was focused elsewhere. I had got engaged in April. Arranged match. She was from Bawana in Delhi. I had again been moved to Planning. I knew the work, there was not much stress at work. I had no problems. Whenever I had time on my hands I spent it talking to her on the phone. We used to talk for hours. Every day we had these very long conversations. That day too, in the afternoon, I had stepped out in the yard to talk to her.

She had called. I was then on duty. But my work day was about to be over. I finished the work and went into the yard. I had heard that there had been some sort of a scuffle on the shop floor but didn't know exactly what had happened. This was a daily occurrence so I did not think much of it. The shift had ended. We were talking on the phone. It was late. The TV was on in her house. Some news channel was on.

All of a sudden she said to me, 'There is a fire in your company!' I was surprised. I said, 'What are you jabbering about? I am standing here and there is no fire.' She said that the news was on TV. 'They are showing a fire in your factory.' So here she was in another city telling me that a fire had broken out in the factory where I was standing.

I quickly went in to check. I did not see much or for long.

What I saw was quite disturbing. The public was beating up the management. When you have a fight, you sometimes get too angry and beat up the fellow you are fighting with. It happens. Sometimes you can't control your anger. It is not right but it can happen. But just thrashing whoever happens to be there is not done. They were simply beating up whoever they saw. Some people were being thrown out of broken windows from upstairs. One person died but many were injured. The police had arrived.

I quickly left the place. I went to stay with Mohan. The next day the factory closed down. There was silence in Gurgaon. Mohan asked me to go back to my village. I went home.

I had never thought that the police would come for me. I had done nothing wrong. I didn't even know what had happened that day. I had not been named in the FIR. The police came for me on 25 September. After so many days! The incident had happened in mid-July. The company had sent me a letter dismissing me from my job. The IO came to the village. He came to me and said, 'You must have definitely beaten up people.' I said that I had not. I did not even know who had. I had seen the fight but I had not recognized anyone in the melee. But they picked me up and carted me away.

They took me to a police station in Sector 17 in Gurgaon. It is not even a proper police station, just a *chowki*. They had already arrested another man from my village a month and a half earlier. The policemen even said to me, 'We have a feeling that you did nothing but there is too much pressure on us. We don't know why but the government is putting too much pressure.'

I was not afraid. I don't know why but my mind was calm. I felt no fear. None at all. That very day we were presented in court and we were sent to a judicial remand of fourteen days. I was sent to Bhondsi Jail. Then the remand was again extended by fourteen days. This kept happening. I spent four years in prison.

The police filed a *challan* after three months. The verdict came on 18 March, four years later. I think it was 2016 or 2017...can't really remember. The court found me guilty. In August 2016 I had got interim bail and had come back home. When the judgement was pronounced in March I was taken away to prison again. I think it was 10 March. Anyway, the sentencing was to be done a week later. That is how it happens. First they decide on the charges. Then they do the sentencing. I had been found guilty so I was taken into custody again. The court sentenced me to three years' imprisonment. I had already spent more than that in prison. So they let me go.

My life had changed completely in that time. I was to be married in November but I had been arrested in September. My engagement was over. They broke off the engagement. I was so unhappy. Till today I have never felt such pain in my life.

In prison I did not have any problems as such, but a prison is a prison. There were another 147 people from Maruti in the jail. We would all be taken out of the barracks in the morning and counted and locked up again. Then they would let us out for lunch. We had no work. We had not been given any work to do. We played volleyball. They would sometimes make us do something, like cut grass in the lawn or some such thing. Actually, jail employees had some sneaking sympathy with us. We were not given any trouble. They had a soft corner for us.

I also feel bad that none of the workers ever came to prison to meet us. The union activists were of course all in prison with me; I am talking of the ordinary worker. Mohan used to visit us. Ajmer Singh used to come. Some activists of the union came too. But I am talking of the ordinary workers—they never came.

Even inside the prison, union people displayed stupidity. Everyone was bothered only about himself. We should have all stayed as a group and fought the case as a group. But nobody was prepared to do so. Our lawyer was Rajendra Pathak. He said that we should let the case hang for a long while. Pressure would build on the government and it would help us.

A provisional committee was set up after we were arrested. That committee would take care of court expenses. Now there were some people like me too who knew nothing about such things and procedures. We did not know what the case would be, how it would be fought, how it was supposed to be argued—we knew nothing.

In fact we did not even know that this was not just a fight between the management and the workers but a fight between the capitalist class and the working class!

It was a class war!

Eight

Solidarity for Ever

Here is power in a factory, power in the land
Power in the hands of a worker
But it all amounts to nothing if together we don't stand
There is power in a union
The union forever defending our rights
Down with the blackleg, all workers unite
With our brothers and our sisters from many far off lands
There is power in a union
Now I long for the morning that they realize
Brutality and unjust laws can not defeat us
But who'll defend the workers who cannot organize
When the bosses send their lackeys out to cheat us?

—'There Is Power in a Union',
originally written by Joe Hill in 1913
and modified later by other activists

At the time when the 18 July 2012 events happened the Maruti Suzuki Workers' Union was in the midst of negotiating a wage revision which was due every three years. The management had offered a wage rise of Rs 1,000 per month a year. But the workers said that it was not enough because they were being worked much harder to make up for the losses during the previous strikes.

The union also was trying to negotiate better conditions

for the contract workers. Apart from the issue of wages, there was the problem of transportation for the contract workers in Manesar and the problem was acute because there was no public transport there unlike Gurgaon. The company had not organized any buses for them in Manesar and they had to make their own private arrangements.

Union leaders say that the management had made it clear that they were not willing to negotiate on the charter of demands submitted by them. At least one study found that the management would try and undermine the confidence of the workers by pointing out the mistakes in spellings and syntax. The workers were assembling one car every 51 seconds and here was the management which would not conclude the negotiations. This made the workers restive. Their repressed rage was on the verge of exploding. (Verma 2014)

The workers kept themselves informed on the negotiations, waiting for a settlement. Yet the management kept denying the very fact that the MSWU had put forward concrete demands and were negotiating with the management in the hope of a settlement. For instance, in the Preface to the paperback edition of his book published in 2013, *The Maruti Story*, R.C. Bhargava writes:

'We recognized that communication with the very young workforce in Manesar had not been as intensive as had been the case in Gurgaon. This workforce possibly did not have enough time to imbibe the Gurgaon work culture. As a result, the Manesar workers felt that they had several legitimate grievances. An intensive process of communication started and senior management members of Maruti had regular discussions with the workers. Maruti helped the workers to get a separate union registered. This union was informed that *the contract workers would be brought on par with regular workers by March*

2013. Other comparatively minor grievances were also resolved to mutual satisfaction. The union made a commitment to solve all problems through discussions and not adopt other means. There were no indications that the union, or the workers, had any serious grievances remaining.

'The events of 18 July 2012, which resulted in the management being violently attacked, with the death of the HR head of the Manesar plant and other ninety persons hospitalized with serious injuries, came as a complete surprise. *The union had given no demands*, nor expressed any unhappiness about any matter. The union members and the workers have not clarified what caused them to become violent. In fact some of them say that the management caused the death and injuries by bringing in goons from outside! The union members are now facing criminal charges for their role in the violence, and since the matter is sub judice, it is not possible to comment further on it.

'However, why the workers and the union adopted this course of action is puzzling...' (Emphasis ours throughout)

There are sharp differences of opinion on who started the fire or beat the managers on 18 July. There is no denying, however, that it grew violent as a result of the workers' mounting anger. The leaders of the Maruti Suzuki Workers' Union had been sitting for long hours and days trying to negotiate with the management and feeling increasingly frustrated by the lack of response.

Ram Meher

I remember the charter of demands that we prepared and gave to the management.

It is true that the first demand we made was of regularizing contract workers. They were getting a really raw deal. Frankly, we had also worked as contract labour and we could feel their pain.

We did not ask for making all contract workers permanent. We only said that they should be treated as trainees. Trainees get regularized after three years on the job. So we said, make those contract workers regular who have sweated it out for three years and designate the contract workers as trainees. This way, gradually all contract workers would get permanent jobs.

The management refused point blank. They said that they would not even want to talk about it. So we asked them to at least provide some facilities to them. We had transport facilities and we asked the management to provide transport facilities to contract workers also. The company bus fetches regular workers and trainees from home and takes them back. We said that contract workers should also be given this facility. The management refused. We kept insisting.

Then they changed tack. See, we used to pay a monthly amount of Rs 280, deducted from our wages, towards transport charges. The management now proposed that if contract workers were to be given bussing facilities they would have to pay double the amount. Contract workers earned less than us and the management wanted them to pay double the amount for the bus service. This was so unfair. How could we agree to it?

There were many other demands apart from increase in wages. Our buses fetched workers only from a radius of fifty kilometres and we wanted the radius to be increased to a 100 kilometres. For everybody, for us regular workers too, the radius should be 100 kilometres, we said. A number of workers live very far off. Some live in Jind, some in Rohtak, and we wanted them to get the bus service. That way getting to the factory is easier. We had demanded the radius to be increased to 100 kilometres because we thought they would then negotiate and probably we could come to an agreement for sixty or seventy kilometres. There were several such demands.

It is true that we were dead serious about the contract workers' issue. They worked by our side. They did everything that we did. They got so little for it. We used to feel terrible about it. For the same work regular workers get 18,000 rupees and contract workers get half of that. That is not a good thing. We did not like it. They were in a majority in the factory. Permanent workers were few, contract workers were many. However, it is not true that we raised their issue only to gain the support of the majority for our union.

For three years there had been no meetings even for a settlement of wages. Salaries had not been raised. Everything was pending. Sonu was trying to make a union. His union never got registered, so how could there have been any negotiations for a settlement? When we launched a struggle in 2011, the contract workers had stood by us, supported us in every way. Many of us had worked on contract earlier and we understood their situation.

After the strike organized by Sonu Gujjar the attitude of supervisors towards the workers changed. They began to speak rudely. Fights would break out. Supervisors frequently abused workers. They would say, the supervisors, that these workers cannot do anything to us, no action will be taken against us, and if workers say anything we dislike we will get them thrown out. The atmosphere in the factory was bad. Very bad.

The new union was under a lot of pressure to deliver, and that was one reason why, as we saw in the testimonies of union office bearers in the previous chapter, they insisted on trying to resolve the matter of Jiya Lal's suspension.

Junaid Khan (name changed)

He was a foreman in Maruti Manesar and a member of the provisional committee formed immediately after the 18 July 2012 events. Now the union has elected new office bearers. Interviewed on phone on 14 February 2022.

I don't want you to use my real name because what is the point? I was a nameless worker for them [the management] and that is how I wish to end that chapter of my life. Yes, I am still fighting a case in the labour court but who knows when it will reach its conclusion? It is possible that I may have to fight all my life.

My father told me to desist. He said there was no use of any union; they all take advantage of the opportunity and then they vanish and you're left with nothing. In Haryana, we have a saying, '*Apna kaam banta, bhaad mein jaaye janta.*' This is what my father says happens. He turned out to be right.

What happened? Sonu Gujjar and others took some twenty-four lakhs or whatever they could get and vanished. That is why poor Ram Meher and all got into trouble. Poor Ram Meher could not answer the people's questions. He could not say that he was unable to get the managers to agree and postpone the decision on Jiya Lal's suspension. Ram Meher went to prison. All those thirteen people were sentenced to life. That was all so horrible. I feel bad for them. They didn't do anything to deserve it.

It is all because of that old union. Nobody trusted the office bearers of the new union. They had to prove themselves. So they could not go to the workers and ask them to postpone the decision on the issue of Jiya Lal.

I don't think Jiya Lal was at fault. I was not there in the 'A' shift. I was in the 'B' shift and when I reached the factory the discussions had been going on for hours. Everything was in chaos. The police was there at the gate but they just stood there, they did nothing. There were bouncers too. There was a massive crowd inside. There is a passageway to the shop floor and it was crowded. The work on the 'B' shift began but it was really not working. It was like a strike. We were at the station but we were not working. Lots of people were talking and there was much confusion.

I never saw that Sangram Kumar Majhi. I never saw him that day or in court. I don't know where he went. How can someone vanish like that? But he did vanish.

Then the fight began and who knows who was beating whom. What happened was that someone said, '*Aaj aar paar ki ladai hogi.*' I heard that but I don't know who said it. Someone in the crowd said it. Then all the beating and fighting started. I really don't know who started it and who was beating up whom. In a crowd you really don't know what's happening.

I left the factory soon afterwards and I went home. Then I went to my village.

For a full one and a half months I was in the village. I was not named in the FIR. They shut down the factory. I used to go to Gurgaon. We had a provisional committee. I was in it. There were seven members in it. For a month or so we continued to help in the legal battle. We organized protest campaigns.

Then what happened was that one day I went to the Gurgaon market and I got a call from someone who said that he was a journalist and would like to interview me. I said fine and asked him to come over to some place, and the police landed up there and took me to prison. A policeman had called me, pretending to be a journalist.

I think that they wanted to arrest me only to suppress and scare the provisional committee. I and Ram Niwas and Khushi Ram—we were very active in it. And they picked me up.

I asked them why they were arresting me. I told them that I had not been named in the FIR.

There is a catch. They have a category called 'others'. They always have names [of primary suspects] and then they have 'others' and they told me that I was one of the others.

I was in prison for ten and a half months. The lower court rejected my bail application. Then the High Court granted me bail. I will never forget the date when I got bail. It was 11, 12, 13...11 December 2013!

I work for a car dealer now, near my village. The work is easier. More relaxed. I told him, the dealer, everything when I came to get the job. I told him that I have a case and I will need time off to go to court. He knows. It is always the best to tell them everything up front. Because they will discover anyway. If they know that you're telling them the truth they know you are trustworthy and they can give you a job. It is okay. They know, a lot of people know, that the factory management was bad. In my village too everybody is sympathetic. Nobody harasses me or my family or taunts me. They don't say that I am a jailbird.

When I worked in the Maruti factory I used to be so tired that once I got off duty I would fall asleep wherever I sat down—in the bus, in a tea shop. I simply could not keep my eyes open.

Yes, we suffered a lot. At least the workers who are working now have benefited. It is all right, it helped someone. I don't feel bad about it. I go to court to attend hearings. Even after I got bail I used to go to court for hearings till I got acquitted. After that I quit going to Gurgaon or Manesar. I don't go there any more. I became inactive in the provisional committee also.

They also chose new office bearers in the union. They have benefited from our struggle.

I have also heard that the permanent workers no longer care about contract workers. You see, my father was right. *Apni daal gal gayi, doosre ki fikr nahi karni...* [People take care of their own needs, not those of other people.]

Ram Niwas

When the interview was conducted, he was a member of the provisional committee chosen to continue the struggle.

I was also in the Maruti Manesar union. I also took part in the strike led by Sonu Gujjar. In 2011, there were three strikes in the company and one of our major demands was to have a union of our own. It was Awanish who persuaded the management to let us form a union. It will not hurt their interests is what he explained to the other managers.

There were three strikes. Maruti had suffered many losses. Awanish Dev told the managers that it wouldn't be possible to explain issues concerning the factory and the workers to so many workers separately. It would be easier to talk to union representatives. If a union were to be formed, then they would have to talk to only twelve or thirteen people. It would then be the job of the union representatives to convince the workers.

By arguing like this, he persuaded the management not to put obstacles in the way of union formation. He even went with us to Chandigarh to register the union.

We all liked him very much. When he fell ill, all the office bearers of the union went to the hospital to meet him.

The tragedy of Manesar was not just a tragedy of the death of a manager. It was a tragedy in the lives of many workers which hasn't ended.

After that incident, when 546 workers were fired, a seven-member provisional committee was set up to continue the struggle. I am one of the seven members. What we did is that we chose one representative from one region or one State from among the workers. So we have a member from Rajasthan to represent workers from that State, one from Rewari in Haryana, one from Himachal. There are no office bearers or any ranks, all are equal. All are active.

Don't ask me how bad the working conditions in Maruti were; they are indescribable. My work station was about 400–500 metres away from the gate. Meaning I had to sprint to reach the work station. I used to work on the sub-assembly.

We had no time for family. When my grandmother died, I could not even attend her funeral. I could not get leave. There was no time to even drink water there; sometimes we did not get a minute or two to even go to the toilet.

I have already told you about how I got a gash on my forehead and about the accidents that take place inside the factory and how callous the company is towards its employees.

In such an environment, a union is necessary just for the safety of the worker. It is necessary for their rights. We were only asking for our rights, we were not asking for something unreasonable.

On 18 July 2012, I was in the 'B' shift. When I reached there for work, the police was standing there at the gate. It was not inside. Above our shop floor was the office of the HR, et cetera. It was on the mezzanine floor. It had these big glass panels and that glass was broken. We heard that too. Our work had continued till about twenty minutes past seven in the evening. Our shop was not that far from the gate. Some shops were even a kilometre away from the gate. It is a very big complex.

Everyone used to think of Maruti as a good employer, a place where salaries were very good. These people are making big money, is what they thought. When we met the labour officer in connection with the formation of the union, he asked us why we needed a union when we were getting high salaries. When we told him how much we were getting and what the reality was, he was very surprised too.

Of course, now the permanent workers are earning seventy to eighty thousand a month. They and their families are happy. Their children are going to good schools. They have ACs in their houses, they have a car. They may even own their houses or have bought it and are paying EMIs. Now these workers have a lot to lose.

When we went to form our union after Sonu Gujjar had been made to take VR, Awanish came with us. He had bought silver utensils to gift them to Sarabjeet's [the general secretary, MSWU] new born daughter. He was very sympathetic to us.

But when we gave the demand letter [charter of demands] after forming the union, the management got very angry. They felt that we were raising political demands. Our demand for the abolishment of the contract labour system annoyed the management. They had assumed that we would only raise issues concerning permanent workers, demand more salaries and more facilities for them. So the other managers got angry with Awanish. They told Awanish that he had helped form the union so he should deal with it.

In fact, had the contract system in Maruti ended, it would have become an example for the industry. There are many automobile factories in this area, they also have vendors. This demand could have arisen in all of them, in the entire belt. That is why the management found this demand political.

Then they began harassing us in various ways. Even for small things they would not heed our complaints. It was exasperating. Once it so happened that a worker in the 'A' shift found a rotten fish in the cargo, in a packing box. This item had not come from the Kandla port. Had it come by sea, we could have assumed that the fish must have entered it somehow and died. The union told the management about it, even showed them the box. The goods had been made here in some other factory and how a dead fish was found in a box of auto parts is still a mystery to us. Nothing happened. No enquiries were made. At least we never got to hear of any enquiries.

Another time, a dead lizard popped out of the tea kettle. They have big kettles there that can hold tea for twenty people. A lizard was found in it. Many boys fell ill after drinking this tea, some even fainted. We told the management. Nothing was done.

Then one day what happened was that some insects were found in the rice served to workers. Not weevils, more like their larvae, like little worms. We collected them and put them in a matchbox which we took to P.K. Roy, the head of Plant B, to show him how substandard food was being served in the canteen. He picked up that rice with the worms, put them in his mouth and swallowed them. Then he said, 'So what happened if you found this? See, I am not dead, it is a very nutritious thing. You eat chicken, don't you? What's wrong with this?' He had swallowed the rice, so the evidence was also lost.

P.K. Roy had just joined the production department in Manesar on 21 August 2011. He was truly one of a kind.

I was one of the 546 workers who got fired from the job apart from those arrested. I have filed a case in the labour court that I should get my job back. In my case, the management has cross-examined my witnesses. Now we have to cross-examine the witnesses of the management. I am waiting for the verdict. I have not found any other job; not even looked for one. If I join some other job I will not get the dues of the past years that Maruti owes me. It will have to pay me the dues for all the eight or more years I have been out of a job unjustifiably. That is if I get reinstated and I have high hopes of that happening.

We have engaged Sanjoy Ghosh as our lawyer for the labour court. We have to pay him forty lakhs as fees for all the 546 cases. That is the total amount and we are hoping that the cases will be over in eight years. Even if it takes longer that is the amount he will get. Every year we pay him a part of the amount.

After that incident in Manesar, the whole union was destroyed. Then a retired judge was made the returning officer and elections were held. The management said that those who had been fired could no longer be members of the union; only those workers who were still working could vote. That way the total strength of the union, its membership number, got reduced. Our team of supporters also contested the election and won. We got 85 per cent of the votes.

After the election of this new team a resolution was passed that notwithstanding who wins in the future, this union will give 2.5 lakh rupees every year to the family of each of the thirteen workers who have been imprisoned for life. This money is not to be given from the union fund. This money is raised separately. Only the workers of the union contribute towards this fund.

The union did this because everyone's salary had increased because of their sacrifice. In three years, their salaries went up threefold. Today, if the Manesar worker takes home ₨ 80,000, the credit goes to the tireless struggle of the union. Everyone acknowledges this.

We have tried our best to ensure that those who fought

so bravely and are now in prison...that their families should continue to have our support. They should not feel abandoned or lonely. Two years after Sandeep went to jail his sister got married. We said in the union that Sandeep may be unable to arrange for his sister's wedding but that we are all his brothers and his sister is our sister. We all have to shoulder the responsibility and do so better than what he would have done. We, 1,100 of us, went to that marriage. We collected and gave Rs 11 lakh in the *kanyadan*. We organized a grand ceremony but none of us ate even a morsel of food in the party because the *gharatis*, the family of the bride, are not supposed to eat at the daughter's wedding. We did not let the sister feel the absence of her brother.

We have maintained this unity till now. It's been eight years. We all meet each other and we keep in touch. We help each other in times of need. Ajmer has a brain tumour. He got out on parole when he had a lot of pain in the head. He got tests done in a private hospital and discovered that he had a tumour. He had two operations. The union raised eight lakh rupees for his treatment and will raise more when it is needed.

We are determined to maintain this unity. It takes a lot of hard work to maintain it.

Today, we can proudly say that we have deposited fifteen lakh rupees in the bank of each of these thirteen people.

When Modiji was contesting elections [in 2014], he had said that by bringing back black money, he would deposit fifteen lakhs in the account of every citizen. If you ask him today, he cannot give you the name of a single person in whose account he has deposited the fifteen lakhs. But we can give you the names of all the thirteen in whose account we, a union of workers, have deposited fifteen lakh rupees.

This is called unity, this is called strength. This is called struggle. Of course many of our people went to jail but we are not defeated. We are fighting. We will keep fighting for justice.

Ram Meher continues...

After we walked out the factory on 18 July 2012, it did not occur to us to call a lawyer. It is true that the legal advisor of the union knows no law. But it never occurred to us to call a lawyer, seek someone's help and surrender in court. We just switched off our phones and went into hiding. We were very scared.

The police were looking for us and harassing our families. We had never imagined that something of this sort could happen. Whom could we have called? Yes, there is a trade union activist, Mohan—we could have called him. But we had switched off our phones and all our numbers were in them. We did not want to switch on our phones.

It was Sandeep's family that sought the help of the villagers [of Dahola village, who spoke to ACP Tomar]. A *panchayat* meeting was held there in his village. ACP Tomar went to that meeting. In that meeting Tomar cupped water in his hands and swore on that water that if we surrendered we would not be beaten or tortured. But he went back on his word.

Jiya Lal, Yogesh and I were the ones who were tortured the most. Whatever they subjected Jiya Lal to they also did me. And in that very place, in the *thana* in Sector 10. The same police officer, Sanjeev Balara, did it. Tore my legs apart. Passed electric current through me. Hung me upside down. Everything. Whatever they did to Jiya Lal, they did to me.

Before they produced me in court, the police had already warned me in the police station that if I dared say anything in court or to the media they would teach me a lesson because, after all, I would have to return to their custody. They beat you in such a way that even doctors cannot figure out that you've been beaten up. They don't break bones. Once they beat me up so badly that I fell unconscious. When I opened my eyes, I was in a hospital. It was a small clinic, not a big hospital. They always take you to such places. They never prepare any report of what happened to you.

It is not as if on that day we had been obstinate or any such thing. We had only been insisting on the revocation of the suspension order of Jiya Lal. Later, the management threw out 546 workers. Why? We had only been demanding our rights.

I used to be a contract worker in the Honda factory in 2005. There too we were made to do all the work that a regular worker does. Still, the conditions there were better. When there was that long struggle of Honda workers...I had just been laid off ten days before the agitation began. The workers were called to the mini-secretariat in Gurgaon, surrounded and beaten up by the police. I knew some of the men who had been thrashed very badly that day. I had worked with them.

On the fifth anniversary of that struggle in 2010, they had had a big meeting of workers and I had attended that too. We used to keep asking them how to form a union. They would suggest we form a union and get affiliated with AITUC. But we decided to remain independent. We did not get affiliated with any big federation. We remained independent.

Awanish Dev used to tell us to remain independent. He always said we should not get affiliated with any federation. He helped us a lot. He used to suggest that we tie up with the management too. He said that if we cooperated with the management, we would never face any difficulties.

We used to consult everyone. We had also talked to some unions in Faridabad. There they had managed to get salaries of up to 90,000 rupees a month. We looked at many such charters of demands before preparing ours. Mathew [Abraham] also said to us that the management would not necessarily accept all our demands. He told us that we should never be too obstinate. We should always be open to negotiations. 'What you ask for and what they will offer will be very far apart and the settlement will be at some mid-point. So be prepared to give some and take some,' he told us. Now, when people seek my advice I tell them the same thing: never be stubborn, leave scope for negotiations and be firm but not unbending. The management never accepts all demands. We have to be clear about that.

Of course, for us things have changed drastically. Earlier, we hardly read anything. We did not have the time to read. Now I do read books. I read what I find in the prison library.

My family was extremely unhappy with the turn of events. They had had high hopes from me when I landed this job. Eventually, I would have managed to get a high salary too. But what has to happen always happens. It is written in our fate. I don't think that if we had simply stopped demanding the revocation of Jiya Lal's suspension this wouldn't have happened. We were not wrong, our demand was not wrong or unjustified. They took advantage of the fact that Jiya Lal had had that fight that day. Who knows, they may have deliberately got Jiya Lal provoked into fighting with the supervisor. Had this fight not happened, something else would have happened. They were determined to do this. They wanted to be rid of us and they threw out 546 workers. They did not give the workers their jobs back even after they were acquitted by the court. I don't think we did anything wrong that day.

The condition of my family is not good now. My wife is not educated. She does not have a job. We have a little land in the family and we make ends meet. My brother does not have a job either. Both my children go to school. They know I am in jail. Everyone in the school knows this. I have also told the principal. But he is a very nice man, he has not told anyone. However, people do discover such a thing. My children face no harassment because of this. Those who know are sure that I have not gone to prison because of something bad that I did. They are sure that I have done no wrong to anyone. If only the High Court would hear our appeal we may perhaps get some relief.

Sumit Nain

An ordinary worker who was arrested and spent four years in jail before he was acquitted, though never reinstated. Anjali interviewed him in his work shed—which is close to a stinking pool of stagnant water with clouds of mosquitoes over it—in Gurgaon, where he makes packing boxes in partnership with his father-in-law. Interviewed on 1 March 2020.

My son was born five months after I went to jail. When he began walking, he was brought to meet me in prison. I saw the face of my little child across the netting of the prison window. He was not even clearly visible.

I joined Maruti Gurgaon as an apprentice in October 2006 after doing a course at the ITI in Narwana from 2004 to 2006. It was a good ITI. They taught us theory. They had practicals too. In October 2007, I was sent to Manesar as a trainee. The assembly shop there had just started working. I used to live in Rajiv Nagar in Gurgaon. I cooked my own meals, went to the factory to work and got back from work.

In October 2010, I became a permanent worker. My salary was good. At the time, I used to get Rs 9,000 a month as incentive. It was a good amount. I used to earn about 22,000 or 24,000 a month. Not bad. This was because there are some deductions towards EPF too and for health insurance and other such things.

Every day I put in an hour and a half as overtime. My attendance was a full 100 per cent. I took no leave whether I worked in the 'A' shift or 'B' shift. Sometimes I even worked the night shift. I had got a uniform too. It was blue. Later, the colour changed and it became a grey uniform.

Then, in 2011, there was talk about forming a union. I had no idea what a union is. When the union was formed I had filled in a slip and become its member. The union fees was Rs 50. I paid it. In June 2011, some forty-five people had been suspended. There had been a thirteen-day strike. I don't remember all that happened.

Perhaps I was in the 'A' shift. We all sat inside the factory and most of us stayed hungry. They used to get some food from outside but it was never enough. Sometimes we ate biscuits. For two days we kept sitting in the corridors of the factory.

We had many grievances. If we took leave for three or four days our entire incentive of Rs 9,000 got deducted. We lost all of it, not part of it. For two days of leave we lost half of it. We got a day off only on Sundays. It is true that the overtime was not mandatory, we could refuse to do it, but the rates were pretty low. We got some seventeen or eighteen rupees an hour for overtime work. After putting in such hard work we could not take a day off even for some urgent work. It is true that the company bus took us to work and dropped us back, but it was not free. We paid Rs 600 a month for the bus pass; later it went up to Rs 2,000 a month.

We had all these issues and we wanted them to be resolved. This was our first struggle. The second one went on for one and a half months. It started in October 2011 and this time the company had a lock-out. The company wanted to throw workers out. We sat at the gate. Every day we would come from home to sit at the gate. There were lots of us, some 1,500 or 2,000 workers sat there from morning till evening. I used be afraid. I couldn't bear thinking what would happen to all of us.

By then I was married. My wife was a homemaker and she lived with my parents in the village. I lived in Rajiv Nagar in Gurgaon. My family never interfered in my matters; they never discouraged me from struggle. They did not encourage me either. They were neutral. They never said anything. But I used to feel scared. And yet I continued with the struggle.

One day the lock-out was over. We don't know why it happened or how it happened. Only that the factory was open again and we had to go work in it. We started working but we did not get paid. So, four days later, the strike began again. Half of the workers had been dismissed and they had not been taken back. All of us had been transferred to new stations. Our speed was slow because the work was new. This is how they harassed us.

Sonu Gujjar was our leader at that time. When I saw one day that others had stopped working I did so too. I called home to tell them I won't be coming home. This time, within ten days, there was a settlement and everybody was taken back except about thirty people. Sonu was among these thirty or so people who had been dismissed. They were all thrown out. Actually, all the union office bearers were thrown out.

Again, work began as usual. The only difference was that now we had no union. We were all united, all together, but we had no union. People from MUKU did not even come to meet us. This time when work began I was posted back on the engine line, my old station. I began to fit chassis again. People began working towards forming a new union. Ram Meher,

Sandeep, Ram Vilas, Sohan, Dhanraj, Yogesh, Suresh, Pawan and Ajmer were the office bearers. I did not know any of them well.

The union was officially formed when it got its registration number on 23 February, and on 1 March we also had a flag raising day. We got a DJ and we danced to songs. We did not eat or drink but we were happy and we danced and sang songs. Some managers also came to the party.

For some days all went well. There are clocks inside the factory and they display seconds and parts of seconds all the time. Whenever there is a break, like a tea break or lunch break, a siren goes off and the same siren sounds when the break is over. We were working according to the clock and hoping that our wages would go up.

I do not remember the date, but it was in July when Jiya Lal had some heated exchange with the supervisor Majhi. Sangram Majhi was his name. He left the factory after that on a half day's leave.

I know Jiya Lal. He is from near my village. Very nice man. We were told that Jiya Lal had been suspended. I don't know what they had said to each other. I was in the 'A' shift that day. But we got to know around 2 pm or later.

Around 3 pm the 'A' shift finishes work. At that time the 'B' shift is entering. Our buses had also arrived. We had finished our work. The 'B' shift had entered and with them the police also arrived. The police did not enter the factory, it stood at the gate. That day Manesar looked like it had turned into some police occupied place, a cantonment of the police. We felt afraid. The workers were frightened and they did not step out. We all stayed inside. I was leaving too and was going out but when I saw the heavy police force at the gate I turned back and ran inside. I was scared. I was inside till 5.30 pm.

The 'B' shift was working. I don't really know what happened after that. Suddenly, there was a sort of stampede. Everybody began running helter-skelter. Glass panes began to break. People began to scream. There was a lot of noise. I ran out and kept running for a while. Then I got home. On TV, at around seven, I saw that the factory had caught fire.

Earlier, when there used to be strikes workers and management people used to get things sorted out among themselves. It used to be an issue only between them. Even when we had sat on a *dharna* outside the factory the police had come, but they just hung around. The police had no role in our negotiations. Why the police came in that day, what they wanted to do inside the factory—I have no idea. I just couldn't understand. After all, the negotiations were happening inside the factory between the management and the union, and it had nothing to do with any outside force.

Awanish Dev used to favour the workers. I never met Awanish but had heard about him. Ram Meher and some others had also been to his house. When he was unwell, all the union people had gone to meet him. We had heard that Awanish had resigned but his resignation had not been accepted. During the conversation, he was probably agreeing with us, but S.Y. Siddiqui, who was there, he was not agreeing.

There were many arrests after that. My name also appeared in the FIR but I was not arrested. I was at my home in Gurgaon then.

The police began visiting Narwana to find me. The factory had my Narwana address so the police used to go there. My wife would be at home. My father and mother had passed away in 2004. I am their only son. We have a bit of land and we do some farming. My father's younger brother and his wife were my guardians. They live in a town near Narwana. The police harassed my uncle and asked him to call me. They threatened to take him into custody if he did not help them find me. Three or four times a week, the police would land up at their house. Finally, my uncle called me. Then I went to the Manesar police station and surrendered.

I surrendered at the police station. The police then took me to the court and from there I was taken back to the police station. They kept me in the police station for all of ten days, beat me up, abused me. They abuse you to your face all the time. The IO, he used to say to me, 'You "sister something", you are so shameless, you killed the manager.' I kept telling them I was not involved at all. But no one was listening to me. No lawyer came to the police station. There was no lawyer in the court either. Till that time the union office bearers had not been arrested.

The court sent me to a three-day police remand. In the Manesar police station, the police beat me up a lot. Then they made me sign on two blank papers too. After three days, they took me to court again, showed those papers and asked for a fourteen-day remand. There my wife came to meet me. No lawyer came during the first remand, no one came the second time either. But by then the union leaders had been arrested. The court remanded me again and after that we were all sent to jail when we were brought to court again.

I was in Bhondsi Jail for four years. There is a barrack for under-trials there. Everyone was kept in it. Sometimes other workers used to come to visit. We couldn't make phone calls from there.

There are stone slabs in the barracks, those were our beds. Place mattresses on them and go to sleep! There was nothing to play with. We couldn't do anything voluntarily. Everything is decided for you. A person goes into depression. For two years

I didn't do anything, didn't even do any work.*

Those who came to meet me stood across a window. Actually, there would be two windows and the wall with the window was so thick that there would be two feet of space in between, a lattice on the inside, a lattice on the outside, a lattice here and a lattice there. You had to shout to talk to the visitor. You could hear some words, you missed some words. Others would also be standing next to you talking to their visitors—all of us shouting together. But yes, there was no beating in jail. Even the officials there did not beat us up. That was a relief.

Jail officials used to treat us with respect. Earlier, there was a hearing every fourteen days. They would bring us out to take us to court. Our family members used to come there. Many workers also came to court. We used to meet people. It felt good. Then the hearings began to happen once in four months. We had to pay lawyers' fees also. The workers of the company helped a lot. The case was heard in the sessions court.

We were accused of hitting the manager with door beams. A door beam is heavy. I don't know what evidence they had. Actually, there was no evidence at all. Had there been any evidence, why would I have been acquitted? There was no evidence. They put me in jail and kept me there for four years without any evidence. I got bail in July 2016. I had applied for bail once before but it had been rejected.

In between, I had been let out on parole only once, only for one day for my aunt's son's wedding, and even then the police went with me and kept me in custody. The wedding was in Punjab and I got only twenty-four hours' leave for that.

Witnesses told the court that they had seen me standing

* As under-trials, they weren't given work. Some imprisoned workers did work inside the jail but they began after their conviction.

with fifteen to twenty labourers but that I had done nothing, just stood around. No one heard me abusing or doing anything. I was acquitted. Simply acquitted. No offence was found to have been committed. I was innocent. That proved to be the case. But I lost my job.

Now a case has been filed for reinstatement on the job. That case is still on.

What I have seen is this, that the entire Haryana government became subordinated to one company. The truth is that the government has done injustice to us.

I got out with great difficulty and now I do not dare say anything more just in case I get into trouble again. I don't have the courage to say anything.

I tried very hard to get a job but didn't get any. I have passed out from an ITI, I have experience of several years. There are many companies that need such skilled workers. But everyone has our biodata, so who will give me a job?

People who worked with me are earning Rs 80,000 a month in Manesar today. I feel awful that even though I did not do anything, I lost out. Had I not lost the job I too would have been somewhere else, earning well and living well. Now I just manage, just go on living. There is no joy in life.

My father-in-law had bought a plot in the industrial area in Gurgaon. He suggested setting up this factory. It's next to a stagnant pool full of mosquitoes. I had to do something, make a living. Even a stone becomes heavy if it never moves, if it is lying around. We set up this shed. We make cardboard boxes for packing. We do get some orders. We make ends meet.

People say all kinds of things. There are people who say that I did something bad that I should not have done! I know that I did nothing wrong. I only stood up for my rights. Shouldn't a person do that? Should you never stand up for your rights? Is that wrong too?

However, it is also true that not many people think I was in the wrong. I do not have a bad reputation. Most people treat me with respect. That's all I have now—respect. At least I have that.

Dhanraj Bhambi

Executive member of the union; sentenced to life imprisonment. Interviewed over phone on 28 September 2020 when he came out on parole.

I am asking you: if the working conditions at Maruti had been good, had the pay been decent, why would we have wanted a union and why would we have fought for our rights?

All I had wanted to do when I joined Maruti was to make a decent living and live with dignity.

I come from Apkol village of Chittorgarh, Rajasthan, and I completed a fitter's course from the ITI in Chittorgarh. Soon afterwards, in 2006, I came to Manesar as a trainee in the Maruti factory. It had just started and there were many trainees. We all believed that after three years of hard work, we would become permanent and get good salaries.

I come from a farming family. I have three elder brothers and three sisters. The sisters are all married. My family did farming and never participated in any *kisan andolan*. In fact, people in my village were completely unaware of any previous farmer agitation or movement. We led a simple life. Ours is a big family and the land is limited, so I wanted to do something else and I chose to acquire a new skill at the ITI.

When I started working here, I realized that the work here was sheer torture. I do not shy away from work and can work hard. But if you cannot spare time for a sip of water when you are thirsty even if you have a bottle of water with you, then that work is not hard, it is deadly. Sometimes your body cries out to stop and drink some water, get a moment's rest. But you cannot do it. It is impossible to pick up the bottle. Why? Because another car is sliding in front of you demanding parts to be fitted into it. You have to stop thinking of everything and work. There is not a moment's respite.

The supervisors there used to talk very rudely. They abused us, used vulgar language. Their whole purpose was to keep workers under control. They talked down to us. Even if you had an upset stomach, they did not give you a break to go to the bathroom. They said it wasn't allowed.

To tell you the truth, I joined the union only to escape this atrocity. If the workers do not get united and speak in one voice why would anybody listen to them? Workers are not treated like humans.

When the union was formed, their attitude changed. Then they started talking nicely. The foreman would even take your place if you needed a break; the supervisor would do the work so that you could quickly run to the toilet. A union is an absolute must.

The union's demand was that we should get relief from this kind of a merciless work environment. We had also asserted that the workers are not careless; they do a good job. That is why the best quality car is made in the factory. And so the workers should get better treatment, some time to drink water, to eat their meals in peace, and not be rushed all the time.

It is true that when the union was formed the attitude of the supervisors softened a little. Even then, if they wanted to harass someone the supervisor would go back to his rude behaviour.

That is what happened with Jiya Lal that day.

I used to be an executive member of the union, and on 18 July, I too was upstairs in the administration block building. There is a big hall in which compartments have been made. Like kiosks. They are so small, literally ten feet by ten. So there are these kiosks in one part of the hall and the other part is open hallway. There are two rooms on one side. Siddiqui and M.M. Singh were not there when I was upstairs.

We were holding a meeting with Vikram Khazanchi, who was the head of production at the Manesar plant. P.K. Roy, who is second to Khazanchi, was also there. The Manesar plant was headed by Birendra Prasad from the HR department and Salil Bihari was a manager of HR. These two were also in the meeting. C.S. Raju, who was head of the HR department, was also there. Anil Gaur of Gurgaon HR had also come and he too was attending the meeting.

I was in the general shift and we have to reach the factory only at nine o'clock. When I got there I heard that Jiya Lal had had some quarrel with the supervisor. This had happened before the union people had reached the factory. We heard about it when we were in the meeting upstairs. We asked the managers to tell us exactly what the matter was. They then suspended Jiya Lal so we said that they should suspend the supervisor too, or not suspend anyone. Our stand was: either take action against both or none.

While this meeting was on, the management had called the police. The 'A' shift was working and production went on. Later, the 'B' shift also came in and they started working. We did not ask anyone to stop work or stay put after work. When the 'A' shift was over, workers stayed behind of their own accord. Even in the 'B' shift, work continued till six o'clock.

To tell you the truth, Jiya Lal was not at fault. If someone abuses you, you are bound to get angry. But the management was not ready to listen to anything.

Later in the evening the place got very crowded. A lot of people had come to that building. I don't know who all were there. I never saw anyone beat anyone up. I do not know how the violence broke out. We were inside the room and all this must have happened outside in the hall.

I don't know how it started. But when the fighting started at around seven all of us said that everyone should go home and that we would talk next day. We got out. We even tried to shout out to the workers to go home. But there was such a ruckus and so much noise nobody could hear anything.

We union leaders left the factory. I didn't see who started the fire. I was not there. We had all come out of the factory.

I used to live on rent in Manesar then. I went to my room and then I went away somewhere. I left my room probably at one o'clock at night. I had got the news that a fire had broken out in the factory and that the police were looking for us. My mind went numb. It got hung like a computer hangs, just like that.

The police picked up two of my brothers and took them to the police station. Then they took them somewhere else. They beat my brothers mercilessly. I got to know about it and finally I surrendered on 25 July.

I did not know the law. I did not know any lawyer. I just went to the police station and surrendered. They called it an arrest, as if they had found me and arrested me. For one day they kept me illegally without putting my arrest on record.

They tortured me no end. They used an iron roller on my legs and rolled it up and down. They hung me upside down from the ceiling and beat me up. I would pass out and then they would pour water on me, bring me back to my senses, and then start beating me and torturing me again. They used to press my head down in water and just when I felt like I would now drown they would pull me out and then again push my head into the water. This went on through the night.

I was nearly dead when I was taken to the court. I even told the judge what all had been done to me but nothing happened. There was no medical examination. Later, my lawyer filed a complaint against the SHO. But nothing ever came of it. Our lawyer was Rajendra Pathak.

The judge had given me into police remand. Since then I have been there. Sometimes I get parole.

I had gone to work in Maruti not to go to prison. Before we formed our union there was the MUKU, but it was useless. It never raised our issues and never listened to anything we had to say.

We had to work hard but they were not satisfied with that. They expected us to reach the factory early. Every morning before work they would get us together in the assembly, give us work targets and make us do some exercise. For this one had to reach half an hour before the shift.

They always said that Maruti is a family. If it is a family, then we are also part of it, the contract workers are also in the family. Why do they pay contract workers less for the same amount of work? That is not justice. We had demanded that contract workers be made permanent too. What was wrong with it? If all of us are a family then all workers are the same and should be treated equally.

Now, I have been convicted and am in jail. During the trial not a single worker came to meet us in prison. Even my family members used to come once in a year. How could they have come more often? Bhondsi Jail is 700 kilometres away from my village. They have only four to five *bighas* of land; it is hardly enough to survive on. They do not have surplus income to come visit me in prison. I was the only one in our family with a regular income and this happened to me. I am not married. I was thinking of getting married when this happened.

In jail, all of us from Maruti are together. We have been kept separately from criminals. There we do office work. We work in two shifts, from eight in the morning to two in the afternoon, then from four in the evening to eight at night. Our daily wage is Rs 40.

The food is not good. The lentils are watery. Sometimes we get out on parole. Then I need two sureties of two lakhs each. Family members stand those sureties.

I have got life imprisonment. It is said that a life sentence means fourteen years in prison. However, other prisoners tell me that in Haryana, life means twenty years in jail.

I have stopped thinking about it. It is their wish, the wish of the authorities. Let them keep us inside for as long as they want.

Jiya Lal continues...

After I left the factory that day on 18 July I went back to my room. I had no idea what was happening at the factory. Then a friend called me. He is the one who had helped me get a job earlier at Honda and now he worked at the Manesar Maruti factory. He works for Maruti even now.

That day this friend was in the 'B' shift. He called to tell me that there was a fire in the factory. I just could not understand what had happened, why there was a fire there. I was tired. I went back to sleep.

At night, at 2 am, my brother called me to tell me that just an hour back the police had come to the village. They were going around looking for Jiya Lal. He was very scared. He asked me why they were looking for me, what I had done. I was petrified. So I ran away.

I went to a friend in Punjab who worked for Bharat Electronics and stayed with him for twenty days. I assumed the name of Sandeep. But news spreads fast and the other workers [the roommates of his friend] got scared and told me to leave.

The police picked up my brother-in-law. They went to my sister's house early in the morning at six or so and dragged away her husband. They slapped him many times and kept him in the police station the whole day. They beat him up. In the evening my brother-in-law told them the name of the Maruti worker I was in contact with. After extracting this information from him they let him go and picked up the worker from Maruti. He is a Lohar by caste. He knew me well. The police thrashed him too. He told them where I was and with whom. This is how the police traced me.

It is very difficult for me to recount how the police behaved with me.

They had a cemented pool filled with water. They would push my face into it. I would begin to drown; I wouldn't be able to breathe. When I would begin to think that I am going to die, they would pull me out. After a while they would push me back again, holding my head under water.

They used filthy language. Without using mother and sister swear words they would not even talk to me. What could I do? I cannot tolerate such abuses. That is why I had had that fight with Majhi. Now, I had to hear them all the time. I felt so helpless.

For four days they kept me in the police station unofficially; without showing that I had been arrested. I cannot even begin to explain what all was done to me in those four days. I thought I would not live. There is a police station in Sector 10, Gurgaon. The station head was called Balara.

He stripped me naked. Then he attached a battery to my

behind—down there... How can I tell you? Just understand what I am saying...down there in my behind [anus]. They passed electric current. For half an hour they kept doing this. They would pass the current, then they would stop and then run it through me again. Then stop, then run it again. It felt like someone had lit a fire inside me there. A flame settled in me there. It burnt so much. It hurt so much. I used to think I would die. I just went numb. I could not even sip water. I was not myself. I lost all consciousness of everything around me.

For so many days I could not use the loo without trepidation. I could not pass stool. Something kept shuddering inside me. I don't know how long they did this to me. It seemed endless. I felt as if it would never end. It possibly went on for over half an hour. It could have been longer. Who knows? I don't even remember how many times they hooked me up to the electric current. My teeth chattered. I would scream. When my condition would turn extremely bad, they would stop and give me water. They stopped when I was only half dead. Then again at four in the afternoon they started all over again. They passed current through me repeatedly.

Once they tore my legs apart. They would make me lie down on the floor, spreadeagle me, then one person each would hold one of my legs and tear me apart. One pulled one way, the other pulled the other way. It used to feel like I would be torn into two from the middle. They would tear me apart. Then they would give me a spoonful of water. Only one spoon. I remember that so clearly. One spoon of water.

The police told me to pay them two lakhs. They said that if I paid them that amount they would reduce the charges against me. They asked me to call my brother and sister. They asked them too, to pay them so that they could reduce the charges against me. Where could they get so much money from? They said they did not have enough money. I did not haggle, did not negotiate for a lesser amount. I had no money. What would haggling gain me? Where would my sister or brother find the money? We are all poor workers.

Let me tell you another thing. On 14 September, they told the press, 'We know where Jiya Lal is. We will get hold of him in a day or two.' When they said this, I was already in their custody. I was there in the police station. It was reported in the newspapers that the police had claimed that they would arrest me in a couple of days. I read it too! In police custody, I read it. After two days they showed me arrested and produced me in court. They produced me in court on the sixteenth after 2 pm. They told the magistrate that I had been arrested that very day.

The judge didn't give me a chance to say anything. Even if he had, what could I have said? When I got caught the police kept me in the *thana* at Sector 40 [before being taken to the *thana* in Sector 10]. I was probably taken away on 13 September but they did not record my arrest. When they produced me in court on 16 September they got a remand for five days. They beat me very badly. They once slapped me so hard on my ear that I still cannot hear properly.

When they took me to court, they had told me that I should remain quiet, not tell the judge that I had been thrashed or tortured. By that time, I was half dead anyway. There was a lot of media there too. The police had told me that if I complained about the torture I would be killed. So, I kept my silence. I was very scared.

After being produced in court I was taken to a doctor in the evening. It must have been around eight at night. When the doctor asked me if I had any complaints, I said no. But if the doctor had examined me physically, he would have discovered what all had been done to me. My whole body was bruised. In some places the skin had turned blue. He did not even touch me. I have noticed that in hospitals they don't examine you physically. They keep their distance and just ask questions. One or two questions—then they write their report. That is all. The police get the doctor to write that all is well. The doctor's job is done and the police get the report they want.

I did not talk to any lawyer. I didn't know anyone. I had no information, no knowledge of such things. There was no union either at that time. I mean there was nobody from the union who was around for me to get in touch with. Everybody was in hiding or had already been arrested. Whom could I talk to?

Those days I really got a lot of beatings. Inside a police station they don't consider us human. Whoever wants can come and beat you. Pound you thoroughly. They would come to the police station drunk, would holler, 'Bring him,' and pull me out of the lock-up and thrash me whenever they wanted to. Sometime at nine o'clock at night, another time at eleven o'clock at night—whenever they felt like beating someone they used me as a punching bag.

They also showed me a roller. It may have been some two and a half feet long and two and a half inches in diameter. An iron rod, like a pestle. It weighs some two and a half quintals, they told me. One person cannot even lift it. Two or three people lift it. It is definitely like a pestle, one they use to pound grain with—that kind but very heavy and made of iron. They told me that if I did not confess to whatever they wanted me to confess to, they would roll it over my legs. I was by then half dead. Had they done this I would have died. What they do is they make you lie down, lift the roller and place it on your thighs, each end being held by one or two persons. Then these people holding the ends of the rod roll it downwards on your legs. Then they roll it back. It is so heavy it crushes your muscles. They would show me the pestle, and say they would give me the full treatment with it. They would use it to scare me. They never used it on me or I would not be alive today.

After five days in remand, they sent me to prison. Once I reached there all the torture stopped. But I never got out of prison. I am still a prisoner, out only on parole.

On 10 March 2017, the Sessions Court in Gurgaon sentenced thirteen of us to life imprisonment. Thirty-three were convicted of lesser offences. The rest of the 101 were acquitted. They had spent several years in jail already; and they were not reinstated.

Our appeals to the High Court are pending.

I do not want to discuss the court proceedings and the law. When the witnesses came to court, not one of them said that Jiya Lal beat anyone. Nobody said that. Four people said that Sohan Kumar and Jalaal and two others set fire to the factory. Nobody said that Jiya Lal started the fire. In the identification parade too, nobody recognized me as Jiya Lal. Even then I got such a severe punishment. Life term. I did nothing and even then I was sentenced to life in prison.

It is clear that the law, the court and the legal process are not meant to protect workers. How else do you explain that the thirteen of us have been given life sentences for something we did not do, and do not even condone?

Now I am in prison. Everybody in the village knows I am in prison. Such a big thing cannot be hidden in a village. Whenever I apply for parole my family has to go to the *patwari*. They have to get him to write a recommendation for my parole. So how can you hide that I am a prisoner?

In a village you cannot hide anything. There is a lot of difference between the city and a village. In the village the social atmosphere is very different. Every caste lives in its own *mohalla*. Chamars live separately and Brahmins live separately. But in my village there are no hostilities.

I don't know what they say about me behind my back but to me they all say that I have not done anything bad. People tell me that that is the general opinion here, that I have done no wrong, that I am a good man and have not gone to prison for anything bad.

Half the village says I should have continued to work in the factory quietly, and not have got involved with the union. To me they all say, 'You have done nothing wrong,' but to each other they say, 'He had landed a good job, was making a decent wage. Why did he have to become a leader? He landed in a mess unnecessarily.' So I have heard. As I told you, in a village everyone gets to know everything. Such people think that I cut my own limbs. Brought the axe down on myself!

Even now they treat my family well. Nobody harasses them. Nobody harasses my children either. My elder son goes to school; the children in his school know that his father is in prison, but they never say anything bad or hurtful to my son or taunt him. There is no discrimination in the school.

Even otherwise, there is no discrimination in my village. Earlier, people used to look at us with disgust. I am Chamar by caste. People used to have a lot of contempt for us. They kept their distance. They did not talk to us properly. Now things have changed. They don't show any disgust. They talk to us nicely... No, they do not eat with us. They don't invite us to weddings and *mundans*. But that is how it is in a village. Chamars invite Chamars, Brahmins invite Brahmins, Yadavs invite Yadavs. Nobody invites people from another caste.

But yes, we are no longer abused. Nobody picks fights with us. They are good people in my village.

I am very ill now. I have got cancer therefore I am on parole.

I fell ill in prison. In February this year [2020] prison officials got my CT scan done. I never got the report of that scan but they had got it done. It is possible that they did not give it to me because the report was not good. Whatever the reason, I don't have it. Then they took me to PGI in Chandigarh for another CT scan. They did not give me that report either. After that they released me on parole.

Only when I got home and went to the hospital did I get to know that I had got cancer. I am getting chemotherapy. I have had six rounds. I can walk a little bit. Otherwise, I was bedridden. Every chemo round, I get medicines worth Rs 10,000. When I need money for treatment, I have to borrow money at 2 per cent monthly interest from moneylenders in the village. The union has helped a lot. They gave us money earlier too. They are always around when we need help to go somewhere for treatment. We even built our house with the money the union gave us. They gave us money for my brother's wedding too. There are many expenses apart from the money needed for treatment. I have to take a taxi to go to hospital. It is a private taxi. The ambulance does not come from the hospital. I have to hire my own cab. It is true that there is an All India Medical Institute in Jhajjar but it is 170 kilometres from here. I cannot go there for treatment.

At least now I can walk up to the bathroom. I must say that my condition is now better. When I was in hospital it was so much worse. I could not do even this much. Everything had to be done in bed. My wife and brother did everything, gave me bedpans. It doesn't feel good.

I don't think I am getting any better than this. I can only walk up to the bathroom. Though even that is welcome. Otherwise, I was dependent on others for everything. My brother is younger than me. I have a wife. They have both done a lot for me. They are still doing a lot for me. I can get up with the support of a stick now but generally I keep lying in bed. What can I do? There is nothing I can do.

Jiya Lal died of cancer at 11 pm on 4 June 2020. He was on parole and died at home. Pawan Dahiya also died of a snake bite while working in the field during parole.

Praveen

When we would be on strike, the media used to arrive, newspapers used to send reporters. They used to talk to us a lot; we would give many, many interviews. We used to talk endlessly till our throats became sore. But the next day we would read in the papers that 500 cars had been produced in the factory.

And you know how they all say that the principle of justice is that not a single innocent should be punished even if a hundred guilty go unpunished? Well, that is all just glibness. A lot of innocents are punished.

When I got out of prison all roads to employment were closed for me. When I went to prison, I was only twenty-eight and I was thirty-two when I got out. At that age, people are married and have two kids. I was simply nowhere. No job. No marriage. No children. Nobody willing to employ me. Nobody cares whether your fight was just or not. I had been stamped a criminal, someone who had been in prison, and that is all that mattered. Nobody has the time to go into the details. They do not want to know that you went to prison because you were fighting for justice. It is enough for them that you have served time. Whether you are truly guilty or not, who cares?

I had to do something. Everyone starts advising you in such circumstances. I thought of opening a shoe shop. I did some research for a week. Some people began to say that I should start selling cement. But I decided that this time I would do only what I feel like doing.

My mother is a very cheerful woman. She always laughs in the face of adversity. She was such a joy to behold. Now even she grew teary-eyed. She had grown sad because of me, for me. She once took me to a Babaji. He placed a slip of paper before me and said that it was written on that paper that I had been in prison for three years. I asked him where it was written. I began to argue because nothing of the sort was written on it. My mother began to cry. Then she sent me to a priest in the village. By now I had begun to think that there was no God. The priest would keep asking me why I would not go to his temple. 'Why don't you come to the *mandir*?' was his constant refrain. One day I asked him, 'If I visit the temple every day and someday I do something terrible—like, suppose I kill someone—will God save me from prison, will the police not arrest me?' He began to bristle and said, 'Of course not.' Then I asked him, 'Suppose I never visit the temple, never pray, and never do anything wrong or bad. Will I still get into trouble with the law?' He said, 'Of course not!' Then I asked him what the role of God is if in either case I am responsible for whatever I do! If I do good, I will remain free of trouble, and if do bad, I will pay for it. So what is God doing for me? Panditji was speechless. After that he stopped bothering me. We still meet. I run into him. But we talk like friends now.

Eventually, even my mother gave up on me. She began to say that I could do nothing. She was very disappointed in me. I had a friend in Kurukshetra who used to sell pizza. I used to visit him once in a while. He suggested that I open a pizza shop.

Those days there were very few pizza shops here. I found this place to rent. It is not far from my village. It is close to a medical college. I pay 8,000 rupees as monthly rent and I sell enough pizzas to make a profit. I have a gas oven, a fridge, an inverter for times when there is a power breakdown or power cut. Two people work with me. We are all happy and content.

It was very difficult to get married. Whoever came to see me rejected me. There came a time when, if the family invited anyone with a daughter to meet me, I would think: okay, here you are for twenty minutes, you will finish your tea and snacks and leave having rejected me. It happened so many times. Some hundred families may have rejected me!

I was on Facebook. One day an ad for Jeevansathi.com opened on my page. I began to surf it. Then I got a call to ask me to become a member. That meant paying them a thousand rupees. I refused. So, they asked me a few questions and created an ID for me. Then they began to call to say that I should make them my friend on FB so that I could get to see who all was there on the website. That sounded reasonable and I befriended them on FB. Now I would send friend requests to people on this Jeevansathi and they would be declined! That was one insult that I had not experienced till now and now I had tasted that too. Rejection on the net! So why would I pay them a thousand rupees and become a member to be insulted like this? You don't get to see many profiles of people on the website without becoming a member, and I thought, what is the point anyway, because I am going to be rejected outright.

One day, I saw the profile of a girl I liked. I called Jeevansathi and told them that I wanted to get in touch with her. She lived in Ambala. We chatted. We liked each other. Now her family began to object. They said that the girl was a city girl and couldn't live in a village. I must say that she turned out to be a woman who knew what she wanted. She stood firm. She is very strong. Finally, everyone had to bow to her wishes and we got married in 2018 and now we have had our first baby. He is only two months old.

I am no longer connected with any organization. I do not even talk to my old contacts much. I have quit being an activist. Every morning I come here to work from my village and return in the evening. I am content.

Unfortunately, we could not interview many of the women, mainly the wives of the workers. However, we did talk to Sushma Devi, wife of Sohan Lal, a worker in Maruti Manesar. She is a woman of exceptional courage and intelligence. Her husband, Sohan Lal, was not named in the FIR but he was arrested and spent three years in jail before he was acquitted. Despite the fact he was acquitted of all charges he was not reinstated.

Sushma Devi

Now an elected sarpanch of Purwala village in Sirmaur district of Himachal Pradesh and wife of Sohan Lal. Interviewed over phone on 10 February 2022.

When that incident in Manesar happened, I was not in Gurgaon but I remember the details. I remember a lot about those days because it was a particularly stressful time in my life. My husband, Sohan, was a worker in Maruti Manesar. I was pregnant and the doctors kept saying that my foetus had no heartbeat. Eventually, I had to have an MTP [medical termination of pregnancy]. That was done on 6 July 2012 in

Gurgaon but my husband could not get leave. His manager had come to see me in hospital too. I don't remember his name but it was not Awanish Dev.

Those days we lived in a rented room in Rajiv Nagar. I was discharged the next day. My husband got leave on 7 July, the day I was discharged. Then my mother came down the next day from Paonta Sahib, where our village is, and he joined duty. My mother brought me back to Himachal with her a day later. I was still recuperating when that incident took place. We used to talk on the phone every day.

On 12 July, I called him half an hour after his shift ended. He worked the 'A' shift and it used to end at 3 pm. He usually got back home in half an hour. When I called around 3.30 pm, and asked him if he had got back home, he said he was still in the factory because some meeting was going on. I called two hours later and he said they were all sitting in the ground of the factory, the whole 'A' shift, because union leaders were holding some meeting in the office and they were waiting for some decision. I was a little surprised. Then when I called again at 6 pm he was still in the factory grounds. I wanted to know what had happened but he said not to worry.

Then, sometime later in the evening, the wife of one of his friends called me to ask me if I had heard the news. I hadn't. She told me that a fire had broken out in the factory. I called him immediately. He said he was in the ground with lots of other workers; yes, there was some fire somewhere upstairs and they were all leaving, so I need not worry.

The next day he came to Paonta Sahib to my mother's place. That is when I heard about the issue of Jiya Lal. I knew about the union. I am telling you, that factory used to make workers work so hard you can't imagine.

I was born and brought up in Purwala village in Sirmaur

district in Himachal Pradesh. It is practically in the plains, near Paonta Sahib, and we usually refer to it as Paonta Sahib. I studied there. I have an MA and a BEd degree from Shimla University. Never got any government job. I got married to him knowing he worked in Maruti. It was a good company. It had prestige and I thought nothing of marrying a worker. He was from Karnal district. His village is Khukhani.

He got leave only for five days for the marriage. To come to Paonta Sahib, get married and get back to Gurgaon where he lived; I too came to live with him in Rajiv Nagar. Lots of workers lived there. My landlady was very nice. She always stood by me and helped out whenever I had some problem.

Don't ask me about my honeymoon. There simply wasn't any. He used to come back home so tired. One look at his face and I would know that we couldn't step out anywhere. All he did was come back dead tired and eat and sleep. He used to keep saying that it was so hard, they made them work so much. He never got any leave. I used to feel very bad.

When they formed a union, only then did things ease a little. They had to go on strikes to do this. The first time they sat on strike inside the factory I had called him and got to know about the union. Of course, he told me a lot about work, and I always stood by him. For months, they sat outside the factory in 2011. He sat there with all the others and did not come home.

Once, during one of those strikes, I had called him to tell him I would not keep the *karava chauth ka vrat* because he wouldn't be coming home. So he said he would and he came for only one evening. They fought hard to get that union. They were then able to get at least some leave when they needed. Even then, when I had that abortion, aunty—our landlady—went with me to the hospital. He got leave for one day only, the next day. My life changed after that abortion. Completely changed.

After 18 July, the factory shut down and he came to be with me in Paonta Sahib. The police came to the village and picked him up on 21 or 22 July. I have forgotten the exact date. For two days we did not even know where he was. My brother and some friends went to the police station in Gurgaon and only after two days did we find out that he was in Bhondsi prison. They had picked him up from here and shown him as arrested from Gurgaon.

What I do not understand is [how he came to be arrested when] he was not named in the three lists the police had of those responsible for the violence. I still have copies of those lists. His name does not figure in any one of them.

There were four Sohans in the factory. One was a union office bearer. He has been sentenced to life and is in prison now. Two other Sohans have never been arrested. They have probably been declared absconders. Obviously, each Sohan had a different father and it was mentioned in the lists. Still, the police came and picked up my husband who did not figure on those lists.

Apparently, when he asked the police why they had arrested him, they told him that they had to show how hard they had worked to get hold of the culprits, that they had gone all the way to Himachal Pradesh to nab someone. I asked the police about it. The police said, now that the paperwork had been done, they could not help us. They said I could try to get him out on bail. He got bail three years later, sometime in 2015!

When this happened, I did not crumble. I decided to fight for him and us. I moved back to Gurgaon. Yes, I lived alone in the room. I used to teach in a school, but it was difficult to manage school teaching and visits to Bhondsi Jail and attending court hearings. Then I heard of a vacancy in a company in Gurgaon. I appeared for the interview and told the

MD everything. What is the point in lying? I thought I would need days off, so it was best to tell them everything. They gave me the job. The MD told me that since I had no other skills, I would first be put on the reception. In schools you have to reach very early and I had to go to the prison in the mornings. I quit the school job. In this job I had to reach office at 9.30 in the morning.

Every Monday and Thursday I would visit Bhondsi prison and reach office fifteen or twenty minutes late. I was allowed to. Many companies in Gurgaon were sympathetic to us. This MD and his wife were sympathetic. Many educated people were sympathetic.

I am very brave. My father used to tell me that I am a courageous girl. I am unafraid and I can do anything in the world. I can learn any new task. In that company too I learnt accounts and in three months they shifted me from the reception to the accounts department. Then the pressure to reach on time eased a little.

Even when my husband had not been arrested, I would do a lot of things on my own. I got up early, I cooked, I went to school to teach, and if I fell ill, I looked after myself. He had no time. I used to feel sad just looking at his tired face. He tried to take leave once when I had fever and he got one day off.

I never missed a single hearing in court. I also went to join a few sit-ins and protest demonstrations after all these people were arrested. I could not go to all the protests like the *pad-yatra* [rally] in Haryana because I had to hold down my job and earn money.

When he was terminated after the violence in the factory, the company gave him three months' salary. The company had opened salary accounts for all workers; I was glad I would now have a little money. We had to do a lot of running around. There were some expenses on account of the court cases too.

I will never forget how much money there was in his account. He had a balance of exactly one rupee and thirty paise. The exact amount!

I was shocked. I did not know such things those days so I asked one of his friends to find out how, after getting three months' pay, he had nothing in the bank. So, he found out. It turned out that Sohan had been a guarantor for someone who had taken a loan in the company and when the company paid him those three months' wages they deducted the whole amount and he was left with nothing.

So, all of a sudden, I had lost his salary, all the money he had in the bank, and I had to fend for myself and also pay for many things like his prison expenses and my visits to the prison. My in laws are not well off and they could not pitch in.

I never lost courage.

He had done nothing and this is what happened to him.

I don't blame Jiya Lal for what happened. He was a worker and he was being treated badly so he reacted. The company is at fault. I am a *sarpanch* now. Suppose something happens in my village, I have to listen to all the people involved in it. I must. Otherwise, what kind of a *sarpanch* will I make? I have to listen to all and then arrive at a decision. Even if Jiya Lal had done something wrong, the managers should have listened to his version. They should have either taken action against both him and his supervisor, or not taken action against any of them. Jiya Lal was not at fault and I don't blame him for what happened to us.

The company is powerful. We are all weak compared to them. So they did what they wanted to.

I never missed a single hearing in court. I met all the lawyers. I met Vrinda [Grover] also. She was very nice. But the company is very powerful.

When we went to protest outside Randeep Surjewala's* house there was a lathi-charge and I also got hit three or four times.

It is interesting that even the police was sympathetic but it was helpless. Before the lathi-charge we had all broken for lunch. When we opened our tiffins to eat, the cops were roaming around, so we invited them to eat with us. They refused the food but they told me that they were sympathetic to us, that they had a job and they had to do what they were ordered to do. I understand their compulsions. I told them that they could do their job and we would continue with our own work of protesting.

My husband was not tortured. He told me that they slapped him a couple of times, that is all.

When he was acquitted, he should have got the job in the company back. At least fifty permanent workers had been acquitted by the court of all charges. They had all spent three or four years in prison despite not being named in the FIR or having been falsely accused. They should have been automatically reinstated. But no, they are now fighting a case in the labour court. This is not justice.

I keep praying to God to ask Him to ensure justice. I tell God that He has to listen to me; I pray every day.

When my husband got out, I told him that we ought to file a case of compensation against the government for falsely accusing him and keeping him in prison when he was completely innocent. I also wanted to file a defamation case. Lawyers would have explained what kind of case we could file and how to go about it. We never got to that stage. I talked to

---

* Randeep Singh Surjewala has been an MLA in the Haryana Assembly, and was the cabinet minister for industries during 2009–14. He was one of the official spokespersons of the Indian National Congress.

all the fifty people also. But they all said no. My husband was so relieved to be out of prison that he did not want to make the rounds of the courts once again.

And now the labour courts are taking their time. I think we should go sit on a *dharna* outside the court to demand that they expedite our case speedily. Nobody agrees with my proposal.

When the criminal case was going on there were hearings every day. My husband was not brought to court every day, only when his part had to be heard. But the hearings were held every day. They can do it for us also, for the workers who lost their jobs.

Those are my demands. They should immediately reinstate all those who were acquitted.

In the High Court also, the hearing of appeals is pending. That should be heard immediately too.

As for the union, I got to know them only after my husband was arrested. Earlier, I knew some of my husband's friends but not the union people. I never met Sonu Gujjar or even go to the *dharna* when they were on strike. Families did not join that protest or even go there. Afterwards, I became close to the union and used to talk to them often and participate in their programmes.

After my husband got bail in 2015, I had a bad experience with the union and the provisional committee. They may say that they have supported all the workers who were arrested. It is true that they helped the people who were in jail. Even now they are supporting the families of those who are in prison. But they did not step up when those who got bail faced problems.

In 2017, I became pregnant again and my pregnancy was very complicated. I had to go to PGI in Chandigarh. No, I did not go to Delhi, which is closer to Gurgaon. We went to PGI and I needed three lakhs. The doctor had told me that if I had a normal delivery my baby would not live and had suggested a surgery. They said to get it done before full term.

I called Khushi Ram and asked him to help us. I told him that I would manage some amount and expected the union to help with some. He refused. He said the union only pays when someone dies, not in any other case. That, he said, was the provision in the union rules or some such thing.

I finally had a normal delivery and I lost my baby girl. It hurt so much. It hurts even today. My *gudiya* died.

I don't have any children. There is some complication. I feel very sad about this.

I no longer feel that close to the union. I do talk to Khushi Ram and others too but only when it is about a necessary matter. It is more of a formal relationship now. My baby died. I cannot forget that.

Pooja (name changed)

The wife of one of the union activists; she was very particular about not revealing her identity. We are, therefore, not disclosing the date of the interview or the name of her village.

I was doing MA in History when a proposal came to marry a worker in the Maruti Suzuki factory. I knew the family since we had relatives in his family. It was *Dadi* [paternal grandmother] who had done the negotiations. Later, I met him. He was concerned about the fact that he was a mere worker while I was so educated, and said that I should think it over before getting married. Honestly, I too was unhappy about the proposal. I did not like it at all. But I convinced myself the elders must have thought it through.

All the same, I was excited at the thought of living in a

big city like Gurgaon, because I live in a small village and had not seen the wider world. I even took cooking classes so I was better equipped for city life.

I finished MA after marriage. I was pregnant when the Manesar violence happened. I learnt that my husband had been arrested. Initially, my family did not tell me the news since I was taking my final exams. They even hid the newspapers from me.

In the beginning I did not take any interest in the union and its activities. I stayed in the village with my parents. Then I started going to jail to meet my husband. I did not go for many demonstrations and protests since my son was small, but when there was a *pad-yatra* from Kaithal to Jind I took part in it for three days.

I started understanding what my husband was doing. He was fighting for his rights and the rights of workers. Their struggle was for justice.

Look around. I did not realize my dream of living in a big city; even now I live in a village with my husband and his parents. I am in my husband's village now. My in-laws are very nice. I do not mind. I also work as a school teacher.

Sarabjeet Singh

I made a major mistake in life, a blunder. I should never have joined the ITI. All my friends in school were going there so I chose to join too. My father asked me not to, but I wouldn't listen to him. My wife is from Patiala and we had been married for only one and a half years when this incident blew up in our faces.

After I passed class 10 I joined a course to become a fitter in the ITI and then I joined as a trainee in Maruti Manesar in 2006. Three years later I became a permanent worker. At that time, I had said to everyone that I did not want to get involved in the *lafdas* of a union or any such thing. At the time there was MUKU. It was a mere formality; it was not an actual union. They would get some small complaints of workers resolved and in the real and big matters they did what the management wanted them to do.

I had a close friend called Naveen those days. This Naveen knew Sonu Gujjar. I would go with him to meet him. It is because of Sonu Gujjar that my mindset changed. I began to feel that one should definitely fight for one's rights, struggle for justice.

For us all workers are the same whether they are casual, temporary, on contract or permanent. We wanted everyone to be paid well and we wanted everyone to live with dignity. We all work together. Would the factory function if we did not work as a team? Would the plant be able to produce anything? We all work hard and as a team. It is our unity that keeps the plant running. We had assured everyone that we wouldn't let anyone lose their jobs. Our unity was supremely important.

Nine

No Justice for Workers

Parliamentary Democracy in standing out as protagonist of liberty has continuously added to the economic wrongs of the poor, the downtrodden and the disinherited classes.

—B.R. Ambedkar

The workers of the Manesar factory and the families of those who were in jail continuously protested against the unjust arrests and the unfair trial, and demanded the release of the workers. The protesting workers and their families and supporters faced police action. It was obvious that the police wanted to ensure that repression acted as a deterrent to protests not only by Suzuki workers but other workers in the Manesar and Gurgaon industrial area as well.

For instance, on 18 May 2013, the Haryana police imposed Section 144 of the Code of Criminal Procedure in Kaithal and arrested around 150 workers peacefully protesting there since 24 March. These workers were demanding the release of arrested workers and reinstatement of terminated workers.

The Maruti workers were faced with opposition, repression and injustice from all sides.

Mahapanchayat

After the events of 18 July, villagers of 200 villages held a *mahapanchayat*. It unanimously criticized the Maruti Suzuki

Workers' Union and condemned the violence that led to the death of Awanish Kumar Dev, the general manager of the Human Resources department at the Manesar plant. The villagers proposed an independent body consisting of local villagers to mediate between the company and the workers. At the same time, they called for the ousting of all existing labour unions.

The villagers condemned the MSWU because they feared that the factory may close down, thus depriving the villagers of their livelihoods. The villagers earn by renting out rooms to plant workers, and through shops from where the workers can buy their daily necessities. In just two villages, Aliyar and Dhalla, for example, more than 5,000 workers, including Maruti workers, live in what have been described as 'sub-human conditions'.

Jitendra Kumar

People of the nearby villages are all with the management. The company has managed to win them over with small contracts of transport and other such works. Kankrola, Bansgaon, Kasan, Bhangrola, Ahir Dhana, Khogaon are some of the villages where the people are against us. They drive trucks for the company. They get contracts to run the canteen and other such small-time jobs or contracts from the management. A number of people from the villages are local goons here.

The *sarpanch* of the Ahir Dhana is a witness against us in our case. He was not even there but he is a witness.

Private Security Forces

Maruti Suzuki employs private security services to guard its factory. From the accounts of the workers and other reports the police had arrived at the factory on 18 July 2012 by the afternoon but did not enter till late in the evening.

The workers and trade union leaders at the Manesar plant have consistently maintained that the violence was started by the 100 to 150 bouncers who entered the plant during the second shift dressed in the uniform of the factory workers but without names. This allegation was reported by several journalists but no one seems to have followed up this lead.

Here is the statement given by Ram Meher, the president of the union at Manesar, a day after the events of 18 July.* It was published in the media and deserves to be read in full:

> The Maruti Suzuki Workers Union (MSWU) is anguished at the recent developments in Maruti Suzuki plant, IMT Manesar where the management has resorted to anti-worker and anti-Union activities in a pre-planned manner leading to the closure of the factory yesterday.
>
> We have had a long tough struggle with the strong unity of our permanent and contract workers to establish and register our Union last year, and had recently as of April 2012 submitted our Charter of Demands to the management of Maruti Suzuki, and the process of negotiation for wages and other demands was underway. However the management has done its utmost to derail the process and break the back of the spirit of unity of the workers and the legitimacy of the Union.
>
> As part of this vindictive attitude and in a pre-planned manner, yesterday, the afternoon of 18th July, a supervisor in the shop floor abused and made casteist comments against a dalit worker of the permanent category, which was legitimately protested by the worker.

* 'What the Union has to say about Maruti standoff', *Firstpost*, 20 July 2012 (https://www.firstpost.com/business/full-text-union-accuses-maruti-hired-bouncers-of-burning-factory-382717.html, last accessed 11 January 2023).

Instead of taking action against the said supervisor, the management immediately suspended the worker concerned without any investigation as was demanded by the workers. When the workers along with Union representatives went to meet the HR to demand against the supervisor and revoke the unjust suspension of the worker, the HR officials flatly refused to hear our arguments, and it was in no mood to resolve the issue amicably.

When the negotiation was going on with the leaders of the Union inside the office, the management called in the entry of hundreds of bouncers on its payroll to attack the workers.

This is completely an illegal vindictive action in the spirit of conspiracy to corner us into submission even as our demands and methods are legitimate. The gates were closed by the security on behest of the management and the bouncers brutally attacked the workers with sharp weapons and arms.

They, joined by some of the managerial staff and police later, beat up a number of workers who have had to be hospitalised with serious injuries. The bouncers, who are anti-social elements on hire, also destroyed company property and set fire to a portion of the factory. The gates were later opened to oust the workers and enforce a lockout by the company.

We have the workers and the company's welfare in mind and have worked towards it after the resolution of the dispute last year, and to blame the current violence on us is unjust. We are still keen to dialogue with the company and want to sit with the company management and the government labour department to amicably resolve the matter and restore industrial peace in the factory.

Ram Meher
President, Maruti Suzuki Workers Union (MSWU)

The workers even filed a complaint in the court stating that it was the bouncers who actually beat up the management officials and set the factory on fire. The complaint was rejected. ('A Pre-Decided Case', PUDR, 2017)

This allegation is important especially in view of the fact that corporations employ security forces from private security companies. Today, there are nearly nine million employed in private security services according to *Private Security Industry: A Report* produced by FICCI and BDO in 2018. Trade union leaders tell us how even the furniture in police stations seems to have been supplied by Maruti Suzuki for you can see the logo of the company on it. This privatization of security forces, with the job of security in private hands, whether bouncers or private security forces, and a police seemingly beholden to the corporates, has far reaching implications for the citizens living in Gurgaon.

Trade union leaders maintain that the company employs local villagers and goons as bouncers; they are encouraged to 'discipline' the workers who are immigrants and therefore looked upon as 'outsiders'. Maruti Suzuki does not employ local people as workers any more, whether permanent or on contract. Almost all of them are immigrants. The company thus seeks to isolate workers by driving a wedge between the workers and local villagers, and between the workers and the security personnel. We have already seen in previous chapters how they do so between the permanent and contract workers.

Criminal Case

The criminal trial which led to the conviction of Maruti Suzuki workers, including life sentences for thirteen workers, was anything but fair. We have not gone into the proceedings in this case but there were some obvious absurdities which illustrate that the workers did not get a fair trial.

The list of the accused workers submitted by the witnesses

to the court, for example, was in alphabetical order, as if they had assembled in the plant in that order; thus, one prosecution witness testified against individuals with names starting from A to G, another against those with names starting from G to P and so on. Deepak Anand, the general manager who filed the FIR had named more than fifty accused, but when he was cross-examined he could identify only one of them. The court was told he had since left his job.

The lawyer appearing for the state as prosecutor was K.T.S. Tulsi. It was discovered that he had charged the government more than eighty-five crores. After the BJP government came to power he was dismissed and an enquiry has been instituted against him.

The workers too had to pay their lawyers. To begin with, they had one lawyer, Raghbir Singh Hooda, or Hooda Saheb as he was called, who fought the case with passion and took little money. He was the former Haryana State secretary of the Communist Party of India (Marxist). But he had cancer and he could not come to the court during the last days. Some workers engaged their own lawyers and had to pay for their services. Even those who professed to appear pro bono charged several lakhs towards costs.

The greatest anxiety the workers suffered while in jail was about the court proceedings; especially the dates for their bail hearings. They would anxiously wait for the date, and then, when the day came, they would be taken to court in jail vehicles, stuffed into them like sheep. And then they would have to wait there all day long in the heat, without food, in a cage—only to find out that their bail application had been rejected.

It was only in 2015 that the first batch of workers, seventy-nine of them, got bail. Others had to wait for longer.

The workers who were sentenced to life imprisonment were

not given bail/parole till much later. Many were not even allowed to attend important family functions, even funerals of their close family members.

The anxiety and stress of being in jail and not knowing what to expect from the courts and not being sure whether your lawyer is truly representing you was perfectly captured by Yadavendra Sharma, a worker who worked in the press shop and spent five years in jail for a crime he did not commit.

Yadavendra is from the Bharatpur district of Rajasthan. He joined the factory in 2006 and became permanent in 2009. We interviewed him on 20 August 2022, when he came to meet us after he heard that we were putting together this book. This is how he recalls Osamu Suzuki's visit to the factory:

'I saw Osamu Suzuki a few times when he visited our factory. He was really small. Only four and a half feet or so in height. He walked like a monkey, jumping around. When he was about to arrive, the factory was cleaned up like never before. It was dusted and swabbed. Preparations were made as if a king was arriving. The factory sparkled. Every corner was cleaned up.

'Not just were many workers hidden away from sight, they were made to hide in different sections. Not in toilets. Suzuki used to open toilet doors to see if anyone was hiding inside; he peered behind doors to check all this. He behaved as if he did not trust the management and always wanted to ensure that they employed more people than they were supposed to. The management used to pretend as if they were getting all the work done with a very small workforce.'

He was active in the union formed by Sonu Gujjar. On that day, 18 July, he was working in the press shop, which is far away from the part of the factory where the incident took place. And yet he was arrested and had to spend five years in Bhondsi Jail before he was acquitted. Now, he is fighting for reinstatement and back wages in a labour court.

He told us:

'I truly did not know what happened that day on 18 July. I had never met Jiya Lal. I met him for the first time only in jail.

'When that incident happened on 18 July, I was in the "B" shift and working in a building that was a kilometre away from the HR building where that incident took place. I used to work in the press shop and that is far away from the HR building.

'I was totally innocent and the biggest injustice here is that I spent five years in prison despite being innocent. This happened because of the management. They gave the names of innocent people too to the police; the state entered the picture later.

'It is the management that is responsible first.

'I think that the apprentices and casuals were very young and this new blood was angry with the management. They thought somewhat on these lines: "What can happen to us? Let us smash some cars and break a few windows and get out of here. We can easily join some other company." That was as far as they could think. In the prison I asked one of them why they had smashed cars and he told me that he had had a lot of fun smashing things! He had done it for fun! When I asked him if he was having fun now, being a prisoner, he said, "How could I have known that it would result in this?"'

He also shared some of his memories of his time in jail:

'In prison we were all together. We used to distribute sweets if anyone of us got good news from the family. If a worker had a child, or it was the birthday of a child, we would distribute sweets. If that worker could not afford to buy sweets for everyone we all collected money and spent it to celebrating together. If someone in the family of a prisoner died we would mourn together and keep silent for two minutes.

'In prison, we Maruti workers earned a lot of respect. We helped not just each other but other prisoners too. We had with us a small-time contractor who had been falsely accused in a rape case, or so he told us. He got bail from court but he did not have Rs 25,000 to pay for the bail. Maruti workers in prison collected that amount and gave it to him and he thanked us tearfully when he was leaving the prison. Even our jailor was impressed. All jail officials praised us.'

Yadavendra kept a dairy in jail, filling up several notebooks. We hope it will be published in its entirety one day. Here we only record a small part to convey the stress, anxiety, disappointments, longing and small joys that a prisoner feels. The diary also shows the workers practising their religious rituals. Being in jail tested Yadavendra's faith in God to a degree which was unbearable.

---

9 March 2013

Today is Maha Shivratri. Most of the boys [a reference to his colleagues] are fasting. We have already informed the kitchen that seventy to eighty of the boys will not be eating so food should not be cooked for them. In our barrack there is going to be a recitation from the *Maha Shiv Puran* for twenty-four hours. In B Barrack, they are chanting '*Om Namah Shivay*' for twenty-four hours. I am also fasting...

11 March 2013

Today, the recitation of *Maha Shiv Puran* was over at eight. In the morning. We worked hard and made a *yagya kund* [sacred fire pit] and the Brahmins among the *lambadar* [i.e. from the landowning class] convicts finished recitations. All Maruti workers gave their *ahuti* [oblation] and later *prasad* was distributed and the programme came to an end.

20 March 2013

This morning I got up late because I had a severe headache. I did not do any exercise. Today was *mulaqat* day* but no one came to see me. Today, at 9 am, two members of Daboo gang beat up Rathi, a *havildar*. That's why the jail was closed. The two members of the gang were beaten up by the jail police. They were beaten so much they could not walk. The other boys told me that the two must have been beaten 1,000 times with a *lathi*.

Since morning my mind has been in turmoil. I keep thinking that people who say there is justice in God's abode are lying. In my memory, I have never harmed anyone. Even if I think of doing harm to anyone my heart and limbs tremble with fear. Even Mummy-Papa [*sic*] can't think of doing wrong to anyone. Today, there are eighteen criminal charges against me. I had never in my worst nightmares thought such a thing could happen to me. I left behind my three-month-old son. He is ten months now. My heart longs to see him. Today, I am being punished for offences I never committed. Is this God's justice?

There are days when hope shines through like a ray of sunlight through dark clouds. In the following excerpt Yadavendra talks about celebrating Eid for the first time when a Muslim prisoner invited him to his barrack.

---

* A day when a prisoner gets visited by members of his family.

10 August 2013

Today is Eid. All of us who have joined the dance classes were invited by Aftab, who is also in our class, to his barrack. We all ate there. We ate biryani made of rice, *zarda*, which is a dessert of sweet rice, and *poori-sabzi*. After that we went for the dance class... This is the first time I have celebrated the festival of Eid in this wonderful manner. Here in the jail there are a lot of Muslims.

The environment in here does not seem like a jail. We have most amenities. But the longing for home is always there. But there is one consolation, which is that we will get out soon—God willing!

Yadavendra's notebooks show how painful it was for this young man to see the distress his incarceration had caused to his family: his father and father-in-law; his young wife, whom he had married barely two years ago, and their baby, who he cannot even hold; and his mother, who cried every time she came to the jail and saw her son behind bars.

---

19 October 2013

Today is my *mulaqat* day. I do not know whether Chachi [his mother] and Jaya [his sister] and Jijaji [brother-in-law] will come. Last *mulaqat*, Papaji [father-in-law] had said they would come to meet me on Sunday. Whenever I wait in anticipation of a *mulaqat* the family arrives late. I tried not to think about it much but my heart was filled with strange emotions. This would be my second meeting with my mother after the first on 8 December 2012...

This time they arrived at 10 am and, as I had hoped, all three came. The moment Chachi and Jaya saw me their eyes filled with tears. Their throats were choked and they could not speak. I also had the same emotions but I controlled myself and I started talking to them as if it didn't bother me. Jijaji's face was still swollen after his accident but he looked better since the last time. Chachi's condition was bad; she looked so weak, her hair had turned absolutely white and her face looked darker. Looking at her, I was shocked and blamed myself for leaving her in that state. Her worries about me have caged her body. Chachi said I looked weak and I told her it was because I did exercise every day. She told me it was better to stop exercising if it made me weak. We did not talk for long but I was satisfied. But for them it was not enough. Chachi said they had now got an electricity connection and that Tanmay [Yadavendra's son] had become very naughty. She said she would spend the entire day looking at him playing. I told her that I too longed to see him. She said she did not want anything else other than that I came back home. Jijaji forced me to accept Rs 2,000. He also gave me a shirt and a jersey.

The heat and humidity inside the jail is unbearable and the prisoners long for a breath of fresh air.

The memories of his family, especially on festivals and the anniversary of his wedding or the birthday of his baby, would choke him up and tears would flow bringing little relief.

And then, as the days, weeks and months turned to years, the family too felt the stress; they too felt stigmatized because their son was in jail. When family members did not come to meet him the anger and loneliness became unbearable. He knew he could not blame them. He prayed to God to at least look after his family and protect them.

By putting one worker in jail the family had lost not only the main breadwinner but also had to find the money to pay his lawyer, apart from giving some to him to pay for his basic needs inside the jail, tea and toiletries, among other things. They would bring him tomatoes, cucumber and onions to make the jail food taste a little better; and of course, some homemade ghee. This was particularly burdensome for a family that found it difficult to bear even the travel expenses from their village to the jail or court, including for the food they had to buy that day.

The workers' greatest support has been their families. One young woman said that her husband had managed to get her a rose from the jail on their wedding anniversary and he had given it to their infant in court. Another said she would never leave her husband because he had always been honest and not even asked for dowry. But we could not interview them in any depth due to various constraints.

The burden on the families, however, has been too heavy for many. Few have anywhere to turn to in this time of desperation.

The workers tried to contact political parties in the hope that they would give them some help. Some of them reached out to Congress leaders, including Sonia Gandhi. She told them that she could not talk to 'guilty' people accused of murder. They got a similar reaction from the big trade unions, who said they would stand by 'innocent workers'. But the families of the workers have said all workers are innocent.

Of the thirteen workers who got life imprisonment, two have died. Jiya Lal died of cancer and Pawan Dahiya while working in his field when out on parole. Most of the others except one have got bail. We were able to talk to some of them, ask them what their plans were for their future, and the problems they faced after being in prison for ten years.

Out on Bail

Suresh Dhull

Former treasurer of the union; interviewed while he was in Delhi on 9 August 2022.

All of us who were in jail did learn a few things while in jail and are trying to build a new future. Some four or five of the prisoners with shorter sentences wanted to learn Japanese and the jail officials organized tuitions. One of them already knew a few words of Japanese and he learnt it well. Now he has landed a job in one of the vendor companies of Maruti and is in the managerial section. He recently went to the Maruti office to meet the managers in his official capacity!

I am doing a course in repairing air conditioners from Delhi. There is a lot of scope in it and I do hope to get some work soon. I also cultivate the land we have in the village.

One of our comrades, Sohan, is still in prison; two died while we were still in jail—Jiya Lal and Pawan Dahiya.

The rest, ten of us, are out on bail and we keep in touch with the union though we are not very active.

Amarjeet is running a garments shop in Rohtak and also a fast food shop.

Ajmer Singh has become a singer. He had a tumour in the brain, had surgery and has recovered. He is quite popular on YouTube. He has recorded and posted at least twelve songs on YouTube.

Sandeep Dhillon

Interviewed over the phone on 31 August 2022.

I got out on bail, perhaps on 24 January 2022. It is a relief to be at home and with my family. It feels very nice to be free. However, there are other problems. I had completed my MA in Sociology from IGNOU in jail but that degree is hardly likely to get me a job.

Now I face the problem of unemployment. I cannot find any job. I did not even bother to try and get a job in any big company. There is no hope of landing a job in the various companies because of my past. There is a crisis of employment here. I tried only in our local workshops but even there I could not find a job.

I have some land and am busy with agricultural work but there is hardly any profit in agriculture. You know that the farm sector is in deep crisis. But what choice do I have?

I still keep in touch with the union. Sometimes, those friends with whom I spent time in jail get together and we sit and chat. That is all there is to life now. There is no chance of my getting married. It is tough to find someone to agree to marry me, a dismissed worker who has been in jail.

Ram Meher

Interviewed over phone on 31 August 2022.

I am so relieved to be out of prison. I did an MA in prison, in Political Science. Yes, finally I had to read a lot. There were some boys with us who had learnt Japanese. I did not take any interest in that. I was always tense in prison, hoping all the time for bail but being continually disappointed. At last, we have got bail. I am not even thinking of the appeal pending in the High Court. Just enjoying my freedom. Those who learnt Japanese were those who were not accused of serious charges. They were among the 117 who got acquitted.

I am still looking for a job. Right now, I am cultivating the little plot of family land we have in the village. Hopefully, I will find some job, or later I may manage to set up some little business of my own.

I do keep in touch with the union and we sometimes meet to chat and have some fun together. I am taking each day as it comes.

Dhanraj Bhambi

Interviewed over the phone on 31 August 2022.

Not all of us are out on bail. Sohan is still in jail and we are concentrating hard on his case, trying our best to get him out too. We are all out now except him and he must be so lonely there.

I got out recently, on 23 April, and it feels so good to be home with my family.

I can't find a job. I went to a few vendor companies. They ask for a character certificate from the police station. The police will record my case and the pending appeal in the High Court. That certificate means: no job.

I cannot start my own business because I do not have the capital. I live in a small town in Chittorgarh district in Rajasthan. The family does have some land. We can only farm in the rainy season. This year, rains in our area have been plentiful so I am growing corn. Hopefully, I will get a good harvest.

I did BA from IGNOU in jail. I studied Political Science and History. That was good to pass the time. A jail is after all a jail. Whatever they may say about the facilities they give us, in the end it is a stressful place.

I have training from an ITI and can of course do a lot of repair work. But that is theory. In fact, I have been out of practice and out of touch with the mechanisms of cars for ten years now. Technology has changed so much in these ten years that I can hardly work those cars. Now I am thirty-eight. I cannot compete with the younger people who are at work in repair shops and workshops.

I am unmarried. The family did try a few times to find me a bride. However, when the family of the girl comes to meet us they do ask about my past. They find out about me and then they fold their hands, say, '*Namaste,*' and leave.

Yes, I am in touch with the union but just barely. This company is very powerful. They just opened a plant in Kharkhoda in Sonipat and the Prime Minister went to the inauguration. If they find out that we are still very active in the union I don't know what may happen to us. So I keep in touch with old friends but I am no longer active.

Somehow, I am making do, picking up the pieces of my life.

Sarabjeet Singh

Interviewed on phone on 31 August 2022.

I stepped out of prison on 1 March. Yes, it was the day our union was formed. It meant nothing more to me except that I was free. Still looking for a job. I have little hopes of landing one. I am looking for a job in some workshop to repair cars. I don't think I can get any other job now. I have no capital to set up any business. Not even a small shop. Sometimes we old friends get together and talk of old times and have some fun. I am on my way to such a get together now. However, it is not a union meeting. We are no longer active in the union, we just keep in touch. The union did a lot for us when we were in prison. It feels good to have friends.

Yogesh Kumar

Former secretary of the union; interviewed over phone on 31 August 2022.

I have a small cloth shop in Jhajjar now. There is hardly any business. The market is sluggish. I spent ten years in jail. In those years the union supported us. They also helped my family financially. I am so thankful to it. I have now taken a loan to set up this business but I can hardly break even. I have to repay the loan too. I have a small son. A family to take care of. We are making do somehow. The family never had any money. That is why I had become a worker, and now, we are in a financial crisis again.

I do keep in touch with our union friends. I am so happy to have such good friends. But I can't depend on their munificence now. I must fend for myself and I am trying my best. Things may change for the better.

Impact of the Convictions

The events of 18 July 2012 were not an isolated incident. There have been many other protests. Incidents of violent protests are in fact growing, according to one of the trade union leaders who wished to remain anonymous.

For instance, in Orient Craft in Gurgaon, workers set several cars on fire after one worker had suffered an electric shock in the factory and was seriously injured. This was in 2015, three years after the Manesar factory violence.

A trade union leader working in the automobile industry told us in an interview on 1 September 2022:

'After 18 July 2012, the management at the Maruti Suzuki factory was a little scared. Not just in Maruti Suzuki but in other factories too around the area, managements began to pay heed to workers. Many wage agreements were signed and workers' demands were met. In those years, workers would tell the management that they had better agree to their demands or "we will do a Maruti to you" (*Maruti kar denge*)!

'*Maruti kar denge*, or doing a Maruti was a common phrase in those days. Workers felt confident. The incident had a wide ranging impact on industrial relations. Many wage settlements were signed. One was signed in the Belsonica auto parts company. It is a fairly big vendor company with a chain of its own vendor companies.

'However, things changed after 2017 when thirteen workers of Maruti got life sentences. The management then began to threaten workers, saying, "We will do a Maruti to you." (*Hum tumhara Maruti kar denge.*) Now that the workers who had got life terms have managed to get bail the managers have begun to say, "The jail is empty!" Meaning we are preparing to send you to jail.'

That verdict of the court had a demoralizing effect on workers; it was an indication of how future struggle too would be criminalized.

The corporations have been innovative in devising ways to exploit the workers and the government has extended all help. For instance, categories of workers are made by which even though the workers may be doing the same work, one category gets much better paid while others get a pittance. This is not only an unfair labour practice but also a way of saving on wages.

There are five categories of workers now in the Maruti Suzuki factory in Manesar:

1. MA or Maruti Associate: These are permanent workers numbering about 1,822 workers. They get approximately Rs 50,000–70,000 a month.
2. CT or Company Trainee: They number only nineteen. They are actually promoted from or selected from among trainees and are on their way to becoming permanent workers. They earn Rs 29,000–31,000 a month with the hope of becoming permanent.
3. Apprentice: There are approximately 850 apprentices and they get Rs 17,500 per month. (Earlier, apprentices were employed for only one year as such and they got their diplomas only after they completed their apprenticeship. Now the Apprenticeship Act has been amended and apprentices can be taken on for three years.)
4. TW or Temporary Workmen: They do all the work that other regular workers do. They number approximately 4,000 and are paid Rs 25,000 per month.
5. CW or Casual Workmen: They number about 3,500 and they also do most of the work that regular workers do. They get Rs 23,500 per month.

Apart from these workers, there are other categories too. In the Gurgaon factory of Maruti Suzuki there are FTE workers, that is, Fixed Term Employees. They are employed for six months and then not employed again. In Maruti, there are about sixty FTE workers.

There are some government schemes for workers such as NEEM, or the National Employability Enhancement Scheme. Workers hired under this scheme get stipends which are less than minimum wages, but in a few weeks after they learn the work they are able to do the same work as the other workers though they do not get the commensurate wage.

There are factories in the automobile hub where they employ up to 300 workers under the NEEM scheme, while other factories still have contract workers who are paid just Rs 11,000 a month.

Apart from these categories of workers are the PMKVY or Pradhan Mantri Kaushal Vikas Yojana workers. They are given a bright red T-shirt with PMKVY emblazoned on the back. They do not get paid at all.

The difference in wages between the categories makes it even more difficult for unions to bring workers together for common struggles.

More than a hundred of the 546 permanent workers who were dismissed did not pursue their cases in the labour courts. One reason was that those workers who came from outside Haryana, for instance, Himachal Pradesh, could not afford to travel so far to attend the hearings. Besides, they had little hope of seeing justice done.

Over 300 of them are still doing the rounds of labour courts in the hope of getting justice. But the entire labour protection mechanism has been subverted to meet the needs of the corporations; and now the laws too are being changed.

The new categorization of workers at Maruti ought to be seen in the light of the drastic changes in labour laws made by the government in 2019 and 2020.

New Anti-Worker Labour Laws

Prime Minister Narendra Modi has proudly announced that India is undergoing the 'biggest labour reform in Independent India' by codifying twenty-nine laws into four codes. The government has brought out a pamphlet celebrating these 'reforms'.*

The People's Union for Democratic Rights (PUDR), which has documented the struggles of the workers at the Maruti Suzuki factories, came out with a critique of the new labour laws passed by the government. In a press release they say: 'The 75th Independence Day of India is practically the first for workers in the country without the official protection of crucial labour laws, like the Industrial Disputes Act, 1947, the Factories Act, 1948 among others.'

A joint action committee of all the central trade unions has been protesting against the new labour codes; more than 200 million workers went on a two-day strike for it in March 2022.

Older trade unions view the changes in labour legislation as an attempt to undo the struggle of the workers' movement that fought hard to win the rights that were enshrined in the earlier laws and in the vision of India contained in the Constitution.

The old labour laws were not ideal but they did offer a degree of protection to the workers and safeguarded their basic rights to organize and collectively bargain, and labour disputes were not criminalized.

What we have now are the four new labour codes: the Code on Wages, the Industrial Relations Code, the Code on Social Security and the Occupational Safety, Health and Working Conditions Code. Trade unions have called these

* Available online: https://labour.gov.in/sites/default/files/Labour_Code_Eng.pdf, last accessed 11 January 2023.

'The Anti-Labour Codes'—which have taken away the legal safeguards to protect workers. In fact they are laws to further the government's pre-existing policy of 'ease of doing business' and the government's Business Reforms Action Plan. The new labour codes will substantially dilute the collective bargaining power of trade unions.*

Many of the key provisions later enacted as part of the new labour codes had already been put into place through executive orders, especially during the COVID-19 pandemic.

There have been countrywide protests against the new anti-labour laws which, according to the unions, undermine workers' rights and criminalize trade union struggles through:

1. extensive discretionary powers to 'appropriate governments' to determine crucial aspects pertaining to labour;
2. reduction in liability of owners/management in case of safety violations;
3. dilution in enforcement mechanisms and employer liability, i.e. employers guilty of violating workers' labour rights will have impunity;
4. denial of access to courts, i.e. civil court jurisdiction barred for industrial disputes; replacement of labour courts by tribunals with one administrative and one judicial member, increasing executive control;
5. serious restrictions on the rights of workers to unionize, take collective action and seek legal redress against violations of their rights.

---

* See Jane Cox and Sanjay Singhvi, 'New Labour Codes dilute workers rights and collective bargaining', *The Leaflet*, 1 October 2020 (https://theleaflet.in/new-labour-codes-undo-the-law-on-workers-rights-and-collective-bargaining/, last accessed 11 January 2023).

Challenge Before Trade Unions

The change in the production process and now the repeal of labour laws poses a challenge to the trade union movement.

Workers are now being driven to take desperate measures. There have been reports of an increasing number of suicides by contract workers who have no jobs while the price of commodities continues to rise. The desperation, the helplessness and the injustice will, many predict, erupt again and this time it will be far more widespread; the violence will be ugly and the consequences far reaching.

This is not a voice of clairvoyance. Our study of the events of 18 July 2012 gives us a glimpse of things to come. The trade union movement faces the challenge of organizing workers in corporate India, which is motivated by profits at the cost of human lives, and where foreign investors are protected by the law at the expense of citizens of the country.

Turning down a plea for bail by jailed Maruti Manesar workers in May 2013, this is what a Punjab and Haryana High Court judge had to say: 'The incident is most unfortunate occurrence which has lowered the reputation of India in the estimation of the world. Foreign investors are not likely to invest the money in India out of fear of labour unrest.'*

The bail plea was rejected to ensure the safety of foreign investment.

* 'The struggle is still on: Life after Maruti's Manesar factory clash', *Business Standard*, 10 March 2017 (https://www.business-standard.com/article/companies/the-struggle-is-still-on-life-after-maruti-s-manesar-factory-clash-115111800857_1.html, last accessed 11 January 2023).

Afterword

The avalanches come. We should help dig each other out.

—Hafiz, Persian Sufi poet,
1325–1390

The Maruti Suzuki workers, both those who are still working at Manesar and Gurgaon, and those who were dismissed, continue their struggle for justice despite the odds stacked against them. Theirs is a truly heroic struggle. The young men involved and their families have shown courage, uprightness and self-sacrifice in their fight for the right to work and live in dignity and to ensure a secure future for their children. It was remarkable to see the spirit of some of the union leaders that we interviewed when they came out of jail after ten years. Almost all of them took the opportunity to study at the Indira Gandhi National Open University and have successfully graduated in social sciences; some have even got post-graduation degrees. Five workers, who were not union leaders, demanded to learn Japanese in jail. One of the workers, who had an operation to remove a brain tumour, is now once again singing for a living by posting his compositions on YouTube.

The young men exercised regularly and one of them excelled in yoga while others joined modern dance classes in the jail. But these degrees or skills are of little use to them. They cannot get jobs. Some have taken to farming on small plots, others have taken out loans to start small business. As one worker said in his interview: 'I am so happy to have such good friends. But I can't depend on their munificence now. I must fend for myself.'

These workers, most of them young men between the age of twenty to thirty joined the Maruti Suzuki factories after passing out of various ITIs. Their parents worked extremely hard, sacrificed comforts to ensure their boys (in this story, there are few girls and women) got a good education. The workers of Maruti Suzuki belonged to conservative families, rooted in a social milieu where hard work was a value to be cherished. They proudly wore the uniforms of the Japanese factory, even adjusted to the new concept of time and eagerly learnt new skills.

But then the workers saw how the management exploited them, how it cheated of them of just and fair wages. To begin with, they made many workers work for depressed wages in the name of training them or hiring them as apprentices even when they were doing the same work as the permanent workers. Most permanent workers in Manesar had worked as contract workers and therefore felt a deep solidarity with them. The Maruti Suzuki Workers' Union insisted on fighting for the rights of the contract workers, adding their issues to the union's charter of demands. It was a heroic act which went against the advice and warnings of larger national trade unions.

When the union leaders were put in jail, the dismissed workers formed a provisional committee and continued to organize meetings, *dharnas* and marches to focus public attention on the injustice being done. The co-ordination committee collected money from workers and unions all over India, not from foreign funded NGOs but from unions, to support the families of those sentenced to life imprisonment. They ensured that the families never felt isolated.

Now, the union in Manesar has decided to support the struggle of the dismissed workers. This has cemented the solidarity among the workers. The dismissed workers are fighting their cases in the labour court. They travel from their villages to Gurgaon to attend hearings, often to simply be given another date by the court. This charade has been masquerading for justice for the past ten years. One worker who won his case in Gurgaon lost it in the High Court.

One of the dismissed permanent workers, who is now a daily wage earner, says that on average there are three hearings in a year before the labour court. In addition, he must come to meet his lawyer too. Every visit to Gurgaon means losing three days' wages. On top of that are the expenses: he spends Rs 500 on the bus fare and then there is the expenditure on food. His stay would be free, luckily, because the workers would accommodate him. Of course, much time was lost on the case with the courts remaining closed for three years during the COVID-19 pandemic. Time was also lost when a judge was transferred. And sometimes things get delayed simply because the lawyers are on leave.

Many of the workers' families were stigmatized because their sons were in jail. People still strongly believe only criminals are convicted, not hard-working, honest workers.

The workers have knocked on the doors of every political party. The ruling party, the Bharatiya Janata Party is committed to supporting foreign corporations at the cost of the Indian citizen. But the Congress party, which accuses the BJP of being a '*suit-boot ki sarkar*', or a party of the rich, has itself shown utter indifference to the plight of these struggling workers.

Yadavendra Sharma, whose interview we have included in chapter nine of this book, told us that the workers had tried to contact Sonia Gandhi through contacts with Sheila Dikshit in June 2013. Sonia Gandhi told them that she could not help those in jail because they have done wrong, they have destroyed property worth crores of rupees. To Yadavendra and his friends, this was yet another example of the kind of political environment we live in.

In this book, we have not gone into the details of the criminal case or the proceedings before the labour courts, choosing instead to focus on what the workers told us themselves. But the proceedings show the extent of injustice done to the workers, how the bias against workers is built into the legal system and institutionalized by bench and bar. The media too, with the honourable exceptions, has seen the entire trade union movement and the Maruti Suzuki workers' struggles from the lens of the ruling class.

There is, thus, a need to go to the other side of appearance and understand and perceive the corporate world from the vantage point of the workers. At least, in a welfare state, the ruling class recognizes the need to protect workers from extreme exploitation. But now the welfare state seems to be rapidly giving way to corporate rule.

Indo-Japanese relations have been growing stronger. In 2006, Indian Prime Minister Manmohan Singh's visit to Japan culminated in the signing of the 'Joint Statement Towards Japan-India Strategic and Global Partnership', and in 2014, during Japanese Prime Minister Shinzo Abe's visit to India, both countries agreed to update their partnership to a 'Special Strategic and Global Partnership'. The question is: what impact will this growing friendship have on ordinary citizens who work in Japanese enterprises?

It is significant that Japanese trade union members gave a statement of solidarity with the Maruti Suzuki workers' struggles. Perhaps the basis of this solidarity will grow stronger in the years to come. For the time being, the workers have understood that they must rely on their own strength and the power of their organization. When they could not go near their factory because there was a curfew order which prohibited gatherings outside the premises, the dismissed workers came together and sat on a *dharna* outside the district magistrate's office. The provisional committee of the union provided a delicious *pulao* with soya bean nuggets and *ghiya chane ki daal.* The workers shared their meal with passersby!

Dr B.R. Ambedkar recognized that the purpose of constitutions has been to limit state power in order to preserve the freedom of the individual. Ambedkar argued that fundamental rights must 'eliminate the possibility of the more powerful having the power to impose arbitrary restraints on the less powerful by withdrawing from the control he has over the economic life of the people'.

The purpose of labour laws was to mitigate the imbalance of power between capitalists and labour. They ought to aim to secure the 'rights to life, liberty, and the pursuit of happiness', in both the public and the private spheres. He said: 'A labourer not only wants equality but he needs liberty also, it is really intolerable and detrimental where system proposes equality but denies liberty. The constitution in which equilibrium, of the both is established...is the ideal constitution for the labourers.'

Today, Babasaheb Ambedkar's name is being evoked in a distorted way, to destroy the edifice of the labour protection laws he built to protect the workers.

The trade union movement is now faced with the challenge of fighting ruthless corporate power with successive governments stripping workers of their rights by making the rights guaranteed to them under the Indian Constitution meaningless. Workers are being disenfranchised.

Bibliography

Aiyar, Pallavi, *Orienting an Indian in Japan*, HarperCollins, 2021

Bhargava, R.C., with Seetha, *The Maruti Story: How a Public Sector Company Put India on Wheels*, HarperCollins, 2013

Chan, Jenny, Mark Selden, and Pun Ngai, *Dying for an iPhone: Apple, Foxconn, and The Lives of China's Workers*, Haymarket Books, 2020

Mehri, Darius, *Notes from Toyota-land: An American Engineer in Japan*, Cornell University Press, 2005

Krishnamurthy, V., *At the Helm: A Memoir*, HarperCollins, 2014

Morris-Suzuki, Tessa, and Seiyama Takuro, eds., *Japanese Capitalism since 1945: Critical Perspectives*, ME Sharpe Inc., 1989

Motohashi, Kazuyuki, *Global Business Strategy: Multinational Corporations Emerging into Global Markets*, Springer, 2015

Nowak, Jörg, *Mass Strikes and Social Movements in Brazil and India: Popular Mobilisation in the Long Depression*, Springer, 2019

Takehiko, Hashimoto, and Kuriyama Shigehisa, eds., *The Birth of Tardiness: The Formation of Time Consciousness in Modern Japan*, 2002

Reports, Monographs and Articles

Amit, and Nayanjyoti, 'Changes in Labour Regimes and Challenges to Collective Bargaining: A Study of the Gurgaon-Neemrana Industrial Belt in the DMIC', State of Working India, Background Paper No. 18, Centre for Sustainable Employment, Azim Premji University, May 2018

'A Pre-Decided Case: A Critique of the Maruti Judgment of 2017', People's Union for Democratic Rights (PUDR), 2018

'Driving Force: Labour Struggles and Violation of Rights in Maruti Suzuki India Ltd', PUDR, 2013

'Freewheelin' Capital: Illegal Dismissals, Forced 'Voluntary' Retirement & Contractualisation of Workforce at Maruti Udyog Limited', PUDR, 2007

'Hard Drive: Working Conditions and Workers Struggle at Maruti', (PUDR), 2001

'Maruti to Mafia: The Sanjay Gandhi Story', Mainstream Publications, 1977

'Merchants of Menace: Repressing Workers in India's New Industrial Belt: Violations of Workers' and Trade Union Rights at Maruti Suzuki India Ltd.', International Commission for Labor Rights, 2013

Nowak, Jörg, 'Strikes and Labor Unrest in the Automobile Industry in India: The Case of Maruti Suzuki India Limited', *WorkingUSA: The Journal of Labor and Society*, vol. 19 (September 2016)

Sen, Ratna, 'Industrial Relations at Maruti-Suzuki', *The Indian Journal of Industrial Relations*, vol. 47, no. 2 (October 2011)

Shibata, Yoshio, 'Governing Employees: A Foucauldian Analysis of Deaths from Overwork in Japan', *Global Asia Journal*, Paper 12, 2012 (https://digitalcommons.pace.edu/cgi/viewcontent.cgi?article=1011&context=global_asia_journal, last accessed 11 January, 2023)

Verma, Priti, 'Maruti Manesar Violence: What Went Wrong?: A Case Study (With Teaching Notes)', in *Case Studies in Management*, edited by Agarwal Nayak and Geetu Wahee, Bharti Publications, 2014

'Workers Autonomy Strikes in India: Maruti Suzuki Strike at Manesar (June, September, October 2011)', Mouvement Communiste & Kolektivně Proti Kapitalu, Belgium, May 2012

'मारुति सुज़ुकी के मज़दूरों का संघर्ष, सबक और चुनौतियां', इंकलाबी मज़दूर केंद्र, 2015

Acknowledgements

This book would not have been possible without the active cooperation of the workers of Maruti industry, both from its Gurgaon and Manesar plants. Especially those who were on parole and still found time to meet and talk about their struggle. Many thanks to all of them whose voices you will hear in these pages.

I am in debt to the trade union leaders named and those who chose to remain unnamed for generously sharing their experience and helping me get in touch with the workers. I hope this book will not disappoint them.

Special thanks to Ravindra Goel, retired lecturer and activist from Delhi University, who accompanied me to interview some of the workers in the beginning and also invited them to his house. His hospitality and his availability for any help till ill health made him inactive got the book started.

Gautam Majumdar, you have been a true friend, providing contacts and hospitality while I chatted with a former employee in your drawing room and also for hunting out other contacts willing to talk.

Some retired managers of Maruti have tied my hands by not allowing to me to thank them by name but they should know that I really appreciate their contribution to my understanding of the issues involved.

My thanks to Vrinda Grover for giving me time to explain

the criminal cases although, unfortunately, we decided not to deal with that aspect of the workers' struggle; perhaps one day we will.

I must also mention here that despite several attempts Suparna Dev, the wife of Awanish Dev, the manager who died of suffocation in the Manesar plant refused to talk. She would break down crying and I owe her an apology for reminding her of what must have been a traumatic even in her life.

Many friends and family members helped with contacts and material. My sister-in-law, Santosh, organized and enabled a very important interview in her house. Many thanks to her. Rukmani Anandani, my sister-in-law Anu Satyal and my brother Anirudh Deshpande must be mentioned for the contacts and material they provided.

Without Nandita Haksar I would not have been able to put together the book and give it its present shape. Her partner Sebastian supported us through the difficult process of editing and re-organizing the book.

My partner Anand drove me to many places for the interviews, sat in on them patiently and also got some of his friends to walk me through the management system of a modern factory. I wish he was here to see the book in print. He said he wanted this book to be a counter to R.C. Bhargava's Maruti story. I hope this book is what he wanted it to be.

ANJALI DESHPANDE

It has been wonderful to reconnect with Anjali and work together after a gap of some forty years. All the interviews, without exception have been conducted by her. She had also done the research and gathered so much material that it had overwhelmed her. My contribution was putting it in some order.

I would like to thank the Maruti Suzuki workers and trade union leaders for trusting me to write their story even before we met.

Anjali joins me in thanking our editor, Nazeef Mollah, whose careful and meticulous editing has made the book much more readable. We would also like to thank Maithili Doshi for her cover design. Our thanks to Ravi Singh for his enthusiastic support from the start.

I must mention that my awareness of the Maruti project began back in 1975 when my father, P.N. Haksar, who had been Prime Minister Indira Gandhi's advisor, objected to it. He was victimized for raising objections. This book vindicates many of his objections.

And my heartfelt thank you to Sebastian, my friend and partner without whose support I would find writing very difficult.

NANDITA HAKSAR

Appendix 1

Maruti to Mafia

THE SANJAY GANDHI STORY

by

ANALYST

MAINSTREAM PUBLICATION

Re 1

In view of the great demand of the article "The Sanjay Gandhi Story," published in *Mainstream* of March 26, 1977, it is being reprinted here in pamphlet form.

First published in *Mainstream*,
March 26, 1977

Published in pamphlet form
April 2, 1977

Second Reprint April 7, 1977

Third Reprint April 11, 1977

Fourth Reprint April 18, 1977

Fifth Reprint May 2, 1977

Printed at Shaheed Prakashan Press, A-794, Amar Puri
Pahar Ganj, New Delhi-110 055

THE SANJAY GANDHI STORY

Maruti to Mafia

THE story of a spoilt child of the Prime Minister of India, petulantly insisting on making a car which he could not produce, provides the clue to many of the major decisions — and mistakes — by the Government of India in the last five years. It is an extraordinary story of a youngman's obsession about car, derailing a mother holding one of the highest positions in the world of politics.

First came the acquisition of land to build the car factory. The land was acquired displacing a large number of poor and middle-class families who were paid scanty compensation for the land that they were forced to leave. And this huge plot is in the vicinity of Defence installations, a location normally denied for any civilian enterprise. In all this, the then Chief Minister of Haryana helped with his strong-arm methods. Thus was laid the foundation for the emergence of Bansi Lal on the national scene, with his meteoric rise under Emergency.

But a car, even a small car — smaller than Volks-wagon — cannot be built without there being a modern assembly line. That meant capital resources of at least Rs 50 to 60 crores. This amount cannot be raised without a detailed project report. The public issue of equity shares is possible only on the basis of a project report, and such a project report is required also to get loans from banks and from public financial institutions.

Sanjay Gandhi, however, is not capable of producing such a project report. He cannot even design a car engine, and without an engine, a car, unfortunately, cannot run. For this, Sanjay cannot be blamed. Because, he does not have the mental equipment and technical knowledge of how to build a car engine, not to speak of a whole car. Many reports have come out in newspapers and magazines in the last two years about his training in the Rolls Royce factory in Britain. What is not advertised is that he did not finish his course there, and came back home without training, and nobody, not even his mother, could persuade him to go back to Rolls Royce to finish his course of training.

Incidentally, this is a noteworthy trait in Sanjay's character: he cannot complete a task which is difficult. As a boy he was sent by his parents to India's first public school, the Doon School at Dehra Dun, where the rich sent their sons for schooling. At the Doon School, Sanjay earned the distinction of not having been able to finish his course, as he was expelled because of his misbehaviour and rowdy conduct. Rowdyism is, in a sense, part of his character.

As a schoolboy on holiday, Sanjay was involved in Delhi along with some of his young friends in car lifting and going in for boisterous drives; once the car was smashed up as the boys were drunk and an attendant at a petrol-pump service station where they had forcibly taken petrol without payment, was badly hurt. The matter came up before police but it was hushed up because the children of VIPs were involved. Sanjay and a friend of his were packed off next morning to Kashmir: this other friend was badly wounded in the car smash-up, leaving permanent injury on his brain. He is the son of Mohammad Yunus who, under Emergency, had become the Prime Minister's Special Envoy.

Recently, in a press interview to Uma Vasudev (who had written a fat biography of Indira Gandhi and is known as a close friend of Mohammad Yunus), Sanjay has denied about this car theft and smash-up pleading that at that time he was in Kashmir. But the fact is that he was hurriedly flown out to Kashmir to hush up the scandal. Many respectable personalities can vouch for this. The question came up in Parliament and the Government could make no convincing denial, but the matter was not pursued out of personal deference to Indira Gandhi.

Let us come back to the story of the car manufacture. Although he is incapable of himself producing a car, this spoilt child of an indulgent mother, insisted on becoming a car magnate. This was his childhood dream, since as a child, he had a little toy car and he was keen on growing up to be a motor-car manufacturer. Recently, Mohammad Yunus, writing an article flattering Sanjay on his birthday, referred to this childhood dream of car-making.

Sanjay spent some time in a junk workshop handling car parts, hoping that he would somehow set up something that would run. This junk workshop where parts of old or stolen cars used to be stored, was owned by one Arjan Das, a well-known leader of toughs of Delhi. Arjan Das became a close friend of Sanjay, and as a reward, he became a Congress member of the Delhi Metropolitan Council. During Emergency, Arjan Das became a powerful person, "controlling" several markets, extorting the shopkeepers. With Sanjay's protection, he became so bold that his toughs were reported to have blackmailed many shopkeepers and traders in Delhi and this way several lakhs of rupees were pocketed. Arjan Das is a typical example of a public figure under the Sanjay *raj*.

Sanjay's ambition of becoming a car magnate naturally could not be satisfied in Arjan Das's junk workshop. So, instead of being able to make a car, he decided to set up a car factory on the Gurgaon Road, near Palam airport, on the land provided by Bansi Lal by evicting a large number of people. Building construction in the huge, high-fenced, compound started with the help of some of his pals, Raunaq Singh, Sagar Suri and a few other adventurers who were clever enough to calculate that if they could cosy up to the Prime Minister's son, they would have easy access to the seat of power.

This was the beginning of the Maruti. The money that Sanjay and his cronies could collect could not amount to much. The declared statement of accounts of the Company toted up to only Rs Two crores by way of equity shares. But almost an equal amount was shown in the accounts as having been subscribed by the so-called car dealers. The question that is worth investigating is whether the money shown under this head, actually came from car dealers; this would be clear if one looked into the list of names and addresses and assets of these so-called car dealers. What is known is that the bulk of this big amount had come from the siphoning of black-money collected in the name of the Congress party. And this operation, pouring in the Congress party's black-money stock into the Maruti, was done with the knowledge and consent of Indira Gandhi.

More money was collected for the Maruti from other sources. By blatant pressure tactics, big loans were obtained from the nationalised banks. The largest chunk was extorted from the Central Bank of India. Soon a point was reached when the banking system including the Reserve Bank of India, could not go on coughing out money to a non-existent car project. The Reserve Bank of India told the nationalised banks not to advance further money to the Maruti, as this would create a financial crisis.

At this stage, the Birlas entered the field. There were, for instance, a number of investments in the Maruti in the name of a large number of small firms; in effect, these were mostly *benami* firms of the Birlas. And day by day, the Birla hold on the Maruti, on Sanjay Gandhi, on the power-centre itself, began to grow. It is not just an accident that in this very period covering the last four years, the Birlas have emerged as the Number One business house in India, both in terms of assets and profits.

But the young man was in a hurry. His imperious nature pampered by the mother's blind support, could not tolerate the restrictions laid down by the Finance Minister, nor the veto of the Reserve Bank, more specially its Deputy Governor, Dr R.K. Hazari, who was at that time in charge of the banking system under the Reserve Bank.

Taneja, the Chairman of the Central Bank, was worried at the persistent demands of Sanjay Gandhi for more loans. He was the first to fall; he was sacked despite the protest deputations by both the Bank's directors and employees, to the Prime Minister.

The Reserve Bank itself was put in charge of an amiable insurance man, K.R. Puri, with no knowledge whatsoever of the banking system but endowed with the virtue of subservience to Sanjay Gandhi. Finance Minister Subramaniam resisted his appointment, and a ding-dong battle followed for months, and ultimately the Finance Minister lost and Sanjay's choice, K.R. Puri, was appointed the Governor of the Reserve Bank of India. Dr Hazari, with all his distinguished record, was moved out to an insignificant assignment, and in his place, a pliable Income-Tax Officer was made the Deputy Governor of the Reserve Bank with the charge of the banking operation in the country.

When the Emergency came, the banking system including the Reserve Bank of India, had fallen into the hands of Sanjay Gandhi. And during Emergency, the entire nationalised banking system was mercilessly abused to benefit Sanjay Gandhi's corrupt friends — be they the Kapadias of the National Rayon, Alok Jain of the Sahu Jains, and, of course, the ever-present Birlas. Only a detailed enquiry into the lendings made during the Emergency can reveal the havoc played by Sanjay Gandhi and his gang with the entire fiscal and credit system of this country.

With all this, it was only a small step to deal the finishing blow to the Finance Minister. Overnight, important Departments of his Ministry — Banking, Income-Tax, Customs, Industrial Development Bank, Credit Policy — were taken out of his charge by the Prime Minister and put in charge of a novice, a political adventurer with roots nowhere, having no standing except as a lackey of Sanjay Gandhi. This was Pranab Kumar Mukherji, who was known not only in his home State of West Bengal, but in the business and financial circles all over India, as a servile waiter of Sanjay Gandhi.

A glaring example of how blatantly the banking system has been subverted during Emergency to enrich Sanjay and his gang, is provided by the case of Talwar, the Chairman of the State Bank of India, who is distinguished as the only professional banker in the country. To remove Talwar, who became a hindrance to getting indiscriminate and irregular loans and credit from the State Bank, a law was hurriedly enacted to enable the Government of India to dismiss any disobliging chairman of a nationalised bank by giving him three months' notice.

In his own way, Sanjay Gandhi is a whole-hogger. He knows he is too deeply involved in financial irregularities to permit any loopholes to put him into trouble. For this, Pranab Mukherji was not sufficient protection. Because a minister, after all, did not himself conduct tax raids, and Sanjay and his gang with their ill-gotten money needed protection from such raids. So, from the Income-Tax Department some of the best officers were shunted out and in their place, the corrupt ones had been installed. And on top of them all was S.R. Mehta, made the Chairman of the Board of Revenue, who had been awarded with a Padma Bhushan, which Sanjay Gandhi would certainly recommend. One of S.R. Mehta's great achievements was the virtual sabotage of the Commission to enquire into the irregularities of the Birlas who were the chief patron and partner-in-corruption of Sanjay Gandhi.

Sanjay Gandhi boasted that he was a firm champion of free-booting private enterprise. He had made no secret of his philosophy of a merchant-adventurer. In his first press interview after Emergency, he attacked the nationalisation of the coal industry which liberated lakhs of coalmine workers from the horrible condition, worse than that of animals, under which the private coalmine owners had kept them.

6

But Sanjay Gandhi was callous about the inhuman plight of such colliery workers: he enjoyed the company of corrupt businessmen.

While the Government had to acknowledge the high level of industrial performance of the public sector in contrast to the poor record of the private business houses — particularly those who were closely connected with Sanjay Gandhi — the manner in which Emergency had been used to disrupt and undermine the public sector, betrayed Sanjay's hand. The entire system of recruitment to the top executive posts in the public sector was changed overnight. Instead of the very distinguished recruitment board under Rajadhyakshya, a new board had been set up under the chairmanship of a venal civil servant, and included among its members two other with corrupt and pliant records.

This had caused widespread consternation in the entire public sector organisation, particularly among its top managemant at a time when the public sector had been showing creditable results.

Even in the matter of sale of valuable public-sector products, Sanjay Gandhi and the clique round him here made good money. In the newspapers it was widely publicised that the Government had sold a large quantity of steel as export to foreign countries. What was not mentioned to the public was that out of this export of steel, a good amount had been sold to an Indian company based in London. This company was reported to have given huge amounts of money as bribe to Sanjay and his nominees. out of the profit they had made out of this deal in Indian steel export. This secret and corrupt deal was done with the knowledge of the Steel Minister while the then Commerce Minister was equally reputed to be an accomplice of many of Sanjay Gandhi's underhand business deals.

His another Doon School pal, Kamal Nath, had made piles through the dealings of his EMC enterprise with the West Bengal State Electricity Board, getting contracts worth huge amounts for which no ten der was called, nor the prescribed rules and procedures followed. This Kamal Nath succeeded, through the good offices of Mohammad Yunus, in securing a huge contract from a UAE country, bypassing normal Government regulations.

Step by step, everything flowing out of Sanjay Gandhi's obsession of Maruti, other developments have flowed to poison and destroy the whole system of the Government.

Civil Service had to be terrorised and made subservient to Sanjay Gandhi. The established practice of the Government until Emergency was that the appointment, transfer, promotion of Joint Secretaries, Deputy Secretaries and other executive officers of the Government of India were made by a Senior Establishment Board of the Cabinet Secretariat. But this was usurped by Sanjay Gandhi's man, R.K. Dhavan, a corrupt officer in the Prime Minister's House and a distant-cousin of the notorious Yashpal Kapur, whom he replaced when Kapur was made Rajya Sabha Member. Dhavan acted along with a few corrupt civil servants, including N.K. Singh (the Special Private Secretary and confidante of Commerce Minister, D.P. Chattopadhyay). In this way, practically all the appointments of civil servants was made contingent on the confession of personal loyalty to Sanjay Gandhi.

Very early in recent history, just before Emergency, one of the most capable civil servants was summarily dismissed at almost half an hour's notice. N.K. Mukherji was the Home Secretary; he was replaced by a pliant civil servant imported from Rajasthan, by the name of Khurana, who qualified himself for the post by virtue of being a close acquaintance of Sanjay's in-laws.

With Khurana had come a police officer from Haryana, the nominee of Bansi Lal. This man, Bhinder, wielded real power as the Deputy Inspector General of Police. The real Minister in charge of Home was not Home Minister Brahmananda Reddy, but Om Mehta (Minister of State) who was close to Sanjay.

It was at Sanjay's insistence Bansi Lal was brought from Haryana and made Defence Minister. He brought with him Misra as his Joint Secretary. This man had become all-powerful in Defence Ministry.

In the Ministry of Information and Broadcasting, I.K. Gujral was removed as Minister immediately after Emergency, on Sanjay's direct interference. Vidya Charan Shukla who became Minister of Information and Broadcasting, is a versatile man with disreputable extra-mural activities. His corruption was sky-high and he used his strong-arm methods to persecute the press, destroyed Samachar and made AIR and Doordarshan the laughing stock advertising Sanjay Gandhi. He had brought with him two police officers into the Ministry, one of whom had been made Additional Secretary. This man was in Central Intelligence in the sixties and was reported to have had CIA training.

Mohammad Yunus, who was made the Prime Minister's Special Envoy under Emergency, is very close to Sanjay. Yunus's son and Sanjay are both failed students from Doon School. It was in Yunus's house that Sanjay's marriage was celebrated. Yunus had written articles praising Sanjay. This Yunus was also an important figure interfering in foreign affairs, Information Ministry affairs and in the Delhi Administration.

It was Yunus who virtually controlled the Samachar, the news agency which now monopolised all news suppressing the old news agencies. Yunus had put R.K. Nigam as the Executive Director of Samachar; this Nigam was a flatterer of Yunus, and had no knowledge of newspaper or news agency work. Being the retainer of the Court, Yunus was made the man incharge of the Indian section of the nonaligned newspool business.

Yunus and Shukla ran a new organisation set up under Emergency called The Communication Centre India, and composed of pliable members. This organisation had got grants from the Government running into lakhs and had other sources of revenue, all with the knowledge of the Sanjay clique. This organisation spent money on subsidising their favourite journals. This organisation also sent out Sanjay's favourites for tours abroad on the plea of "explaining" the situation in India. Actually, this organisation is believed to be a sort of under-cover outfit for Sanjay Gandhi's clique in foreign countries, and has handsome resources at its disposal.

So, in all key sectors of the Government, ruled Sanjay and his clique.

The Finance Ministry was managed by Pranab Mukherji, K. R. Puri in Reserve Bank, S. R. Mehta in Income Tax.

The Commerce Ministry was in the hands of D. P. Chattopadhyay and N. K. Singh. The Steel Ministry was controlled by Sanjay through Chandrajit Yadav, whose rapport with Sanjay bore the stamp of his genius.

The Home Ministry was managed by Om Mehta, Khurana, Home Secretary, while the Central Bureau of Investigation was in charge of D. Sen, who also took orders from Sanjay.

The Defence Ministry was managed by Bansi Lal, Misra and J. B. Patnaik (Deputy Minister) who was Sanjay's agent and conducted the operation in Orissa for the removal of Nandini Satpathy from Chief Ministership. It is to be noted that the previous Defence Secretary, Govind Narain, was not given extension because he objected to commission agents infiltrating into Defence Ministry purchases. Most of these commission agents were Sanjay's nominees.

Among other Ministers under direct control of Sanjay, the most conspicuous was Raghuramaiah, known for his corruption. It was Raghuramaiah who at a public meeting in Andhra swore allegiance like a bonded serf, declaring that he, having served two generations of the Nehrus, pledged his service to the third, that is, Sanjay. He put Sanjay in touch with rich tobacco merchants of Andhra. Another Sanjay man was H.K.L. Bhagat, a worthless Minister who had played many antics in Delhi.

An example of how operations were conducted by Sanjay Gandhi and his gang was provided by the case of Delhi Administration. His early exercise in power began in 1972 when he started interfering in the posting of Station House Officers in many police stations under Delhi Administration. This brought Sanjay into conflict with the then Lt Governor of Delhi, Baleshwar Prasad, who was forced to retire even before his term was over. In his place, a spineless civil servant of no distinction was inducted; the new Lt Governor Kishan Chand had been supplied by Sanjay with an adviser, Navin Chawla, a pathological case of an administration officer with total subservience to Sanjay Gandhi personally.

The Commissioner of Delhi, B.R. Tamta, carried out all orders of Sanjay Gandhi and the Delhi Development Authority was monopolised by Jagmohan, responsible for the entire demolition operation of poor resident's huts and tenements and also of shopkeepers in Karolbagh. Chief Executive Councillor Radha Raman had reduced himself to a flattering sycophant of Sanjay Gandhi.

It is in Delhi that one can get an idea of the type of oppression that the whole country would have had to suffer if Sanjay Gandhi and his clique were allowed to continue. The jhuggis of the poor were demolished in monsoon, and this operation was conducted by Sanjay p rsonally, together with Jagmohan, Tamta and Yunus. Men, women and children were herded like cattle and sent off miles away in bogus colonies where nothing was ready to house them. They were ruined both economically and physically and many had turned paupers.

When the people, both Hindus and Muslims, resisted as at the Turkman Gate area (where Sanjay's car was once attacked and he fled under police protection), the Border Security Force was called and they indulged in indiscriminate firing under curfew where nearly 200 were killed.

Side by side went the drive for forcible sterilisation.

Young men picked up from cinema houses, teashops and bazars were rounded up and sterilised. Many died as a result of infection. In this work, Sanjay Gandhi appointed as his lieutenant, Ruksana Sultana, a social butterfly of dubious reputation. She was made the heroine of the sterilisation drive. Subhadra Joshi, the well-known Congress leader who protested, was turned out of the area and earned the displeasure of the Prime Minister.

The Old Delhi is largely populated by Muslims, and Sanjay seemed to have had a particular grouse against the Muslim community. He has expressed his theory among his friends that if the Muslim resistance could be broken, then others would also cow down. So, it was not only in Old Delhi but in the entire UP, his vicious sterilisation campaign continued. Many brutal incidents occurred as in Moradabad district, Sultanpur, Agra and the worst of all in Muzaffarnagar where police atrocities and firing were on a scale larger than Jallianwala Bagh. It is known that there were hundreds of cases of police firing in UP only to enforce sterilisation drive, mainly among the poor people.

Middle-class employees in Delhi and UP also suffered, as no promotion, or ration card, or even licences and loans would be granted without sterilisation certificates. It was a patent lie that the Indira Government had uttered that there was no compulsion in the sterilisation programme.

Sanjay Gandhi made the Youth Congress his political platform. Overthrowing its leader, Priyaranjan Das Munshi, he captured it with the blessings of his mother. He turned it into a variant of the Brown Shirts — no ideology, only loyalty to the leader.

Since it became known to Congress leaders that Sanjay was being groomed by his mother, many started paying court to him. The Chief Ministers of Punjab, Haryana, Rajasthan, Madhya Pradesh, Uttar Pradesh and Bihar, behaved like his door-mats, demeaning themselves in the eyes of their own people.

Those Chief Ministers who refused to kowtow were removed. First came Bahuguna and then Nandini Satpathy. Siddhartha Shankar Ray was almost in dog house, but the resistance of the youth in West Bengal scuttled the toppling game there.

In Maharashtra, Chief Minister Chavan took him as his master and paraded him at different centres. Sanjay Gandhi had, in this fashion, discredited the Congress in the eyes of the people particularly in the Northern and Western States.

Sanjay Gandhi was not only against the declared national policies, such as nationalisation of basic industries. He had amassed huge amounts of money through loot and foreign business connections.

Maruti itself could produce no car. So, it went to assembly of road rollers in collusion with a well-known swindler, Wahi of UPC Corporation. This man, married to a rich Swiss heiress, had cheated the Government of India for Rs 2 crores about which there was CBI investigation and his passport was impounded. Today, Wahi was a close confidante of Sanjay Gandhi. These road-rollers were forcibly sold to Government Departments like the PWD and Defence.

Maruti had also started body-building of buses. This was merely carpentry work, but the State Government like Haryana, Rajasthan, Punjab, UP, Madhya Pradesh were forced to place the body-building of State Roadways buses to Maruti without any calling of tender, violating all the rules of the Government.

Now, Sanjay Gandhi had turned openly to foreign collaboration. The giant US company, International Harvester had negotiated with Maruti which had become its Indian agent. The Government of India was negotiating with Poland for setting up a harvester manufacturing unit in public sector; but the agreement with Poland was not signed because Sanjay's Maruti had taken the agency of selling the harvester of the US company, International Harvester.

The Defence Ministry under Bansi Lal decided to take heavy vehicle trucks fron Maruti which would produce these in collaboration with International Harvester. This was being done in violation of the Government rules for foreign collaboration. The International Harvester Company had openly stated that the Maruti "sought us out" offering collaboration.

Also, it is known that two European aircraft manufacturing companies, a Western electronic company and a big Japanese company were negotiating for collaboration with Maruti which was ready to act as their Indian agent. The Boeing aircraft company was mentioned as one of the companies with which Maruti was negotiating for agency.

Another American Company, The Piper Aircraft, had signed agreement with Maruti which would act as its Indian agent. Sanjay Gandhi himself had disclosed this in an interview published in *New York Times* of January 11, 1977. It is now known that the State Governments and public sector companies had been asked to buy Piper Aircraft for their executive purposes.

The Maruti had recently signed agreements with West German companies M.A.N. and DEMAG for building heavy trucks and cranes. Also, a Maruti Aviation Company was being set up to take over some of the lines now run by the Indian Airlines and Air India.

The Pure Drinks (Private) Ltd., "one of the franchised bottlers of Coca Cola in India", was close to Sanjay Gandhi. Its man, Charanjit Singh, had got the Congress ticket for Lok Sabha from South Delhi. Charanjit Singh acted as Sanjay Gandhi's go-between with many foreign companies collecting commission on sales to the Government of India departments. Since Emergency, Sanjay's rate of commission on all important foreign purchases, particularly of the Defence Ministry, was at least one per cent on all deals.

Washington Post of November 10, 1976, with dateline New Delhi, quoted a man with good contacts in Government of India: "The public believes a vast swindle is going on. The bureaucrats say they can do nothing. Sanjay calls up Ministers and Secretaries and says, 'give the contract to so and so'. He has Ministerial sanction and the Prime Minister supports him. Whether it is Defence Ministry contracts or civil service appointments, the hand of Sanjay is visible."

The most modest estimate that could be made of Sanjay's loot in collusion with his gang including Bansi Lal and Yunus (who handled Arab contracts) would be a fantastic sum, running into tens of crores.

For a long time, many people wondered how Sanjay could do all this without the help of his mother, the Prime Minister. For a time, many felt that possibly this was a case of a mother's totally blind affection and attachment for her son. But with every day that passed during Emergency, it became clear that there was something more than that until Indira Gandhi herself revealed first at Chandigarh Congress (January 1976), then at Delhi AICC (June 1976) and finally at Gauhati AICC (November 1976) how totally she backed Sanjay Gandhi in all his nefarious deeds. She said repeatedly in clear, unambiguous language — even after the announcement of the election — that she subscribed to Sanjay Gandhi's outlook and activity. She had said that she firmly believed that it was not the people of India who had given her unbounded love, affection and support in 1971-72, but this little darling son of her who saved her in 1975, and so she had paid tributes not only to him but to his close comrades-in-thuggery such as Bansi Lal and Mohammad Yunus.

Through blackmail by CBI and income-tax; by open terror through para-military forces like CRP, BSF and other armed gangs under Home Ministry; through bribery and coercion of mass media and debasement of AIR, TV and Samachar; by destroying the political organisation of the Congress; an edifice of tyranny was being built. The

Emergency was used as a cover for this grand design.

It was left to the people of this great country to destroy this edifice built around Sanjay Gandhi and protected by Indira Gandhi. This country would never tolerate the installation of a corrupt clique running the vast machinery of Government, subverting democracy and freedom which had been won with blood and toil of the millions of Indians.

Appendix 2

Press Note

Subject: The Pending Ownership Rights of Flats/Land of the Maruti Employees Co-Operative Housing Building Society Ltd. since 2010 at Bhondsi, Gurugram, Haryana.

Most Respected Sir,

Regarding the above stated subject we most humbly wish to submit the following facts and issues for your kind perusal.

1. Maruti Udyog Ltd./Maruti Suzuki India Ltd. (The Company) had purchased approx 107 Acres of land at Bhondsi, Gurugram in 1989 for the purpose of an employee's housing building project. on more than six fold.

2. In 1990 a Maruti Employees Co-Operative Housing Building Society (The Society) was formed and a loan was taken from HDFC Bank. The Society paid the total price of the land in 1992.

3. The Society constructed 916 flats, 1 shopping complex, 1 hospital and other infrastructural facilities in an area of approx 53.5 Acres in 1994. The Maruti Employees Education Trust (MEET) had constructed 2 School buildings on approx 2.5 acres and approx 8 acres respectively and remaining approx. 43 acres of vacant land remained in the possession of the Company.

4. The loan taken by the Society from HDFC Bank had been paid back by the Society members in 2001, 2003 (VRS employees) and by 2010 (All other employees) completely and the company had issued No Dues Certificates to the members but still the land has not been transferred in the name of the Society and due to this the registry of flats has been pending.

5. In the last few years some meetings have been held between the Company and the Society to resolve the issue but nothing significant has come out mainly because of 1) The lack of financial explanation/ the audit 2) Clearance of the land titles/issues, which needs to be done by the Company.

6. This issue of pending ownership has been also brought to the notice of the Honorable Chief Minister of Haryana in the District Grievance Committee Gurgram in 2020 but nothing has moved forward despite his clear directions.

7. During this period some parts of the vacant land have been encroached & the Company is burdening the Society with unjustified financial obligations by the way of incurring expenditure to secure the vacant land and adding exorbitant interest on such expenditure. The Company likely to impose unjustified terms and conditions on the gullible members of the Society.

8. In order to accept unjustified financial obligations & unclear land titles/issues, the Society is being disordered frequently by the officials of the Co-Operative Dept. of Haryana. The Society members are facing issues even about day-to-day maintenance.

9. Frustrated with the Company's approach & the state of affairs, the members of the Society started an indefinite peaceful dharna (with their Families) on the Main Gate of the Society complex since 1 May 2022.

In view of the above facts and circumstances, we, most humbly, request to your Honorable Self to intervene in the matter so that the total land with clear land titles will be transferred to the Society so that registry of flats has to be done in the name of the Society members.

We shall be grateful to your Honorable Self.

Best Regards

20/12/22

Yours sincerely

On the behalf of the Maruti Employees Co-Op Housing Building Society Members